2002–2016　TOYO ITO

TOYO ITO 2002-2016

Edited by Yoshio Futagawa, Yoshikazu Sugita
Photographed by GA photographers
Text by Toyo Ito
Designed by Takuya Seki

Copyright © 2016 A.D.A. EDITA Tokyo Co., Ltd.
3-12-14 Sendagaya, Shibuya-ku, Tokyo 151-0051, Japan
All rights reserved. No part of this publication may be reproduced,
stored in a retrieval system, or transmitted, in any form or by any means,
electronic, mechanical, photocopying, recording, or otherwise,
without permission in writing from the publisher.

Copyright of photographs
© 2016 GA photographers
Copyright of drawings, renderings
© 2016 Toyo Ito & Associates, Architects

Logotype design (GA): Gan Hosoya

Printed and bound in Japan

ISBN978-4-87140-435-8 C1352

TOYO ITO
2002-2016

A.D.A. EDITA Tokyo

TOYO ITO

1941	Born in Seoul Metropolitan City
	and grew up in Nagano where the hometowm of his father
1965	Graduated from the University of Tokyo, Department of Architecture
1965-69	Worked at Kiyonori Kikutake Architect and Associates
1971	Started his own studio, Urban Robot (URBOT) in Tokyo
1979	Changed its name to Toyo Ito & Associates, Architects
1986	Architectural Institute of Japan Prize for Silver Hut
1992	Mainichi Arts Award for Yatsushiro Municipal Museum
1998	Ministry of Education Award for the Encouragement of Arts for Dome in Odate
1999	Japan Art Academy Prize for Dome in Odate
2000	Accorded the Title "Academician" from the International Academy of Architecture
	The Arnold W. Brunner Memorial Prize in Architecture
	from American Academy of Arts and Letters
2001	Grand Prize of Good Design Award
	from Japan Industrial Design Promotion Organization for Sendai Mediatheque
2002	Golden Lion for Lifetime Achievement
	from the 8th International Architecture Exhibition "NEXT" at the Venice Biennale
2003	Architectural Institute of Japan Prize for Sendai Mediatheque
2004	ADI Compasso d'Oro Award for Ripples (furniture design)
2006	Royal Gold Medal from the Royal Institute of British Architects
2008	ADI Compasso d'Oro Award for the Stand Horm 2005
	Austrian Frederick Kiesler Prize for Architecture and the Arts
2009	Medalla de Oro from Circulo de Bellas Artes de Madrid
2010	The Asahi Prize
	The Praemium Imperiale in Honor of Prince Takamatsu
2012	The Spain Japan Council Foundation Prizes
	Golden Lion for Best National Participation for the Japan Pavilion
	13th International Architecture Exhibition
	at the Venice Biennale (served as Commissioner)
2013	Pritzker Architecture Prize
2014	Thomas Jefferson Foundation Medal in Architecture
2016	The Grand Prize of Architectural Institute of Japan

1941	京城市(現・ソウル市)生まれ。父の郷里の長野県下諏訪町で育つ
1965	東京大学工学部建築学科卒業
1965-69	菊竹清訓建築設計事務所勤務
1971	株式会社アーバンロボット(URBOT)設立
1979	事務所名を株式会社伊東豊雄建築設計事務所に改称
1986	日本建築学会賞作品賞(シルバーハット)
1992	毎日芸術賞(八代市立博物館)
1998	芸術選奨文部大臣賞(大館樹海ドーム)
1999	日本芸術院賞(大館樹海ドーム)
2000	国際建築アカデミー・アカデミシアン賞
	アメリカ芸術文化アカデミー・アーノルド・ブルーナー賞
2001	グッドデザイン大賞(せんだいメディアテーク)
2002	ヴェネツィア・ビエンナーレ「金獅子賞」(生涯業績部門)
2003	日本建築学会賞作品賞(せんだいメディアテーク)
2004	金のコンパス賞(Compasso d'oro ADI)(木製ベンチ "ripples")
2006	王立英国建築家協会(RIBA)ロイヤルゴールドメダル
2008	金のコンパス賞(Compasso d'oro ADI)(HORM社のブースデザイン)
	オーストリア・フレデリック・キースラー建築芸術賞
2009	マドリード美術協会金メダル
2010	朝日賞
	高松宮殿下記念世界文化賞
2012	スペイン日本評議会賞
	ヴェネツィア・ビエンナーレ「金獅子賞」(コミッショナーを務めた日本館が受賞)
2013	プリツカー建築賞
2014	トーマス・ジェファーソン財団建築メダル
2016	日本建築学会大賞

Contents

8   Essay: "On Creating Architecture" by Toyo Ito

22   **Brugge Pavilion** *Bruges, Belgium, 2000–02*
26   **Architects Competition Vestbanen** *Oslo, Norway, 2002*
30   **Serpentine Gallery Pavilion 2002** *London, U.K., 2002*
34   **Shinonome Canal Court CODAN Block 2** *Koto, Tokyo, Japan, 1999–2003*
38   **Matsumoto Performing Arts Centre** *Matsumoto, Nagano, Japan, 2000–04*
48   **TOD'S Omotesando Building** *Shibuya, Tokyo, Japan, 2002–04*
52   **Forum for Music, Dance and Visual Culture Competition** *Ghent, Belgium, 2004*
58   **Gavia Park in Madrid** *Madrid, Spain, 2004–*
60   **Island City Central Park "GRIN GRIN"** *Fukuoka, Japan, 2002–05*
66   **Dormitory for SUS Company Fukushima Branch** *Sukagawa, Fukushima, Japan, 2004–05*
70   **MIKIMOTO Ginza 2** *Chuo, Tokyo, Japan, 2003–05*
74   **'Meiso no Mori' Municipal Funeral Hall** *Kakamigahara, Gifu, Japan, 2004–06*
80   **VivoCity** *Singapore, 2003–06*
88   **Hôpital Cognacq-Jay** *Paris, France, 2000–06*
92   **Tama Art University Library (Hachioji campus)** *Hachioji, Tokyo, Japan, 2004–07*
100   **"Les Halles" Competition** *Paris, France, 2007*
104   **Extention for "the Fair of Barcelona Gran Via Venue"** *Barcelona, Spain, 2003–*
112   **ZA-KOENJI Public Theatre** *Suginami, Tokyo, Japan, 2005–08*
120   **SUMIKA PAVILION / SUMIKA PROJECT by TOKYO GAS** *Utsunomiya, Tochigi, Japan, 2007–08*
122   **The New Deichman Main Library Competition** *Oslo, Norway, 2009*
128   **BAMPFA University of California, Berkeley Art Museum and Pacific Film Archive** *California, U.S.A., 2009*
132   **White O** *Marbella, Chile, 2004–09*
138   **Facade Renovation "Suites Avenue Aparthotel"** *Barcelona, Spain, 2003–09*
140   **Kaohsiung National Stadium** *Kaohsiung, Taiwan, R.O.C., 2006–09*
148   **Belle Vue Residences** *Singapore, 2006–10*
152   **TORRES PORTA FIRA** *Barcelona, Spain, 2004–10*
156   **Toyo Ito Museum of Architecture** *Imabari, Ehime, Japan, 2008–11*
162   **House H** *Hokkaido, Japan, 2009–11*
164   **Ken Iwata Mother and Child Museum, Imabari City** *Imabari, Ehime, Japan, 2009–11*
168   **Yaoko Kawagoe Museum (Yuji Misu Memorial Hall)** *Kawagoe, Saitama, Japan, 2009–11*
172   **Tokyo Mother's Clinic** *Setagaya, Tokyo, Japan, 2009–11*
174   **ITO JUKU Ebisu Studio** *Shibuya, Tokyo, Japan, 2012–13*
176   **"Home-for-All" Projects** *Tohoku and Kumamoto, Japan, 2011–*
180   **Hermès Pavilion** *Basel, Switzerland, 2011–13*
182   **Products**
183   **Set design**
184   **New National Stadium Japan International Design Competition** *Shinjuku, Tokyo, Japan, 2012*
188   **Crematorium and Akayama Historic Nature Park in Kawaguchi** *Kawaguchi, Saitama, Japan, 2011–*
192   **National Taiwan University, College of Social Sciences** *Taipei, Taiwan, R.O.C., 2006–13*
200   **Songshan Taipei New Horizon Building** *Taipei, Taiwan, R.O.C., 2008–13*
204   **New Athletic Field and Sports Park in Aomori** *Aomori, Japan, 2013–*
208   **Museum + / West Kowloon Cultural District Competition** *Hongkong, China, 2013*
212   **Interior Design for the Reconstruction Project of Jikido in Yakushiji Temple** *Nara, Japan, 2013–*
214   **The Shinano Mainichi Shimbun Matsumoto Head Office** *Matsumoto, Nagano, Japan, 2014–*
216   **CapitaGreen** *Singapore, 2007–14*
220   **Residential Hall at Nanyang Drive, Nanyang Technological University** *Singapore, 2011–14*
224   **K-port / Isoya Suisan Minatomachi 1chome Branch** *Kesen'numa, Miyagi, Japan, 2012–14*
226   **New National Stadium Japan Proposal** *Shinjuku, Tokyo, Japan, 2015*
232   **'Minna no Mori' Gifu Media Cosmos** *Gifu, Japan, 2011–15*
242   **Yamanashi Gakuin University International College of Liberal Arts** *Kofu, Yamanashi, Japan, 2013–15*
246   **Fubon Sky Tree** *Taichung, Taiwan, R.O.C., 2010–16*
250   **Miyagi Gakuin Preschool "Mori no Kodomo-en"** *Sendai, Miyagi, Japan, 2014–16*
254   **Museo Internacional del Barroco** *Puebla, México, 2012–16*
264   **Mito Civic Hall** *Mito, Ibaraki, Japan, 2016–*
268   **National Taichung Theater** *Taichung, Taiwan, R.O.C., 2005–16*

280   List of Works *2002–16*

8	エッセイ：建築をつくるということ　伊東豊雄		
22	ブルージュ・パヴィリオン　ベルギー, ブルージュ　2000-02		
26	オスロ・ウェストバーネン再開発計画コンペティション応募案　ノルウェー, オスロ　2002		
30	サーペンタイン・ギャラリー・パヴィリオン 2002　イギリス, ロンドン　2002		
34	東雲キャナルコートCODAN 2街区　東京都江東区　1999-2003		
38	まつもと市民芸術館　長野県松本市　2000-04		
48	TOD'S 表参道ビル　東京都渋谷区　2002-04		
52	ゲント市文化フォーラム コンペティション応募案　ベルギー, ゲント　2004		
58	ガヴィア公園　スペイン, マドリッド　2004-		
60	福岡アイランドシティ中央公園中核施設 ぐりんぐりん　福岡県福岡市　2002-05		
66	SUS福島工場社員寮　福島県須賀川市　2004-05		
70	MIKIMOTO Ginza 2　東京都中央区　2003-05		
74	瞑想の森 市営斎場　岐阜県各務原市　2004-06		
80	VivoCity　シンガポール　2003-06		
88	コニャック・ジェイ病院　フランス, パリ　2000-06		
92	多摩美術大学図書館(八王子キャンパス)　東京都八王子市　2004-07		
100	レ・アール国際設計競技応募案　フランス, パリ　2007		
104	バルセロナ見本市 グランビア会場 拡張計画　スペイン, バルセロナ　2003-		
112	座・高円寺　東京都杉並区　2005-08		
120	SUMIKA パヴィリオン, SUMIKA PROJECT by TOKYO GAS　栃木県宇都宮市　2007-08		
122	オスロ市ダイクマン中央図書館 コンペティション応募案　ノルウェー, オスロ　2009		
128	カリフォルニア大学 バークレー美術館/パシフィック・フィルム・アーカイブ計画案　アメリカ, カリフォルニア州　2009		
132	White O　チリ, マルベーリャ　2004-09		
138	スイーツアベニュー アパートホテル ファサード リノベーション　スペイン, バルセロナ　2003-09		
140	高雄国家体育場　台湾, 高雄市　2006-09		
148	ベルビュー・レジデンシズ　シンガポール, オクスレーウォーク　2006-10		
152	トーレス・ポルタ・フィラ　スペイン, バルセロナ　2004-10		
156	今治市伊東豊雄建築ミュージアム　愛媛県今治市　2008-11		
162	洞爺湖H邸　北海道　2009-11		
164	今治市岩田健母と子のミュージアム　愛媛県今治市　2009-11		
168	ヤオコー川越美術館(三栖右嗣記念館)　埼玉県川越市　2009-11		
172	東京マザーズクリニック　東京都世田谷区　2009-11		
174	伊東建築塾 恵比寿スタジオ　東京都渋谷区　2012-13		
176	東北と熊本の「みんなの家」　東北地方と熊本県　2011-		
180	エルメス パヴィリオン　スイス, バーゼル　2011-13		
182	プロダクツ		
183	舞台デザイン		
184	新国立競技場基本構想国際デザイン競技応募案　東京都新宿区　2012		
188	(仮称)川口市火葬施設・赤山歴史自然公園　埼玉県川口市　2011-		
192	台湾大学社会科学部棟　台湾, 台北市　2006-13		
200	松山 台北文創ビル　台湾, 台北市　2008-13		
204	(仮称)新青森県総合運動公園陸上競技場　青森県青森市　2013-		
208	Museum + / West Kowloon Cultural Distrit Competition　中華人民共和国, 香港　2013		
212	薬師寺食堂復興計画(内部)　奈良県奈良市　2013-		
214	信濃毎日新聞社松本本社　長野県松本市　2014-		
216	CapitaGreen　シンガポール　2007-14		
220	南洋理工大学学生寮　シンガポール　2011-14		
224	K-port / 磯屋水産港町一丁目店　宮城県気仙沼市　2012-14		
226	新国立競技場整備事業公募型プロポーザル応募案　東京都新宿区　2015		
232	みんなの森 ぎふメディアコスモス　岐阜県岐阜市　2011-15		
242	山梨学院大学 国際リベラルアーツ学部棟　山梨県甲府市　2013-15		
246	富邦天空樹　台湾, 台中市　2010-16		
250	宮城学院女子大学附属認定こども園「森のこども園」　宮城県仙台市　2014-16		
254	バロック・インターナショナルミュージアム・プエブラ　メキシコ, プエブラ　2012-16		
264	(仮称)水戸市民会館　茨城県水戸市　2016-		
268	台中国家歌劇院　台湾, 台中市　2005-16		
280	作品リスト　2002-16		

On Creating Architecture
建築をつくるということ

Toyo Ito
伊東豊雄

Erecting Pillars

For the first time in several decades, I went to the Onbashira Festival at *the Suwa Grand Shrine (fig. 1)*. *Suwa Grand Shrine* consists of four shrine buildings: *Hon-miya* (lit. main shrine) and *Mae-miya* (old shrine) at *the Kami-sha* (upper shrine) and *Haru-miya* (spring shrine) and *Aki-miya* (autumn shrine) at *the Shimo-sha* (lower shrine). The festival involves new *Onbashira* (honored pillars) being re-erected at the four corners of each shrine building once every seven years.

What is unique about *Suwa Grand Shrine* is that it is a shrine without a main building, its holy precincts being symbolized by pillars on the four corners *(fig.2)*. Born and raised near *the Shimo-sha*, I have been familiar to this festival since childhood. It is no exaggeration to say that the locals spend their days for seven years waiting for *the Onbashira Festival*: it is an integral part of everyday life.

Giant fir trees grown in the mountains are cut down and dragged along the mountainside to be erected at the four corners of the shrines. In the process, the highlight of the festival is an event called *'Ki-otoshi'* (tree dropping) in which parishioners ride the pillars as they glide down steep slopes. Even at the occasional risk of injuries and fatalities, people are intoxicated with the event's vehemence.

This year, witnessing this festival which is said to have continued for more than a dozen centuries up close for the first time in many years, I was once again impressed by the locals' passion for the pillars.

The ancient belief that the sole act of erecting a set of pillars generates a special inner 'field' can also be found among archaeological sites from the Jomon period. It is said that 'wooden circles' defined by giant trees were found at such neolithic sites as *Mawaki (fig.3)* and *Shinbo Chikamori* in Ishikawa Prefecture and *Inokuchi* in Toyama Prefecture. As we let our imagination roam around *Izumo Grand Shrine* and structures found at *the Sannai-Maruyama* site we become overwhelmed by their magnitude. Since the ancient times, our ancestors have developed a special feeling for pillars.

When I started to conceive *the Sendai Mediatheque* (2001), I did not particularly evoke the image of ancient pillars onto the thick vertical structure named 'tube.' Rather, it was about organic pillars such as simulated rows of zelkova trees along the front road or seaweed swaying in water. I proposed a structural model with thirteen tubes (twelve at the time of competition) supporting seven thin sheets of flat floor that erase the presence of walls *(fig.4)*, hoping to create a variety of 'field' using only a sequence of tubes rather than creating rooms by partitioning space with walls *(fig.5)*. My idea of creating 'fields' instead of rooms comes from my desire to create, based on spaces found within nature, different places according to their relationships with the surroundings, rather than creating an enclosed artificial environment, to allow people to establish a place where they belong driven by animal instinct instead of signs.

Spaces that fill the seven layers that compose *the Sendai Mediatheque* are integrated by means of thick, powerful tubes that run through all seven floors.

Pillars rise from the ground and reach for the sky; it

柱を立てる

数十年ぶり「諏訪大社」の御柱祭を見た(fig.1)。「諏訪大社」は上社が本宮と前宮，下社が春宮と秋宮という四つの大社から成り，7年に一度各社殿の四隅に立つ御柱を立て替える。

「諏訪大社」には本殿がなく，四隅の柱によって神域を象徴するという珍しい神社である(fig.2)。私の故郷は下社に近く，少年時代からこの祭りを身近に感じてきた。地元の人々は御柱祭をひたすら待ちながら7年間を過ごしている，と言ってもよい位，生活に深く浸透している。

山奥で育てた樅(モミ)の大木を切り倒して曳行し，社殿の四隅に建てるのだが，その過程でのハイライトが「木落とし」と呼ばれるイベントで，氏子が柱に跨ったまま急斜面を落下させる。時に死者や怪我人が出ることを厭わず，その激しさに酔い痴れる。

千数百年にわたって継承されてきたと言うこの祭りを今年，久々

に間近で見ながら，人々の柱にかける熱い想いにあらためて感動を覚えた。

複数の柱を立てるだけで，その内側に特別な「場」が形成される，と考える風習は縄文遺跡にもうかがわれる。石川県の「真脇遺跡」(fig.3)や「新保チカモリ遺跡」，富山県の「井口遺跡」などでは巨木による「ウッドサークル」がつくられたと言われているし，「出雲大社」や「三内丸山遺跡」などの建造物も想像をめぐらすだけでその巨大さに圧倒される。古来，私たちの祖先は柱に格別の思いを寄せてきたのである。

「せんだいメディアテーク」(2001年)を考え始めた時，「チューブ」と呼ぶ太い垂直の構造体に古代の柱を重ね合わせたわけではなかった。前面道路のけやき並木を模したとか，水中で揺らぐ海藻のような，といった有機的な柱をイメージしていた。13本のチューブ(コンペ

ティション段階では12本)で7枚の薄くフラットな床を支え，壁の存在を消した構造モデルを提案したのだが(fig.4)，壁によって仕切られる部屋をつくるのではなく，チューブの配列だけでその間に様々な「場」をつくりたいと考えていた(fig.5)。部屋でなくて「場」をつくりたいと考えるのは，閉ざされた人工環境ではなく，自然のなかのような空間を前提にしながら，周辺との関係によってそれぞれに違った場所をつくりたいからである。その時，人はサインによって居場所を定めるのではなく，動物的本能によって居場所を定めるのである。

「せんだい」は7層のフロアから成り立っているが，7層の空間は各階を貫く太く力強いチューブによって統合される。

柱は大地から立ち上がり，天空に向かって伸びる。その象徴的な姿を人は崇めるのである。

「新国立競技場整備事業公募型プロポーザル応募案」(2015年)にお

is for such symbolic aspect that people develop a sense of reverence.

Likewise, we proposed a contemporary 'wood circle' in our *Design B for the New National Olympic Stadium competition* (2015), which consisted of 72 wooden pillars supporting a seating bowl for 80,000 (68,000 for the Olympics) topped by a roof *(fig.6)*.

Its truss structure, called the 'balance truss,' require cantilevers stretching to a maximum of 65 m inside the stadium. In order to maintain balance, steel pipes are pulled down to the ground from the tips of 10-m cantilevers that stretch outward in the opposite direction *(fig.7)*. Our concept was to uphold the points of support of a truly balance-like truss by a colonnade of 72 wooden pillars.

Each pillar is a giant rectangular column with a side measuring 1 m 32 cm to 1 m 52 cm and a height of nearly 20 m. As featured in our proposal, the 1-hour fire rated pillars would have been of laminated lumber of homegrown larch clad in mortar plastering, three layers of allowance for loss of

いても，我々は現代の「ウッドサークル」を提案した。8万人(オリンピック時6.8万人)の観客を収容するスタンドとその上部に架けられる屋根を，72本の純木製の柱で支えようというものである(fig.6)。

「天秤トラス」と呼ばれるトラス構造では，スタジアムの内側に最大65mも伸びるキャンティレバーが求められる。それを逆方向，すなわち外側に伸びる10mのキャンティレバーの先端からスティールパイプで地上に引きおろし，バランスをとる(fig.7)。正しく天秤のようなトラスの支点を，72本の純木製の柱で支えようという構想である。

この柱は一辺が1m32cm～1m52cm，高さ20m近い巨大な角柱である。国産カラマツの集成材の周囲にモルタル層，燃え代3層，耐候層を巡らせ，1時間の耐火認定を受けられる柱で，火災は勿論のこと，傷や変色，カビ等にも二重，三重に安全性を考慮した提案であった(fig.8)。

世界のアスリートが集結して競い合うフィールドは，72本の巨大

fig.1

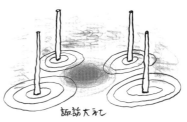
fig.2

fig.3

fig.4

fig.5

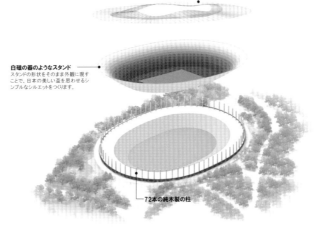
fig.6

fig.7

material charring and a weatherproof layer, designed with double and triple-checked safety considerations for fire as well as damages, discoloration and mold *(fig.8)*.

Its track and field where athletes from around the world gather to compete are a 'field of power' surrounded by 72 gigantic pillars *(fig.9)*. Athletes receive the energy that bursts from the earth to feed their own strengths and transmit them to the spectators in the seating terraces. Red ochre coloring of the tracks is transmitted to the seating area, and gradually changes to white as it climbs up the terraces.

Meiji Shrine Gaien (outer park) where the stadium is to be constructed is an extremely special place in Tokyo. Located in the heart of a city brimming with global economy, the two forests *(fig.10)*— *Naien* (inner park) and *Gaien* (outer park)—have been protected as holy sanctuary along with *the Imperial Palace*. How will it be possible for Tokyo, where history is being eradicated one by one by large-scale redevelopments, to inherit history and tradition and pass them onto the next generations?—ought to have been the question to be asked in this case with the stadium. The issue should not

have been addressed with such a frivolous term as 'Japanese-style.' Our team tried to substantiate the keyword 'New Tradition' by erecting 72 pillars. I believe that what is required for contemporary architecture is the passing down of powers and strengths inherited from ancient times to the future.

Putting on a Roof

'Minna no Mori' Gifu Media Cosmos (2015) is characterized by its undulating roof and 11 'globes' suspended from the rooftop. A 'globe' is a huge umbrella-like object made of polyester layered on semi-transparent fabric *(fig.11)*. They are scattered about a vast, almost wall-less space, reminiscent of a village dotted with houses. Since these globes were born out of a concept of 'small houses' within a 'large house,' it is no wonder that the scenery with a cluster of 'small houses' looks like a village.

Such attempt of creating a nesting space comes from an idea of taking the inside/outside partitioning with walls in contemporary architecture and wanting it to 'partition at least in two steps': it is pursuant to the idea of saving energy by partitioning the inside and outside in stages like in a traditional Japanese house from long ago.

I have always thought that the Western way of energy saving by placing a thick wall as a boundary between the inside and outside as heat insulation was inappropriate in Japan, a region prone to seasonal climatic changes. More

な柱に囲まれた「力の場」である(fig.9)。アスリートたちは大地から噴出するエネルギーを受け取って自らの力に変え，スタンドの観客に伝える。フィールドを染めるベンガラ色の赤はスタンドにも伝えられ，上方へいくにつれて緩やかに白く変わる。

スタジアムの建てられる明治神宮外苑は，東京のなかでも極めて特別な場所である。内苑−外苑という二つの森(fig.10)は，グローバル経済に覆い尽くされた都市にあって，皇居とともに聖地として護られてきた場所である。大規模な再開発によって次々に歴史が消されていく東京から，いかに歴史や伝統を継承して次代に伝えていくのか。今回のスタジアムでは，この問題こそが問われるべきであった。「和風」などという軽薄な言葉で片付けられる問題ではなかったはずである。我々は72本の柱を立て，「新しい伝統」というキーワードを実体化しようと試みた。現代建築に求められるのは，古代から伝えられる力の継承であり，その力を未来に伝えていくことであると思う。

屋根を架ける

「みんなの森 ぎふメディアコスモス」(2015年)を特徴づけているのは，波打つ屋根とその頂部から吊られた11ヶ所の「グローブ」である。「グローブ」は，ポリエステルと半透明の布を重ね合わせてつくられた，大きな傘のようなオブジェクトである(fig.11)。壁のほとんどない広い空間の中にグローブが点在する姿は，民家の建ち並ぶ集落のように見える。元々，グローブは「大きな家」のなかの「小さな家」というコンセプトから生まれたのだから，「小さな家」が建ち並ぶ風景が集落のように見えても不思議はない。

このような入れ子状の空間をつくる試みは，内/外を1枚の壁で隔てる現代建築に対して「せめて2段階に仕切ろう」と考えたからである。つまり，かつての日本家屋のように，内/外を段階的に仕切ることによってエネルギー・セーブを図ろうという考え方に準じている。

私は以前から，1枚の厚い壁によって内/外の境界を設け，断熱

性能を上げて省エネ化を図る西欧流は，日本のように季節毎の変化に富んだ気候の地域にはふさわしくないと考えてきた。何よりも，日本人は四季による自然の微妙な変化を愛でてきたのだから，厚い壁で内/外を隔てることを好まないはずである。

「大きな家」の中の「小さな家」という構想は，かつてオフィスビルで考えたアイデアに基づいている。広い工場のようなオフィス空間内に，独立した木造の小部屋を点在させる，というアイデアである。このプロジェクトは残念ながら実現しなかった。「メディアコスモス」の敷地は広く，低層の建築が可能であった。コンペティションのスタート時点から，このアイデアで再度チャレンジしようと考えていた。

そこで，切妻の工場が連なっているスケッチからスタートした(fig.12)。「大きな家」は半屋外に近いイメージで，壁にも屋根にも大きな開口を設け，内部でも大きな樹木が育つような空間である

than anything, the Japanese, who have always been in love with the subtle changes in nature of its four seasons, would have little appreciation for separating the indoors from the outdoors with thick walls.

My concept of 'small houses' within a 'large house' is based on an idea that I once came up with when working on an office building, which consisted of a vast factory-like office space sprinkled with small independent wooden rooms, for a project that was unfortunately never realized. *Media Cosmos*' site was vast, and a low-rise building proved to be an option. Hence my second attempt on this idea that I had in mind right from the beginning of this competition.

I started out from a sketch of a sequence of gabled factory buildings *(fig.12)*. The 'large house' has an almost semi-outdoor image, with large openings on its walls and roof, a space in which tall trees would be able to grow *(fig.13)*. The real challenge came with the 'small houses.' As I drew my sketch with an imagery of independent wooden houses in mind, they became apparently self-enclosed and uninviting,

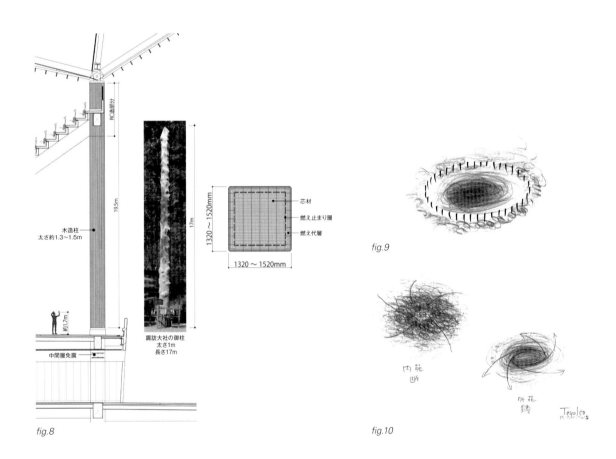

(fig.13)。しかし「小さな家」が難しかった。独立した木造住宅のようなイメージを描くと、いかにも閉鎖的で入りにくい。他人の家に本を読みに行くような印象を与えてしまう。

試行錯誤の時間が続いた。コンペティションで最もクリティカルな時間である。参加したスタッフが夢中になる時間でもある。スタディの中で切妻の連棟は消え、フラットスラブのワンルーム空間に変わった。しかし「小さな家」の解決法が容易に見つからない。試行錯誤が再び続く。そんなある日、突然に大きな傘のような覆いを吊ろう、というアイデアが浮かんだ。

そこから、波打つ木造の曲面屋根、その頂部から吊られる傘といった一連の構想がまとまるまでには、わずか数日しか要しなかった。今回の提案にはARUPのエンジニアとして構造家の金田充弘氏、環境設備設計家の荻原廣高氏（現在、在ロンドン）に加わってもらっていたのだが、二人からのアイデアが実に素晴らしかった。

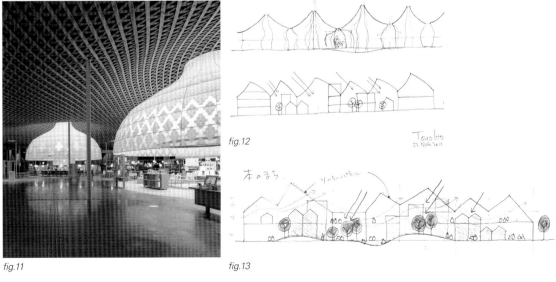

almost like going to someone else's house to read a book.

Some time for trial and error was required, which usually is the most critical in a competition, as well as the most exciting for those who participate in a project. As a series of rough sketches were studied, the row of gabled buildings vanished, giving way to a flat slab one-room apartment space. But a solution for 'small houses' was not an easy find. Days of trial and error continued, then out of the blue came the idea of suspending a huge umbrella-like cover.

From then on, it was a matter of days until a string of ideas such as the undulating wooden curved roof and umbrellas hung from the summits were brought together. This time, structural engineer Mitsuhiro Kanada and environment facility designer Hirotaka Ogihara (now London-based) joined us from ARUP in the preparation of our proposal, whose contributions were truly outstanding.

An uninterrupted shell roof is made of alternating layers of thin local cypress sheets; natural light is introduced from the summits; at the same time, huge umbrella-like objects are suspended, which were later named 'globes.' The base of each globe is an opening and closing device that moves up and down to discharge head according to the interior environment. Ideas for structures and facilities came almost simultaneously.

At *Media Cosmos*, various types of natural energy are used for energy saving such as natural light through solar panels and skylights. Particularly worth noting is the air circulation in the entire building. In close proximity to Nagara-gawa River, the site is abundant in groundwater. Air conditioning is realized through radiant floor heating/cooling system by pumping up groundwater that is stable in temperature all year round. In addition, cool/warm air radiating from the floor is slowly and naturally circulated throughout the building. Warm air is ultimately discharged from the top of globes during summer, or, further circulated inside the globes by closing the apertures during winter. Groundwater is discharged into the stream by the promenade after air-conditioning use, to be finally returned to the ground *(fig.14)*. When experienced in reality, this idea has proved to be very much effective. Gifu is famous for its stifling summer heat in Japan. My visit to the facility right after its opening which coincided with summer vacation, the building was teeming with visitors as in the hustle-bustle of an amusement district. Under such circumstances, with indoor temperature of about 28 °C, humidity was kept as low as 40%. I was amazed how much comfort a little bit of soft breeze under the globe contributed to the indoor environment.

That was how the goal of 'reducing energy consumption to half of that of conventional buildings in the same scale' from the competition came to be achieved, to which the existence of globes was indispensable.

Originally conceived as 'small houses' within a 'large house,' the globes may be compared to the tubes in *the Sendai Mediatheque*, since these globes create 'fields.'

A globe is a big umbrella-like space. An umbrella covers the human body like an extension of clothing. Similarly, a globe covers our body like an extension of clothing. My greatest concern was about 'cover,' which has to do with the relationship with the body: I wanted it to provide a sense

地場産のヒノキ薄板を互い違いに重ねて連続するシェル屋根をつくり，頂部から自然光を採り入れる，と同時に後に「グローブ」と命名された大きな傘のオブジェクトを吊る。グローブの吊り元を上下に動く開閉装置として，暖気を室内環境に応じて排出する。構造と設備のアイデアがほとんど同時に生まれたのである。

「メディアコスモス」における省エネのためには，太陽光パネルやスカイライトを通しての自然光の利用など，様々な自然エネルギーを利用しているのだが，特筆すべき点は，館内全体にわたる空気の循環である。敷地は長良川に近いため，地下水が豊富である。通年にわたって安定した水温の地下水を汲み上げて，床輻射の冷暖房を行う。さらに床から上がってくる冷気や暖気を自然の力で館内をゆっくりと循環させ，最終的に夏季はグローブ頂部の開口から排気し，冬季は開口を閉じてグローブ内で循環させる。また，利用した地下水はプロムナードのせせらぎに注がれ，最終的には地下に還される(fig.14)。このアイデアは，現実に体感してみると実に効果的であった。岐阜は日本でも猛暑で知られた地域である。しかもオープン直後の夏休みとあって，館内は雑踏の盛り場のような賑わいを見せていた。そのような状況で室内温度は28℃程度でも，湿度を40%程度に抑え，グローブ下で微風を感ずるだけで心地良い室内環境が整えられていることに驚いた。

かくしてコンペティション以来の，「消費エネルギーを既存同規模建築の1/2とする」という目標は達成された。その達成のためにグローブの存在は不可欠であった。

「大きな家」のなかの「小さな家」として発想されたグローブであるが，グローブは「せんだい」におけるチューブに例えられる。すなわちグローブによって「場」がつくられているのである。

グローブは大きな傘のような空間である。傘は人の衣服をひとまわり拡張したように身体を覆う。グローブも拡張された衣服として身体を覆う。この「覆う」という身体との関係に最大の配慮が払われた。何故なら包み込んでしまう程の閉鎖感がなく，しかし「内に居る」安心感があって欲しかったからである。グローブの形状，光や空気の透過度，サイズ（グローブの直径）と吊られる高さの関係など多くの条件を統合してグローブ下の居心地の良さは決まる。

このグローブの製作に関してテキスタイル・デザイナーの安東陽子氏，グローブ下の家具デザインに関しては藤江和子氏が大きな貢献をしてくれた。このような素晴らしいチームの力を結集して，「小さな家」は実現したのである。

「せんだい」でチューブとチューブの間に「場」が形成されているのに対し，「ぎふ」ではグローブの下に特別な「場」がつくられる(fig.15)。「場」のつくられ方は異なるけれども，それらはいずれも「流れのなかに生じる渦」のような場所である(fig.16)。壁に囲まれた部屋のよ

of security of 'being inside' without being totally enclosed. Shape of globe, light and air permeability, relationship between size (globe's diameter) and height of suspension define the degree of comfort that can be felt under a globe.

Textile designer Yoko Ando and furniture designer Kazuko Fujie contributed to the production of globes and to the design of furniture placed under the globes respectively. 'Small houses' came into being as a result of such wonderful teamwork.

While in *Sendai Mediatheque* a 'field' is formed between tubes, in *Gifu Media Cosmos* special 'fields' are created under the globes *(fig.15)*. Although the way they are created are different, each of these 'fields' is a place similar to a 'vortex generated in a flow' *(fig.16)*. Unlike a space cut off from the surrounding environment like a room enclosed in walls, it is an open place that is based upon its relationship with the surrounding environment. It is a place where people cannot help but want to stay. People are comfortable when they are in a place that feels free, where nothing is forced. That is the kind of place I wish to create.

うに周辺環境から断ち切られた空間ではなく，周辺環境との関係において成り立つ開かれた場所である．人々が思わず自ら留まりたくなるような場所である．強制されない自由な場に居る時，人は心地良さを感じる．そんな場所をつくりたい，と考えている．

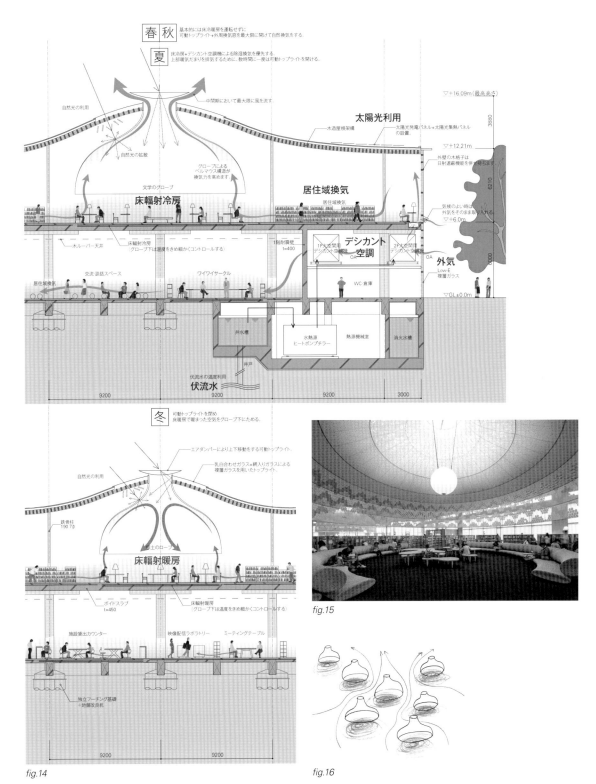

fig.14

fig.15

fig.16

Erecting Walls – 1

Walls were devised to protect humans from natural threats. To create a place that is independent from the outside world by surrounding it with walls was what was asked of architecture. Therefore a wall's original role is to 'separate' and 'build a border between inside and outside.'

Modernistic thinking aimed to establish individualism and consolidated, both physically and mentally, the presence of walls. As a consequence, solid walls were built between humans or the man-made and nature, as well as between individuals. Even if they were transparent as glass, the thought behind them remains the same.

Upon the recovery efforts following the 2011 Great East Japan Earthquake, despite calls for 'bonds' among people, newly-built temporary housing and public housing were just about walls, in the name of 'privacy,' a scheme for the independence of the individual. The fact that massive walls of coast levees are now being built in the afflicted areas reveals how recovery plans are fixated on modernistic walls that separate humans from nature and rely solely on technology under the 'security and safety' dogma, contrary to the locals who have always respected nature all the while being in awe.

Because Japanese traditional architecture has always been based on pillars and beams of wood structure, the concept of 'wall' was an unfamiliar one. The concept of privacy and concern over spatial separation for the sake of function were almost non-existent.

But in order to build an architecture that lives up to programs imported from the Western world such as concert halls and museums, use of walls is imperative. In what way then should we Japanese perceive walls and how should we build them? Is it possible that walls would connect humans with nature, people with people?

Most contemporary museums is composed of a series of pure exhibition spaces called 'white cubes' that provide homogeneous lighting that is as close as possible to natural light suitable for any type of artwork on display. As a result, however, an exhibition room inevitably becomes an enclosed space surrounded by walls. The expected type of uniform lighting consists of natural light from the sky above, whatever the weather, mixed with artificial light. Consequently, access to exhibition rooms and around the museum can only be made through holes in the walls.

Museo Internacional del Barroco (2016, *fig.17*) in Puebla, Mexico is a museum dedicated to architecture, art, literature, music and drama from the Baroque period, hosting eclectic exhibitions and performances. Puebla was chosen as the site for the museum because the city is home to an exceptionally charming Baroque church: in the 16th century when the Spanish colonized Mexico they destroyed pyramids to build churches in their attempt to convert citizens to Christianity. In the process, they used indigenous craftsmen to create statues of black Jesus and black Maria and decorate the church interior. Excessive ornaments of rustic reliefs of angels and plants that fill the interior touch people's heart. Visitors are captivated by its charms, and I was no exception.

So when I took charge of the design of a museum dedicated to Baroque art, I wanted to take the challenge of creating exhibition spaces that are not white cubes.

壁を立てる－1

壁は人を自然の脅威から護るために考えられた。壁を巡らすことによって，外界から自立した場所をつくることが，建築に求められたのである。したがって「隔てること」「内/外の境界を築くこと」が，壁の本来の役割と言える。

近代主義思想は「個」の確立を目指して，壁の存在を物理的にも精神的にも強化した。したがって人，あるいは人工物と自然の間にも，また個人と個人との間にも堅固な壁を築いた。ガラスのように透明な壁であっても，その思想は変わらない。

東日本大震災の復興に際しても，人と人の「絆」が叫ばれたにも拘らず，「プライバシー」という個の自立を楯に取って，仮設住宅や公営住宅に壁ばかりが築かれた。防潮堤という強大な壁が各被災地に次々に建設されている姿からも，自然を畏れ，崇めてきた住民の意に反して「安心安全」神話の下，いかに復興計画が技術に頼って自然と人とを隔てる近代主義の壁に固執しているかが見てとれる。

しかし日本の伝統的な建築は，木構造の柱・梁をベースに考えられていたから，「壁」という概念は稀薄であった。プライバシーという概念や，機能という概念によって空間を隔てる意識もほとんど無かった。

だが，コンサートホールやミュージアムなど，西欧から輸入されたプログラムに従って建築をつくるには，壁が不可欠である。では，日本人として我々は壁をどう受け止め，どのような壁を立てれば良いのか。果たして人と自然，人と人を結ぶ壁はあり得るのだろうか。

現代のミュージアムは多くの場合，「ホワイト・キューブ」と称するピュアな展示空間を連ねて成立している。いかなるアートワークが置かれても，自然光に極力近い均質な光が望まれるからである。しかしそのためには，展示室は壁に囲まれ，閉ざされた空間にならざるを得ない。上空からの自然光も天候に拘らず，人工照明とミックスされた均質な光を求める。したがって，展示室への出入りは壁に開けられた穴に従うしかない。

メキシコ，プエブラ州の「バロック・インターナショナルミュージアム・プエブラ」(2016年，fig.17)はバロックと呼ばれる時代の建築やアート・文学・音楽・演劇などを，広いジャンルにわたって展示したり，演じるミュージアムである。プエブラの地が選ばれたのは，この街に実に魅力的なバロックの教会が存在しているからである。16世紀にスペイン人がメキシコを植民地化した時，彼らはピラミッドを破壊してその上に教会を建ててキリスト教への改宗を企てた。その際，先住民族の職人を使って黒いキリストや黒いマリア像を置いたり，内部の装飾をつくらせた。素朴なエンジェルや植物のレリーフによって内部を満たす過剰なまでの装飾が，人々の心を打つ。私もその魅力の虜になった一人である。

そんなバロックをテーマにしたミュージアムの設計を任された時，

However, since a museum is a sequence of segmented exhibition spaces, it is simply impossible to avoid surrounding each exhibition space with 'walls.' I therefore came up with an idea of 'shifting walls out of alignment' and 'bending walls' *(fig.18)*. That is, by shifting walls that intersect at right angles to form a fylfot, a small square space is produced; by inflecting both ends of the walls, the small square spaces become fluid, drawing spirals, as they serve as buffer spaces that provide smooth connection between exhibition rooms. Openings to the patio and introduction of natural light from the sky above are realized through manipulating the four ends of the walls to open and close in the perpendicular direction like a camera diaphragm, out of consideration to the visitors' comfort.

Walls can be given plant-like, upward-climbing vital forces just by adding such manipulation. Despite starting out from grid geometry, the end product draws closer to the system of the natural world.

Erecting Walls – 2

The National Taichung Theater (Opera House) (2016) is finally brought to completion. The competition having started at the end of 2005 *(fig.19)*, it took in fact 11 years to be finished. We have been put in charge of the design even before we had any vision on the amount of time and construction cost needed for completion, which is something unimaginable in Japan.

Even after we began working on the design, the material and method for realizing a structure composed of a continuum of three-dimensional curves still remained to be worked out. After reviewing the economic efficiency and buildability, the truss wall system was adopted: reinforcing steel would be assembled at the factory, and concrete would be cast on site into the mesh mould. However, with the design in progress, no contractor would show up to take on the project. Just as we were about to give up, a local firm finally agreed to join in.

The construction process was one hardship after another: it is almost a miracle it eventually came to be

fig.17

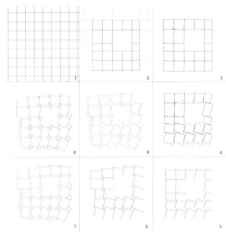

fig.18

私はホワイト・キューブではない展示空間にチャレンジしたかった。

しかし，分節された展示空間が続くミュージアムであるからには，各展示空間を「壁」で囲むことは避けられない。そこで考えたのは「壁と壁の間をずらす」こと，及び「壁を曲げる」ことであった(fig.18)。すなわち直交しながら交叉する壁を卍型にずらす操作によって，交叉部に小さな正方形平面の空間を生み出す。さらに壁の両端を湾曲させることによって，小空間はスパイラルを描く流動的な空間となる。展示室と展示室をスムーズに結ぶ緩衝空間となるのである。そして，4方向からの壁の先端を，カメラの絞りのように，垂直方向に拡げたり狭めたりする操作を加え，また中庭への開口を設けたり，上空からの自然光を導くなどして，ビジターが精神の安らぎを得られるように配慮した。

このような操作を加えるだけで，壁は上昇する植物のような生命力を持つ。グリッドの幾何学からスタートしながらも，自然界のシステムに近づくのである。

壁を立てる－2

「台中国家歌劇院(オペラハウス)」(2016年)がようやく完成を迎える。2005年末のコンペティション(fig.19)以来，実に11年を要した。コンペティションの時点から，完成までにどれくらいの時間と工事費を要するのかの見通しもつかないまま設計を任された。日本では考えられないことである。

設計を始めてからも，3次元曲線の連続体から成る構造体を，いかなる素材と工法でつくるのかさえ決まっていなかった。経済性と施工性を検討した結果，鉄筋を工場で組み上げ，現場でメッシュを型枠にしてコンクリートを打つという，トラスウォール工法が選択された。しかし，設計が進んでも請け負ってくれる建設会社は現れなかった。実現をあきらめかけた頃に，やっと地元の会社が重い腰を上げた。

完成したのが奇跡的とも言える位に，苦難の連続であった。何

fig.19

completed. Why was it so important for me to realize this architecture against such difficulties?

It all started with *the Ghent Forum for Music, Dance and Visual Culture* competition in 2004 *(fig.20)*. I wanted to propose an architecture as 'an extension of a street' where people can relax and enjoy as if they were at a street concert, in the same imagery as *Andrea Palladio's Teatro Olimpico* (1585) where its stage looks to lead up to the streets. My idea for the proposal was a concert hall in which several performances would be given at various places besides the Main Hall at the same time within the building, where people can move from place to place between acts and possibly hear a mix of sounds from different places.

Unfortunately, during the selection process this idea was completely lost on the jury. So I wanted to resolve that disappointment through *Taichung*.

However, the site conditions at *Ghent* and *Taichung* differed considerably. In the former case, the architecture was planned to fill an irregular-shaped site surrounded by a promenade, where it was possible to be accessed from

various directions, hence the proposal for an architecture as an extension of a street. On the other hand, the site for *Taichung* was a vast public park. My plan was to design a promenade inside the park along with three theaters arranged as extensions of the path. That is to say, the theater is incorporated in a tube with apertures that open toward various directions. The resulting facade consists of a box whose four sides and top are cut off and tube sections are exposed outside the box.

This architecture can also be compared to the human body. While a human body is individually independent from nature, it is linked to nature through many of its tubes that open to the outside such as eyes, nose, mouth and ears among other organs. Apertures in architecture are not as good at delicate control as the human body, but the goal is the same.

"The inside of the digestive tract is generally considered the 'inside of the body'," says molecular biologist Shin'ichi Fukuoka, "but biologically speaking, it is not the inside of the body: it is the outside. Human digestive tract

passes inside the body through the linkage of the mouth, esophagus, stomach, small bowel, large bowel and anus, but is connected to the outside in terms of space, reminiscent of 'chikuwa,' the tube-shaped fish sausage. In other words, it is a hollow tube that pierces through the body. (*Dynamic Equilibrium*, 2009, Kiraku-sha)" *Taichung* was an attempt for an outside tube that pierces through the inside of an architecture.

Apart from the importance of its function, *Taichung's* tube structure brings up a more fundamental issue about 'architecture and nature.'

This project's structural system composed of complex three-dimensional curved surfaces is derived from a geometry involving circles drawn in a checkered pattern on two flat surfaces arranged alternately so the upper circle do not overlap with the lower one, and curved surfaces that connect the circles. As this basic pattern is layered vertically and morphed according to the programs, a complex tube structure is shaped *(fig.21, 22)*.

Usually in theater design, the type of theater such as

故それ程までの苦労をして，この建築をつくりたかったのか。

発端は 2004年の「ゲント市文化フォーラム」のコンペティション（fig.20）にまで遡る。ストリートコンサートのようにリラックスして楽しめる，「道の延長」としての建築を提案したかったのだ。アンドレア・パラーディオの劇場「テアトロ・オリンピコ」(1585年)のステージが，街に通じているのと同じイメージである。メインホールだけでなく，建築内の様々な場所で同時にコンサートが行われ，観客は幕毎に場所を変えて館内を巡って歩けたり，あるいは複数の場所からの音が複合されて聞こえてくるような，そんなコンサートホールを提案したかった。

だが，審査会では全く理解されないまま落選してしまった。その無念さを「台中」で晴らしたかったのである。

しかし，「ゲント」と「台中」では敷地の状況がかなり違っていた。前者では建築は周遊路に囲まれた不定形の敷地いっぱいに計画

され，様々な方向からのアクセスが可能だった。したがって道の延長としての建築を提案できたのだが，「台中」の敷地は大きな公園であった。そこで公園内の園路をデザインして，その延長上に三つの劇場が存在するという設定としたのである。すなわち，外部の各方向に口を開けたチューブのなかに劇場が組み込まれている，という構成である。その結果，四周と頂部を切り落とした箱の外側は，チューブの断面が露出した。

この建築は，人体に喩えることもできる。人体は人それぞれに自然から自立しているが，外部に開かれた多くのチューブ，目，鼻，口，耳などの器官によって自然と結ばれている。建築の開口は人体のように微妙なコントロールはできないが，目指すところは同じである。

分子生物学者の福岡伸一氏は「消化管の内部は，一般的には〈体内〉と言われているが，生物学的には体内ではない。つまり体外である。人間の消化管は，口，食道，胃，小腸，大腸，肛門と連なって

身体の中を通っているが，空間的には外部と繋がっている。それはチクワの穴のようなもの。つまりからだの中心を突き抜ける中空の管である。」（『動的平衡』：2009年，木楽舎)と語っている。「台中」も建築内を貫通する外部のようなチューブを目指したのである。

「台中」のチューブ状構造体はその働きも重要だが，「建築と自然」に関わる，より本質的な問題提起をしている。

このプロジェクトの複雑な3次元曲面から成る構造システムは，2枚の平面上に市松に描かれた円を上下でずらしつつ，その間を曲面で結んだ幾何学に由来する。この基本パターンを垂直方向に重ね，プログラムに従って変形していくと，複雑なチューブ状の構造体が形成される（fig.21, 22)。

通常，劇場の設計では，アリーナ型とかプロセニアムステージ型など，まず劇場の形式を決定し，その上で全体の構造が決められる。しかし「台中」では，まず3次元曲面体の構造システムを設定

arena-type or proscenium stage-type has to be chosen prior to determining the type of overall structure. But in *Taichung*, we first established the structural system made of three-dimensional curved surfaces, then attempted to fit the theater in this system. Here, the overall structure was determined by applying some change in shape on a regular geometric format. We used to call such transforming manipulation 'emerging grid' in an attempt to dismantle the geometric format and move closer to an organic, natural system.

Besides *Taichung*, such method that makes use of algorithm (programmed method of determining geometry using computers) was also applied to *Tama Art University Library on Hachioji Campus* (2007, *fig.23*) and *National Taiwan University College of Social Sciences Library* (2014), as well as the recently-completed *Museo Internacional del Barroco* in Puebla, Mexico, out of belief that fluidity of space can be created by applying change in shape in that manner.

Recently, however, I discovered that this transformation has a meaning that is much more critical, thanks to an important hint found on my second reading of Shin'ichi Nakazawa's essay "Ethica of Architecture" (1983), published as part of *Snowflake Curve Theory* (1985, Seido-sha), a collection of his early writings on the train of thought of esoteric Buddhist priests when they were building their monastery in Tibet, where Nakazawa has once submitted himself to Buddhist discipline.

Just like us, people in Tibet also have to rely on geometry when building an architecture. But generally, the ground on which architecture stands is not particularly based on geometry. The earth constantly swirls and swells in dynamic movements. Tibetans attribute it to the goddess called 'Sa Tak' who has the face of a beautiful young girl and the lower body of a serpent. She usually nurtures humans with motherly tenderness and patience, but occasionally goes on a rampage on a girly whim. So when building an architecture, Tibetans do not celebrate human accomplishment: they rather beg forgiveness to the earth

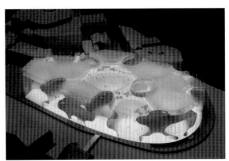

fig.20

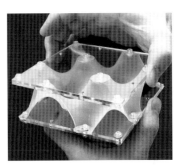

fig.21

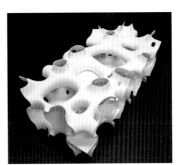

fig.22

し，そのシステムの中に劇場などをはめ込もうと試みる。規則的な幾何学の形式に変形を加えて，全体の構成が決定されるのである。この変形操作を我々は，かつて「エマージング・グリッド」と呼んだ。幾何学の形式を崩して，有機的な自然のシステムに近づけようと考えたのである。

このようにアルゴリズム（コンピュータを用いて幾何学を決定する定型的手法）を用いる方法は，「台中」だけでなく，「多摩美術大学図書館（八王子キャンパス）」（2007年，fig.23）や「台湾大学社会科学部棟図書館」（2013年），最近完成したメキシコの「バロック・インターナショナルミュージアム・プエブラ」等でも試みられている。そうした変形を加えることによって，流動的な空間が生まれると考えたからである。

しかし最近，この変形にはもっと重要な意味があることに気が付いた。再読した中沢新一氏の「建築のエチカ」（1983年）が大きな示唆を与えてくれたからである。この文章は中沢氏が最初期に出版した『雪片曲線論』（1985年，青士社）の中に収録されていて，氏が修業したチベットで密教の僧院を建てる際，彼らが何を考えたかについての考察が綴られている。

チベットの人々も建築をつくるに際しては，我々と同じように幾何学に頼らざるを得ない。しかし，建築が建つ大地は幾何学によって成り立っている訳ではない。大地は常に渦を巻き，うねりを生じてダイナミックに変動している。それは大地に「サ・タク」と呼ぶ女神が住むからだと，チベットの人々は考える。「サ・タク」は，顔は美少女だが蛇のような下半身を持つ。そして通常は，母親のように穏やかな包容力で人々を育むが，時として少女の気まぐれで荒れ狂う。だから建築を建てる時，チベットの人々は人間の営みを誇るのではなく，平穏を祈って大地に許しを乞うのだと言う。だから彼らは，人工的に手を加えて大地を均したり，削ったりすることは決してない。

fig.23

in their prayer for serenity. That is why they never try to level or scrape the ground.

Another observation of deeper interest is about the fact that while the exterior of Tibetan temples show direct expressions of geometry, the latter disappears once inside, leaving people with a feeling of being inside a mother's womb. Nakazawa describes how fluidity of natural world permeates the building, filling the interior with smells of oil and incense and richly-colored Buddha statues in flickering lamp light. (from Chapter 3 "Spinozists in the Highlands" in the aforementioned *Snowflake Curve Theory*; or from the addendum for *The Great Shift in Architecture*, a 2015 recompilation published in the Chikuma Bunko series)

This description successfully captures the true essence of Asian architecture. In Western history since the discovery of geometry, it has been considered a virtue to build architecture that are independent from the world of nature. In the modern times onward, the world reinforced orderly geometric expressions based on the advancement of industrial production technologies and emphasized its diversion from the natural world. The sight of contemporary cities with rows of high-rise buildings looks as though people are proudly showing off human accomplishment based on advancement in technology—a far cry from begging forgiveness to the earth. There is a certain arrogance, as if implying that with modern-day technology, nature can be kept under total control.

Reminiscent of a white cave, the continuum of curved walls is found everywhere inside the completed *Taichung*: the higher the floor the less segmentalized are the floor, walls and ceiling that make up the continuum of curved surfaces. Light and sound travel long distances as they are transmitted along the walls. It is hard to imagine that the space is made based on geometry, as it appeals to not only visual but also auditory and tactile senses.

Like it was named 'emerging grid' when *Taichung* was conceived, rational space created using algorithm—transformation of geometry—is converted to suprarational space, with an aspect of an underground space placed over the ground: the experience of the cave-like interior comes with a view of the surrounding high-rises through the openings in the facade. Such contrast gives a feeling of watching at the lamination of orthogonal grids of the contemporary city from inside the maternal womb.

This disparity and discomfort are exactly what we have spent 11 years looking for. At the cost of far more effort, time and energy than expected, I now find myself slightly closer than before to the minds of those Tibetans who built temples. In other words, I feel like I was able to transmit the earth's swelling force to the architecture.

さらに興味深い考察は, 寺院の外部には幾何学がそのまま表現されているが, 内部に入ると幾何学が消え, 母胎の内にいるような感覚にとらわれる, と言う件である。極彩色に塗られ, 灯明に揺らぎながら照らし出された仏像や, 油や線香の臭いなどが充満した内部は, 自然界の流動性がそのまま建築内に浸透していると言う。(前出の『雪片曲線論』の第3章「高原のスピノチスト」所収, あるいは2015年に出版されたちくま文庫の『建築の大転換』補論として再録)

この描写は, 見事にアジアの建築の本質を衝いている。西欧の歴史では, 人間が幾何学を発見して以来, 自然界から自立した建築をつくることを美徳としてきた。近代以降の世界は, 工業生産技術の発達に基づいて規則的な幾何学的表現を強化し, 自然界からの乖離をより明確にした。高層ビルの立ち並ぶ現代都市の姿を見ると, 大地に許しを乞うどころか, 技術の進化による人間の営みをいかにも誇らし気に示しているように感じられる。現代の技術を以ってすれば, 自然を完全に支配できる, といった驕りが感じられるのである。

完成した「台中」の内部は白い洞窟のようである。いたるところに曲面の壁が連続し, 上階にいくにつれて, 床, 壁, 天井も分節されずに連続した曲面を形成している。光も音も遠くから壁伝いにやってくる。およそ幾何学でつくられている空間とは考えられない。視覚だけではなく, 聴覚や触覚など五感に訴えかける空間である。

「台中」では「エマージング・グリッド」と命名されたように, 幾何学の変形, アルゴリズムによってつくられた理性的な空間が, 理性を超えた空間へと転換されている。その様相は, まるで地上にある地下空間である。その証として, 洞窟状の内部を体験していると, ファサードの開口を通して, 周囲に立ち並ぶビルの風景が目に入る。そのコントラストは, 直交するグリッドを積層した現代都市を, 母胎の内から眺めているように感じられる。

この対立, 異和感こそ, 我々が11年もの歳月を賭して求めてきたものであった。予想をはるかに超えた労力と時間とエネルギーを費やして, 私はチベットの寺院をつくる人々の気持ちに少しだけ近づけたように思う。すなわち, 大地のうねる力を建築に伝えることができたように感じているのである。

On Creating Architecture

From a certain point in time on, I came to believe that what is expected in contemporary architecture is 'strength' rather than 'beauty.' This because as urban architecture continues to update pure, transparent geometry, it keeps amplifying nothing but homogeneous artificial environment, and in the midst of it, people just seem to be exhausting their vivid sensitivity.

Such feeling grew stronger after I saw Le Corbusier's architecture in India three years ago: they felt definitely different from those that were built in the Western world.

For instance, *Notre Dame du Haut* is said to have been completed in 1955, and *Sainte Marie de La Tourette* in 1960, both recognized as masterpieces. Around the same time, Le Corbusier made frequent trips to India—23 times in total between 1951 and 1964, a year before his death. Since *the Palace of Justice* was completed in 1956 and *Palace of Assembly* in 1962, both in Chandigarh, it would be safe to say that all of them were built around the same period.

Every one of them is an exceptional masterpiece, but in my eyes, those in India are more rugged and stronger. Is it not because in India, people's lives are much more open to nature than in Europe? Walking through the old town of Ahmedabad, I saw people and cows, dogs and birds living and blending together. Then there were those giant trees that grow under the sunshine. The painting on the door of *the Palace of Assembly* wonderfully expresses the joy of those blessed with life in the nature under the intense sunshine. *The Palace*'s interior spaces separately painted in shocking red and yellow would not have been conceived if it were not for the land of India. It appears to me that in his final years, the architect, advocate of the beauty of geometry, touched the land of Asia and acquired his 'freedom of architecture' that transcends the format of geometry.

40 years after the creation of my earliest work *White U* (1976, *fig.24*), *Taichung* is about to be completed. All that time I have gone through every kind of trial and error. *White U* was once called a 'white cave.' Back then, though unconsciously, I was focused single-mindedly on creating a beautiful tube of light.

fig.24

建築をつくるということ

ある時から私は，現代建築に求められるのは「洗練」ではなく「粗々しい強さ」であると思うようになった。都市の建築はピュアで透明な幾何学を更新するにつれ，均質な人工環境ばかりを増幅している。その中で人々は生き活きとした感受性を衰弱させているように感じるからである。

3年前，インドでコルビュジエの建築を見てから，そうした想いはますます強くなった。コルの建築が，西欧世界でつくられる場合と決定的に違っているように感じられたのだ。

例えば，名作と言われている「ロンシャンの礼拝堂」は1955年，「ラ・トゥーレットの修道院」は1960年に完成したとされている。その同じ時期，コルはインドに通っていた。1951年から亡くなる前年の1964年にかけて23回もである。チャンディガールでの「高等裁判所」は1956年，「州議事堂」は1962年に完成したのだから，ほぼ同時期と言ってよい。

いずれも素晴らしい名作だが，私にはインドでの建築の方がより粗々しく力強く見える。インドでは，人々の暮らしがヨーロッパよりも，はるかに自然に開かれているからではないか。アーメダバードの旧市街を歩いていると，人や牛，犬や鳥が混然一体となって生きている。そして太陽の光を受けて育った巨大な樹木。議事堂の扉に描かれた絵画は，強い太陽の光と自然の下で生命を授けられたものたちの喜びが見事に表現されている。そして強烈な赤と黄色に塗り分けられた議事堂内部の空間は，あのインドの大地の存在なくしてはあり得なかったに違いない。幾何学の美しさを主張していた建築家が，その晩年にアジアの地に触れ，幾何学の形式を超えた「建築の自由」を獲得し得たように思われる。

私にとって最初期の作品「中野本町の家(White U)」(1976年，fig.24)

Taichung, which is about to be completed, is called a 'sound cave' *(fig.25)*. 'Light cave' versus 'sound cave'—it turned out that both are 'caves.' In other words, I started out with a 'cave' and after nearly half a century came back to the 'cave.' I came full circle with my own history of architecture, reaching *'kan-reki'* thus completing a cycle of 60 combinations of signs and elements in the old Japanese calendar.

This fact shows that the most corporal space for me might be the 'cave,' that is, a space that resembles the mother's womb. In the time between those two caves, I made a variety of attempts in order to escape the maternal womb and head outside. But every time I try to lift from the ground and float, I always feel myself being pulled back to the ground. Looking back, the reason might be that while wanting to take root in the world of reason through geometry, there always exists a force within me that can not be satisfied, pulling me to the opposite direction.

I am now attracted to 'strength' over 'beauty' perhaps because I am in need of a 'freedom of architecture' upon my return to the ground that resides in my own body. Today, many conscious architects are intensely consumed with their search for delicate and abstract beauty. Nevertheless, what is asked of us now is to pull our body, which remains unchanged since ancient times, back toward architecture, instead of dragging it away from architecture.

Just like Le Corbusier has succeeded to do so in India, I also want to liberate myself from the geometric format and acquire my 'freedom of architecture.' That about sums up the significance of 'creating architecture.'

Written on 12th August, 2016

fig.25

をつくってから40年の歳月を経て,「台中」がまもなく完成する。この間さまざまな試行錯誤を繰り返してきた。かつて「中野本町」は「白い洞窟」と呼ばれた。当時ほとんど無意識であったが,ひたすら美しい光のチューブをつくることに集中していた。

今完成しようとしている「台中」は,「サウンドケーブ(音の洞窟)」と呼ばれている(fig.25)。「光の洞窟」に対する「音の洞窟」,いずれも「洞窟」である。言い換えれば,私は「洞窟」に始まり,半世紀近くを経て「洞窟」に還ってきた。私自身の建築史は一巡した。「還暦」を迎えたとも言える。

この事実は,私にとっての最も身体的な空間が「洞窟」,すなわち母体の内部のような空間なのかもしれないことを示している。この二つの洞窟の間に,私は母胎の外部へ脱出するための様々な試みを行ってきた。しかし大地から浮遊しようと試みる度に,いつも大地に引き戻される自分を感じる。振り返れば,幾何学によって理性の世界に定着したいと思いつつ,そこでは満たされない逆方向の力が自分の内に常に働いているからであろう。

今,「美しさ」より「力強さ」に惹かれるのは,自らの身体に宿っている大地への帰還に「建築の自由」を求めているのかもしれない。今日多くの意識的な建築家たちは,ひたすら繊細で抽象的な美しさの追及に身を焦がしている。だが,今我々に求められているのは,建築から身体を引き剥がすことではなく,建築に古来変わらぬ身体を引き戻すことではないのか。

コルがインドで成し遂げたように,私も幾何学的形式から解放されて「建築の自由」を獲得したい。「建築をつくるということ」の意味はここに尽きる。

2016年8月12日筆

Works 2002–2016

Brugge Pavilion
Bruges, Belgium
2000–02

Overall view

Longitudinal elevation

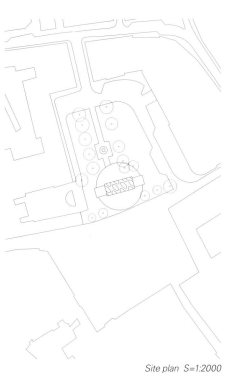

Site plan S=1:2000

Bruges is a medieval city of beauty graced by waterways. It has been designated as the Cultural Capital of Europe for the year 2002. This pavilion was built to occupy a plaza symbolical of this Belgian city for the limited time of one year, in 2002.

Like many other ancient cities, Bruges is now wavering between two contradictory issues: the preservation of historical urban landscape and the acquisition of potentials for a modern city. What we were expected to demonstrate here were possibilities for a new architecture in the midst of a historical landscape. No specific functions were requested, but it becoming a symbol worthy of a 'Cultural Capital'.

We have decided to build a pavilion of aluminum, against the quaint streets of stone.

A gate-shaped tunnel is constructed by means of a honeycomb structure. Since this frame is too fragile to stand on its own, aluminum panels are fixed on both sides where most necessary for reinforcement, so that the architecture can barely exist as a structure. These panels are mounted as floating islands. Loads in-between the island pattern are minutely transmitted to each aluminum honeycomb. Despite the compulsive structure analysis prepared behind, the figure formed by these oval floating islands is reminiscent of children playing with paper cutouts.

Water fills the circular basin that takes after the shape of a medieval church's foundation resting several score centimeters below ground, where drifts a floating bridge made of resin. The site prepared in such manner and the translucent aluminum frame softly placed onto it, are what this pavilion consists of. A translucent object, with floating island pattern resembling to the famous traditional laceworks of Bruges, emerges among the many facades of various styles that surround the plaza.

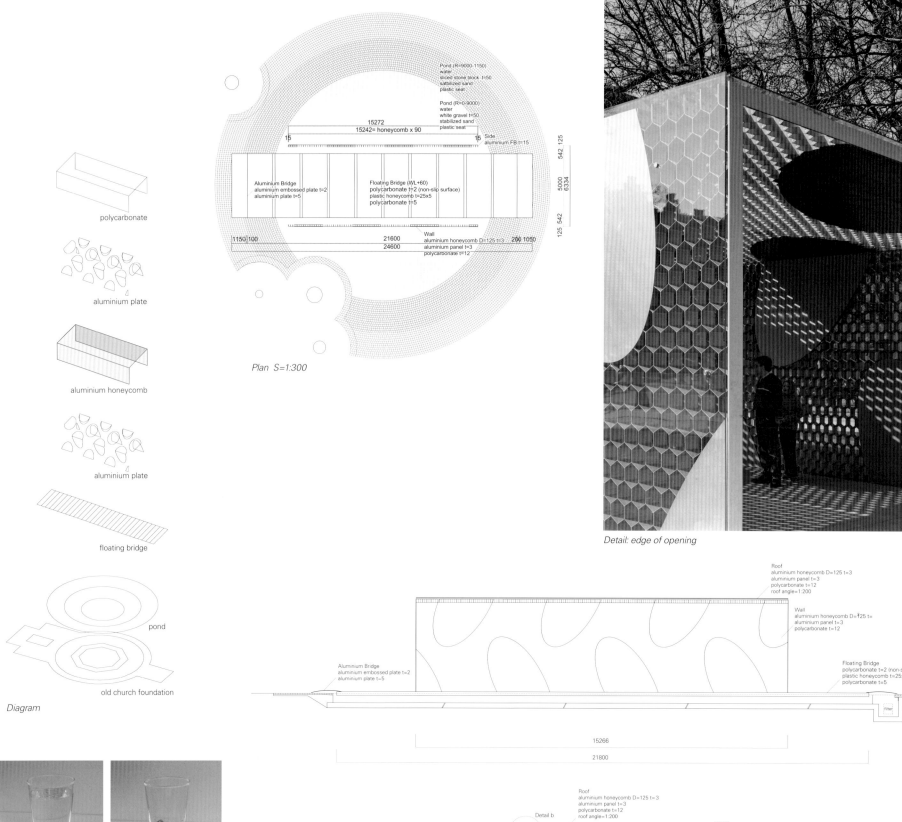

polycarbonate

aluminium plate

aluminium honeycomb

aluminium plate

floating bridge

Plan S=1:300

Detail: edge of opening

pond

old church foundation

Diagram

Structure

Sections S=1:150

△▽ Interior

ブルージュ・パヴィリオン

ベルギーのブルージュは中世の街並みを残す水に囲まれた美しい都市であり、ヨーロッパの2002年度「文化首都」に指定された。これは、この都市を代表する広場の中心に、2002年の1年間だけ存在したパヴィリオンである。

ブルージュも、他の多くの古都と同様、歴史的都市景観の保存と、現代都市としてのポテンシャルの獲得という二つの矛盾する課題の間で揺れ動いている。ここで我々に求められたのは、歴史的景観の中で新しい建築が持ちうる可能性を、他に先行って示すことである。特定の機能は要求されず、「文化首都」にふさわしいシンボルとなることのみが求められた。

石でできた古い街並みに対して、我々はアルミのパヴィリオンを建てることにした。

ハニカムと呼ばれる、蜂の巣状の構造体で門型トンネルをつくる。この架構は脆弱で、そのままでは自立しない。そこで、最低限必要な部分にのみ両側からアルミパネルを取り付けて補強し、構造上ぎりぎりの地点で成立させる。パネルは浮島状に貼られ、島模様の間の荷重は個々のアルミハニカムが微細に伝達する。背後に想定されている構造解析の生真面目さとは裏腹に、楕円形の浮島たちがかたちづくる模様は、切り絵遊びのようにも見える。

地下数十cmに眠る中世の教会の基礎形状を反映して円形に水が薄く張られ、そこに樹脂製の浮橋が浮かべられる。このように準備された敷地の上に、アルミの半透明なフレームをそっと置くことによって、このパヴィリオンは成立している。ブルージュの伝統工芸であるレースのような、浮島状の模様をともなう半透明な物体が、広場を囲む様々な様式のファサードをバックに浮かび上がる。

**Architects Competition
Vestbanen**
Oslo, Norway
2002

This is a proposal for a competition held in 2002, as the redevelopment project of the former *West Oslo Station*, facing to the Oslo Bay. The program is a large complex includes a public city library, a city art museum, a commercial section with a hotel and a cinema complex, the section of the office spaces, and the section of the residences. It was required to house the entire programs in 130,000 m² on the site space of 27,000 m².

After the initial, rather orthodox configuration providing a few high rise wings for the office and residential spaces, and the low rise wings containing commercial facilities, a library, and a museum, we suddenly shifted to a design configured only by two massive volumes. The larger volume of the two even has a scale with 160 m x 160 m in dimension, providing more than 20,000 m² of the space on one floor.

The reason of this change to suggest an 'urban scale project' in a 'super scale architecture' was derived from the experience when we worked on *Sendai Mediatheque* project. We expected to produce a space continuously expanding in horizontal direction by providing different program for each floor. In other words, we thought it might be possible to create a futuristic city completely different from the conventional configuration, by providing a unique, different city appearing on each floor—such as the city of books as if the space is unlimitedly extending out with books and DVDs, or the city of cinema with the series of lined up movie theaters, or the city of a hotel with a large interior garden space on its roof area.

After the collaboration work with the structural engineer Cecil Balmond, this enormous architecture utilizes the structure system supporting eight floor levels by 23 tubes. Those tubes have quadrangle or pentagonal planar shapes, and they stand up high as they continue change their forms. Those columns of tubes are networked at the roof level to enclose the building, while the network is directly appearing as the elevation of the exterior. We intended to produce an architecture, which continues to grow and transform as an organic body, by combining the systems of *Serpentine Gallery Pavilion (pp.30-33)* and *Sendai Mediatheque* to produce the enormously exaggerated structure system.

It was the attempt to manage the entire building by an architectural system even in such case of expanding a building scale into a larger urban scale.

1 PLAZA	20 LOBBY
2 INFORMATION	21 CONFERENCE
3 TEMPORARY HALL	22 RECAEPTION
4 NOBEL PEACE CENTER	23 RESTAURANT
5 TEMPORARY GALLERY	24 SPORTS
6 BOOK SHOP	25 SERVICE STATION
7 MUSIC STORE	26 MEETING ROOM
8 24H LIBRARY	27 GUEST ROOM
9 MUSEUM SHOP	28 POOL
10 CAFE	29 POND
11 OFFICE CIRCULATION	30 CRYSTAL GARDEN
12 COMMON CIRCULATION	31 BOARD ROOM
13 SHOWROOM	32 TECHNICAL GALLERY
14 OFFICE	33 SCREEN
15 LIBRARY	34 COMMERCIAL MARKET
16 MUSEUM / PERMANENT GALLERY	35 COMMERCIAL
	36 CAFETERIA
17 LOUNGE	37 KIOSK
18 EDUCATION	38 BAR
19 CHILDREN	

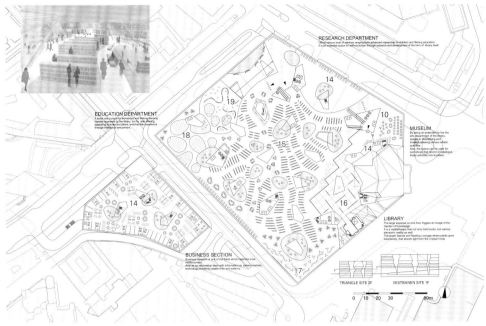
First floor

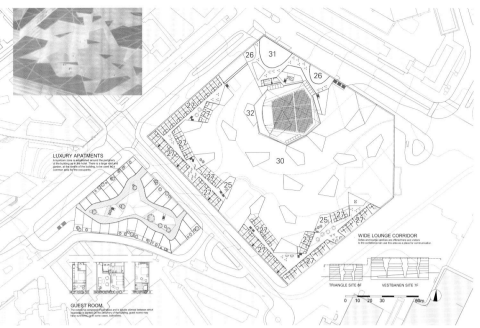
Sixth to seventh floor

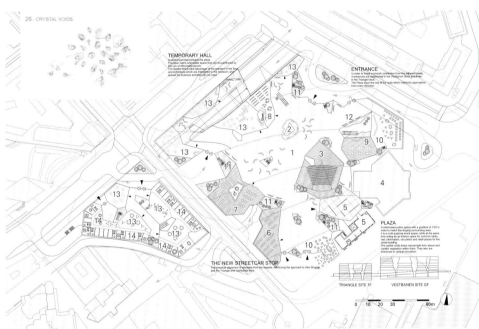
Ground floor S=1:3000

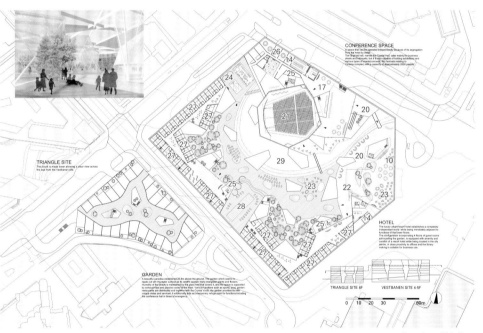
Fourth to fifth floor

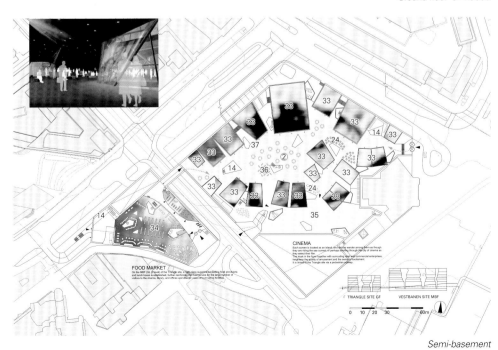
Semi-basement

Second floor

Plaza on ground floor

オスロ・ウェストバーネン再開発計画
コンペティション応募案

2002年にコンペティションが行われた、オスロ湾に面する旧オスロ西駅の再開発プロジェクトである。プログラムは市立図書館、市立現代アート・ミュージアム、ホテルやシネマコンプレックスを含む商業施設、オフィス、ハウジングなどのコンプレックスであり、約130,000m^{2}の延床面積を約27,000m^{2}の敷地に収めることが求められていた。

オフィス、ハウジングなどからなる数本の高層棟と、商業施設、ライブラリー、ミュージアムからなる低層棟というオーソドックスな構成のスタディを続けた後、突如二つの巨大なヴォリュームのみで構成する案へと移行した。とりわけ大きなヴォリュームの方は、160m四方でワンフロア 20,000m^{2}を超えるスケールを持っていた。

都市的スケールのプロジェクトを、敢えてスーパースケールの建築として提案したのは「せんだいメディアテーク」での経験に基づいている。つまり、ワンフロア毎に異なるプログラムを与え、水平方向に連続する拡がりのある空間をつくりたいと考えたのである。例えば、どこまでも本やDVDなどの並ぶ本の都市、映画館ばかりが並ぶシネマ・シティ、屋上には大きなインナー・ガーデンを持つホテル・シティといったように、不思議な都市がフロア毎に現れることで、オーソドックスな構成とは全く異なる未来的な都市をつくることが可能に思われた。

構造エンジニアであるセシル・バルモンドとのコラボレーションにより、この巨大な建築は23本のチューブで8層の床を支えるという構造システムを採用することとなる。チューブは四角形、または五角形の平面を持ち、変形を繰り返しながら上方に向かって伸びている。それらが屋根面でネットワーク化され、そのまま外周の立面ともなり建物を包み込んでいる。「サーペンタイン・ギャラリー・パヴィリオン」(pp.30-33)と「せんだいメディアテーク」のシステムを複合し、巨大化したストラクチャー・システムにより、生成変化し続ける有機体のような建築をつくろうとしたのである。

それは、都市的スケールに拡張された場合でも、建築的なシステムによって全体をカバーしようとする試みであった。

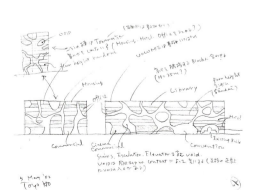
Sketch

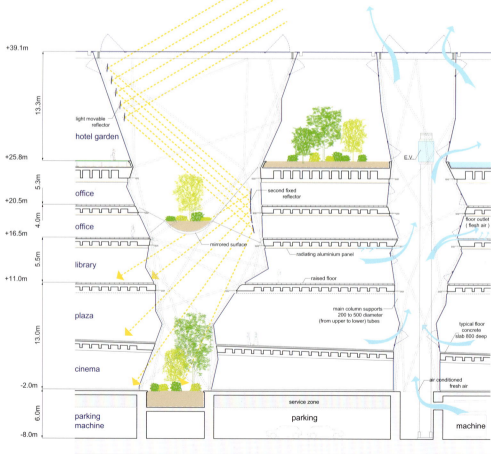
Diagram: transfer system

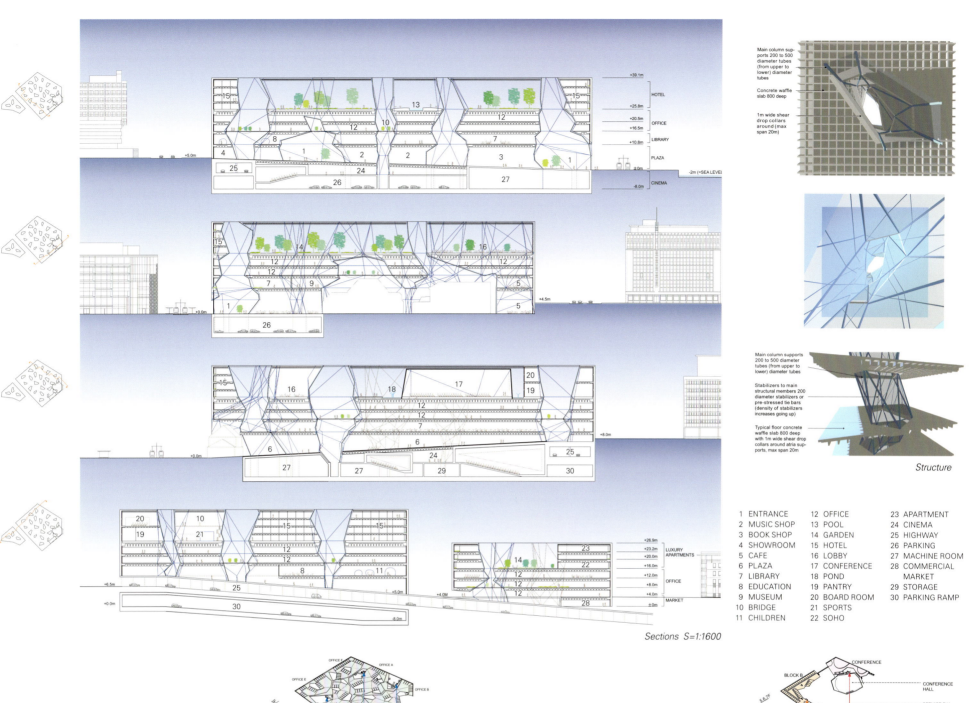

1 ENTRANCE	12 OFFICE	23 APARTMENT
2 MUSIC SHOP	13 POOL	24 CINEMA
3 BOOK SHOP	14 GARDEN	25 HIGHWAY
4 SHOWROOM	15 HOTEL	26 PARKING
5 CAFE	16 LOBBY	27 MACHINE ROOM
6 PLAZA	17 CONFERENCE	28 COMMERCIAL MARKET
7 LIBRARY	18 POND	29 STORAGE
8 EDUCATION	19 PANTRY	30 PARKING RAMP
9 MUSEUM	20 BOARD ROOM	
10 BRIDGE	21 SPORTS	
11 CHILDREN	22 SOHO	

Sections S=1:1600

Structure

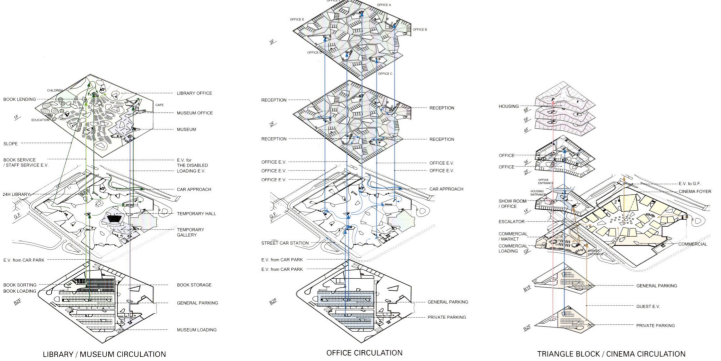

LIBRARY / MUSEUM CIRCULATION

OFFICE CIRCULATION

TRIANGLE BLOCK / CINEMA CIRCULATION

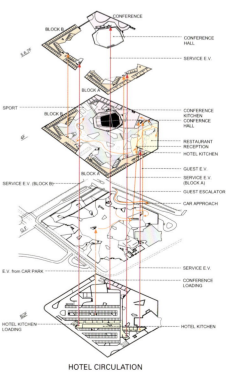

HOTEL CIRCULATION

Diagram

Serpentine Gallery Pavilion 2002
London, UK
2002

View from southeast

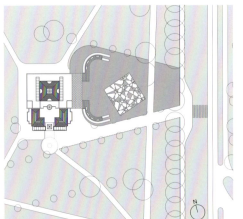

Site plan S=1:2000

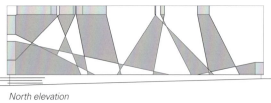

North elevation

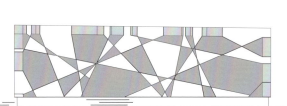

East elevation S=1:250

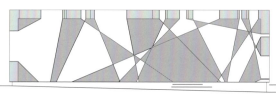

South elevation

West elevation

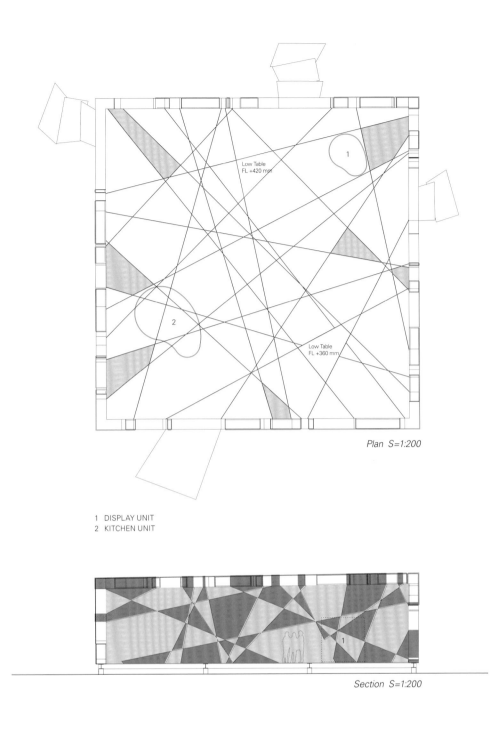

Plan S=1:200

1 DISPLAY UNIT
2 KITCHEN UNIT

Section S=1:200

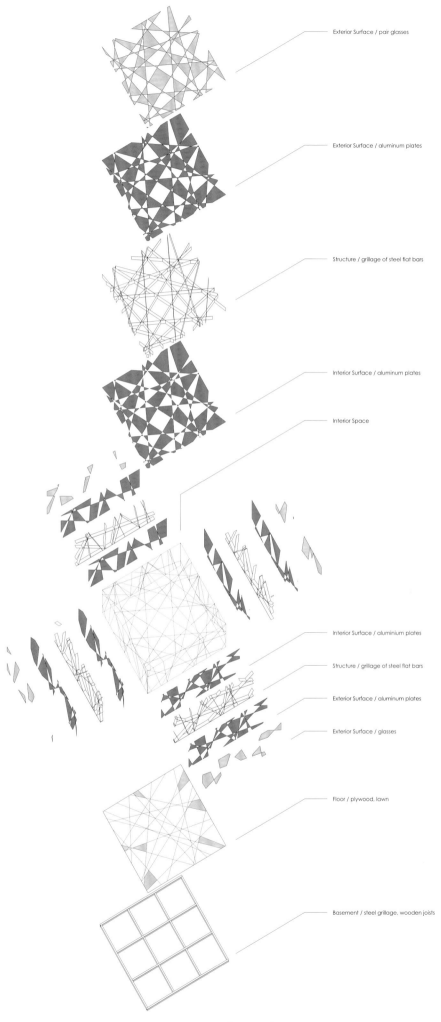

Axonometrics

We challenged to make an experimental architecture in London that could only be achieved as a temporary pavilion that exists for only 3 months in summer. We were faced by fundamental questions concerning the shape and surface that architecture has.

Firstly, an 18 m x 18 m x 4.5 m simple geometry shape is established and then covered with random crossing lines for its structural configuration. In response to our idea, structural engineer Cecil Balmond suggested us to adapt a fractal form of a rotating square.

Normally, square-shaped roofs are segmented at the perpendicular intersections of a grid, but his proposal was to repetitively link the center of the sides and to embed back into the original square while rotating it. By using the rotation as a precondition rule, the rotation of the square will grow out of the boundaries of the original square, and a square can be created on the extension line through developing a rule to link the center points of the sides to 1/3 of the respective sides next to it. As a result, the straight extended line creates a pattern that can draw a spiral limitlessly. On this pattern, the expansion plan of the cube was made 3-dimensional. The beams that are made of 550 mm steel plates compose the roof and walls as a continuous structure, with thicknesses varying between 12 mm - 50 mm according to the stress at each point. Aluminum panels and glass are set separately for the surface of the structure.

As with the richness of the changes in nature due to simple processes of growth, spaces with diversity emerged in this architecture based on a rotation algorithm. The architecture seizes these changes, and allows human activities to be carried out as if it was within a body of dynamism that is free and open.

サーペンタイン・ギャラリー・パヴィリオン 2002

夏の3ヶ月のみ存在するという短期間の仮設パヴィリオンだからこそ可能な，実験的建築への挑戦がロンドンで行われた。建築のもつ形式や，表層に対する根源的な問い掛けがなされた。

まず18m×18m，高さ4.5mの単純な幾何学形態を設定し，その表面をランダムに交錯するラインによって構造を成立させる。これに対して構造家セシル・バルモンドは，入れ子状に回転運動する正方形のパターンを提案した。

通常，正方形の屋根は直交グリッドの梁によって分節されるが，彼の提案した方法は，各辺の中点を結ぶ操作を繰り返し，正方形を回転させながら元の正方形の中に埋め込んでいく。これらの回転のルールを前提とし，辺の中点と隣り合う辺の1/3点を結ぶという操作へと発展させると，正方形は回転しながら元の正方形の境界を越え，延長線上に正方形が見出される。その結果，延長された直線が無限に螺旋を描きながら続く運動のパターンが現れる。このパターン上に，キューブ展開図を描き立体化する。屋根と壁は連続する構造体で，梁成550mmのスティールプレートからなり，その部位の応力に従って厚みは12mm～50mmになる。構造体の表層は，アルミパネルとガラスによって交互に貼り分けられた。

単純な成長のプロセスにより自然が変化に富むのと同様，回転運動のアルゴリズムにより，建築に多様で密実な世界が現れる。建築はあらゆる変化を受け入れ，人々に運動のダイナミズムの中に身体をおいているかのような感覚を与え，自由で開放的な振る舞いをもたらした。

View toward Serpentine gallery

Interior

Entry on west

View from southwest

Shinonome Canal Court CODAN Block 2
Koto, Tokyo, Japan
1999–2003

View toward Ito's block from Yamamoto's block

View from southeast: Yamamoto's block on left and Ito's block on right. S-curved avenue is running through all six blocks

Shinonome Canal Court is a 2000-unit apartment complex developed by the Urban Development Corporation (UDC, now Urban Renaissance Agency (UR)) and built from 1999 to 2005 over landfill in the Shinonome area of Koto, Tokyo.

Six teams of different architects and UDC members designed six distinct residential blocks. Discussion meetings were held to adjust the design to achieve consistency within each block. We established basic rules so that the residential buildings, with a maximum 47 m in height, were to be arranged around an S-curved avenue running through all six blocks, while low-rise commercial facilities and a day-care center were to be arranged to face the main avenue.

The second block, for which our team was responsible, consists of 290 residences and low-rise section that houses commercial facilities, a children's day care center and public facilities for the residents.

For the low-rise section, we collaborated with Riken Yamamoto & Field Shop, who were also responsible for the design of Block 1. We connected the second floor with a bridge to make it more open. This rooftop plaza created a proper sense of distance between the different residential buildings, achieving a pleasant living environment despite the high population density.

By using a central corridor style for the two residential buildings, we achieved a large floor area within a compact volume.

In the 14-story building, we used a structure subdivided into 3 m-spans which became the unit measurement of the rooms. On the S-curved avenue side, we arranged terraces with a 6 m-width and height in a rhythmical pattern. These terraces, which are used as private gardens by the residents, create cadence in the space, and pull light and breezes into the otherwise closed central corridor. These terraces also helped generate over 50 different floor plans, with units that connect vertically or horizontally through the terraces.

In the 10-story building, we made use of the 6 m-spans and designed units with fewer partitions, so the residents can freely enjoy a greater feeling of open space.

Different unit designs in this project suit various lifestyle requirements in order to accommodate the ongoing problems of the modern city, which include the increasingly blurred line between office and residence, and evolving family structures.

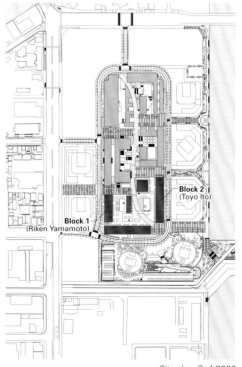

Site plan S=1:8000

Connection of low-rise

Corridor

Duplex

東雲キャナルコート CODAN 2街区

「東雲キャナルコート」は，東京都江東区東雲に位置する埋め立て地に都市基盤整備公団(現・都市機構)によって1999年から2005年にかけて計画された2,000戸規模の集合住宅である。

異なる建築家チームと公団とで，都市居住をテーマに六つの街区をデザインした。街区の調和を図るためにデザイン会議で議論をし，設計の調整が行われた。六つの街区を貫くS字アベニューを中心に，最高高さ47mの住棟を周辺に配置すること，低層の商業施設や保育園などがS字アベニュー側に開かれることなどが基本ルールとなった。

我々が担当する2街区は，290戸の住宅と，商業施設，保育園，住宅共用部などからなる低層部によって構成されている。

特に低層部については，隣の1街区を担当する山本理顕設計工場との協働で進められた。2階レベルをブリッジで繋ぎ，開かれた場所とした。この屋上広場によってそれぞれの住棟に程良い距離が保たれ，高密度ながらも快適な居住環境を実現した。

また2棟ある住棟は，どちらも中廊下式を採用したことで，コンパクトなヴォリュームで大きな床面積を確保することができた。

14階建ての住棟では，個室の単位となる3mスパンの構造体を採用し，S字アベニュー側に幅と高さとも6mのテラスをリズミカルに配置した。居住者が専用の庭として利用できるこのテラスは，空間に抑揚を与え，本来なら閉鎖的になってしまう中廊下にも適度な光や風をもたらした。そしてテラスを介して上下または左右に繋がる住宅など，50種類をこえる多彩なバリエーションが生まれた。

一方，10階建ての住棟では，6mスパンを活かして間仕切りの少ない住宅とした。居住者は，平面的な広がりを自由に利用することができる。

いずれの住宅も，オフィスと住まいの境界の曖昧化，多様な家族のあり方など，現代都市がかかえる問題を意識しながら，様々な住まいのあり方を提供している。

Typical floor S=1:600

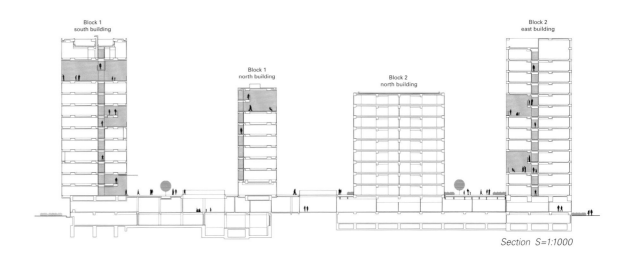

Duplex with private terrace

Section S=1:1000

Unit plan (duplex)

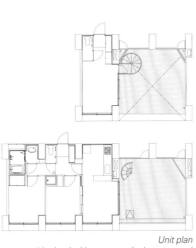

*Unit plan
(duplex / with annex and private terrace)*

Unit plan (SOHO)

*Unit plan S=1:300
(with see-through entrance)*

Unit plan (with annex and private terrace)

37

Overall view from northwest

Matsumoto Performing Arts Center
Matsumoto, Nagano, Japan
2000–04

This Arts Center is the main facility for Japan's largest musical event: the Saito Kinen Festival (since 2015, Seiji Ozawa Matsumoto Festival). The complex consists of a large, 1,800-seat hall that can be used for opera performances, and a 250-seat theater. In 1999, our proposal was selected through a competition process.

The site is unusually deep and narrow compared to its frontage, so we decided to take a drastic approach in the arrangement of the theater. We configured the facility so that the large hall is turned backwards to the front of the building, and built a gently sloping staircase around the site, as well as a foyer in the deepest part of the building. This design alleviated the inherent difference between the front and back sections of the site.

Our idea of making the whole building into a theatrical space was emphasized by the three-dimensional circulation, which made one feel as if he was being drawn into the facility from the streets. Beneath the foyer, we were able to create a dressing room that captures light from the outside. The back-to-back configuration of the large and small halls not only made the services from the center of the site possible, but also put the maximum volume of flytower at the center of the building, which helped to reduce volume impact at the edge of the neighboring residences and a nearby shrine. Thus a single layout solution enabled us to achieve multiple effects beyond our imagination.

The entire building is wrapped in a gentle GRC panel curtain wall inlaid with numerous glass pieces of various shapes. By reinforcing interiority and controlling light, we attempted to physicalize the experience of gradually melting into the thick darkness of the stage.

The curving balconies and gradations of wine red amplified the elegant and sensual aspects of the large hall. We filled the spaces with metaphors of fluctuating waves and water surfaces, such as the curved lines that cover the entire surface of the walls. Here, different materials become exposed, as if to orchestrate a grand symphony. During the 20th century, abstraction was achieved by selecting plain and clear materials, and minimizing the presence of the building itself. This project embraces a change in direction from such philosophy by exploring a new kind of abstraction that appeals to our sense of touch.

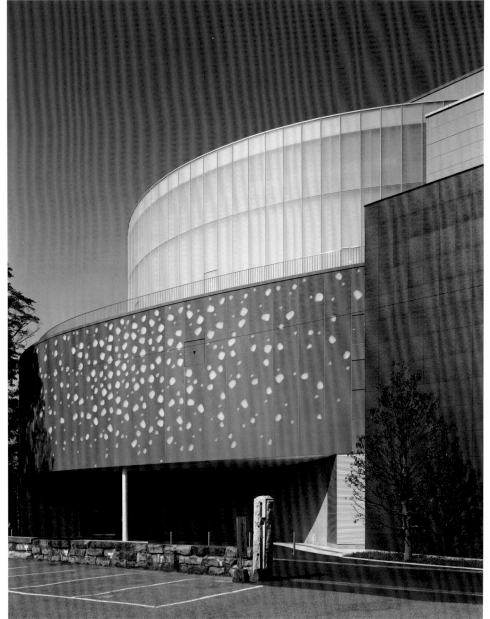
Backstage entrance

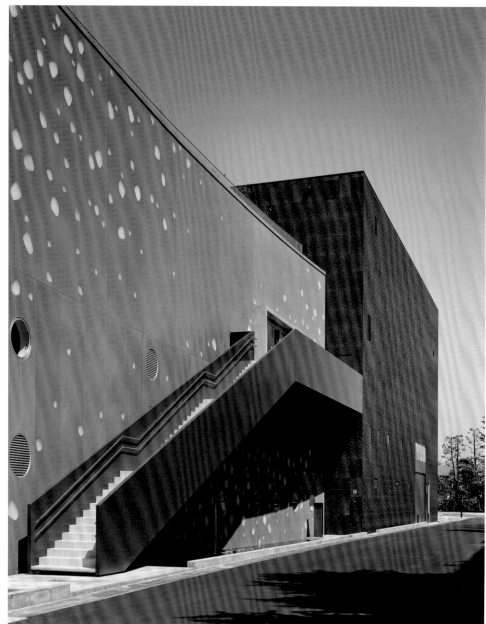
Staircase on east

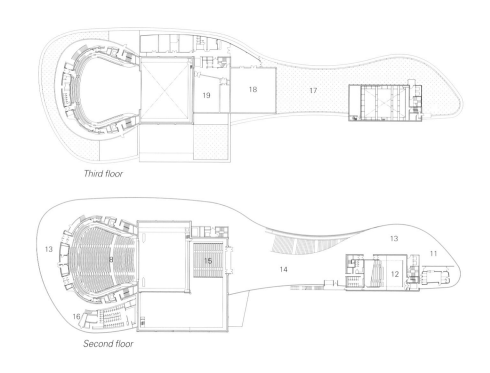
Third floor

Second floor

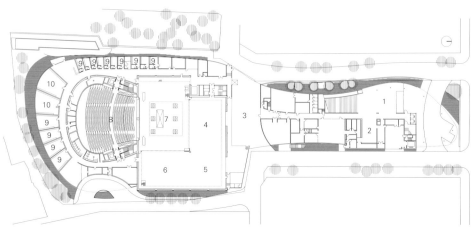
First floor S=1:1600

Evening view from north: space behind glazed wall above main entrance is restaurant

1 ENTRANCE HALL
2 INFORMATION
3 DELIVERY ENTRANCE
4 REAR STAGE
5 REAR SIDE STAGE
6 SIDE STAGE
7 STAGE
8 LARGE HALL
9 DRESSING ROOM
10 ATELIER
11 RESTAURANT
12 SMALL HALL
13 FOYER
14 THEATER PARK
15 ROLL BACK SEATS
16 BUFFET
17 ROOF GARDEN
18 REHEARSAL STUDIO
19 STUDIO

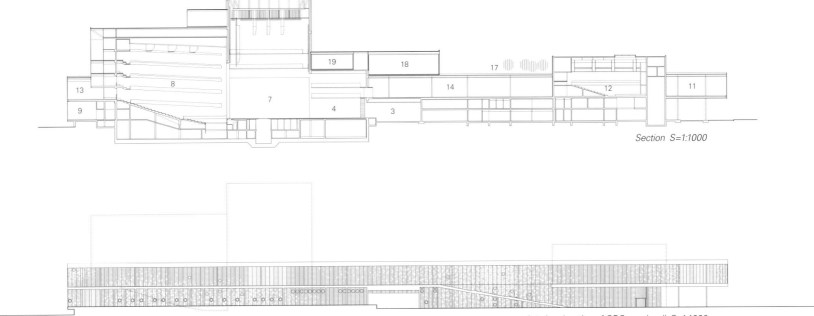

Section S=1:1000

Interior elevation of GRC panel wall S=1:1000

まつもと市民芸術館

日本最大級の音楽イベント，サイトウ・キネン・フェスティバル(現セイジ・オザワ 松本フェスティバル)のメイン会場。オペラにも対応可能な1,800席の大ホールと，250席の本格的な演劇ホールのコンプレックスで，1999年にプロポーザルコンペティションで選ばれた。

敷地は間口に対して異様なまでに細長く奥行きがあり，通常考えられる劇場の配置をあえて裏切る手法を採用した。つまり，大ホールを前面から反対向きに配置することで，敷地の外周を巡るような緩やかな階段状のアプローチと最奥部にホワイエを設け，これが功を奏し敷地が持つ表裏の区別を相対化した。

街から引き込まれたかのような立体的な街路のイメージは，建物全体を劇場化する私たちの構想を後押しした。ホワイエの下階には，外光を積極的に取り込む楽屋を設けることができた。大小二つのホールが背中合わせになることで，敷地の中央からサービスが可能になっただけでなく，最大ヴォリュームを生むフライタワーが中央に寄り，背後の住宅地や隣接する神社への圧迫感も和らいだ。ひとつのレイアウトの展開が，思わぬほど大きな波紋へと広がった。

建物全体は，無数の不定形のガラスを象嵌したGRCパネルのカーテンウォールによる，柔らかい形状で包み込んだ。内部性を強化し光を制限することで，舞台の濃密な闇へと次第に溶け込む体験を空間化しようと試みた。

大ホール内も波打つバルコニーやワインレッドのグラデーションによって，優美でいて官能的な側面もつくり出した。他にも，壁面を埋め尽くす曲線のレリーフなど，至る所にゆらめく波や水面のイメージを満たしていった。ここでは様々な素材感が露わになり，それらがシンフォニーを奏でるがごとく饗宴している。素材をプレーンで透明にし，存在そのものを希薄にすることで獲得してきた20世紀的抽象性に対して，触覚に訴えかけるような新しい抽象性を探求する大きな転換となった意義がそこにはある。

GRC panel wall: some openings with clear glass give exterior views to foyer

GRC panel wall: sectional details S=1:120

Entrance hall: grand staircase to foyer on second floor

Large hall

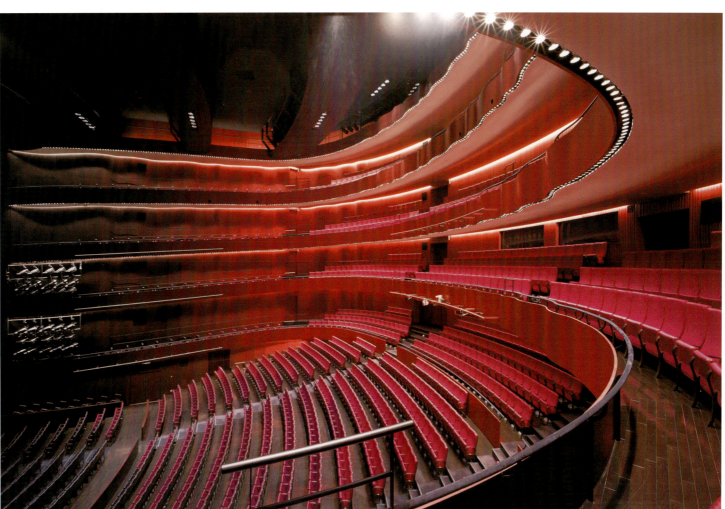

Large hall: curved walls given color gradations

Foyer on second floor: staircase to balcony level of large hall

TOD'S Omotesando Building
Shibuya, Tokyo, Japan
2002–04

Not only do the best brands gather and compete with each other on fashion mecca Omotesando, this is also a place for new creations. Even though *TOD'S* is a global brand, this Italian shoes and bags maker is well known for its traditional craftsmanship, with almost all its products made by hand. For this project, we wanted to build a concrete building that displays a strong vitality within the rows of inorganic glass buildings that line up on Omotesando. This is a challenge to express a new type of abstraction.

During the 20th century, it was taboo to show a specific icon in abstract architecture expressions. However, we wanted to consider materialized objects as a "new icon", and we tried to pursue abstraction by using a method that is different to the conventional way of strengthening pure geometry. We achieved this by overlapping abstract patterns of zelkova trees on Omotesando, and wrapping the building with it as the exterior wall of exposed concrete. Because of the narrow width of front elevation facing the street, the symbolic meaning of the architecture is strengthened by wrapping this zelkova pattern around all four sides of the building. From the exterior, the pattern can be observed like the silhouette of the rows of zelkova trees that line up along Omotesando, while from the interior, it creates a space like being in a forest covered by trees. An important characteristic is the expressions of the concrete and glass that sits on the same surface. Glass is inlayed into concrete with a thickness of 300 mm, and each side supports slabs that have a span of 10-15 m. The columns, beams, brace and skin that make up the properties of the building are all integrated together to create a boundary against the exterior. The pattern also fulfills the demands of the program by putting large openings on the lower sections that correspond to the street below, and smaller openings on the higher sections. Overlapping the zelkova patterns forms a network-skeleton structural body, and we were able to realize a building body that is suitable, but different to the structural mechanism of trees.

View from north.
Relation between row of zelkova and wall pattern

TOD'S 表参道ビル

ファッションブランドの聖地である表参道は，ブランドビジネスが集結・競合する一方，新たなクリエーションの場ともなっている。「TOD'S」というイタリアの靴・バッグのブランドは，世界的なブランドでありながら殆どが手づくりで，職人芸に支えられているという特徴がある。ここでは，美しいが無機質なガラス張りの建物が林立する表参道に，力強く生き活きとしたコンクリートの建物をつくりたいと考えた。これは，新しい抽象性を表現する試みである。

20世紀の抽象的な建築表現においては，明確なアイコンを表現することはタブーであった。しかし，ここで我々はあえて具象的なものを「新しいアイコン」として想定し，従来のような純粋幾何学を強化する方法とは違った抽象性を追及しようとした。表参道のケヤキを抽象化してオーバーラップさせ，コンクリート打放しの外壁として建物を覆い込む。前面道路に面した間口が狭いので，ケヤキ・パターンを四周に巡らすことによって，シンボル性を高めている。ケヤキ・パターンは，外部においては表参道のケヤキ並木をシルエットとして象ったように見え，内部においては樹木に覆われた森の中のような空間をつくる。ここで重要なのは，コンクリートとガラスがひとつの面となった表現である。厚さ300mmのコンクリートにガラスが同面で象嵌され，できた1枚の壁面がスパン10〜15mのスラブを支えている。柱，梁，ブレース，外皮という建築を構成する要素が，一体化されて外部との境界をつくっている。これらの面は，下方はストリートに対して大きな開口を設け，上方は小さな開口を多様に展開するという，プログラム上の要望も満たしている。ケヤキ・パターンがオーバーラップすることによって，ネットワーク状の構造体が形成され，ここには，木とは違う構造力学的な合理性にかなう躯体が顕れる。

Evening view

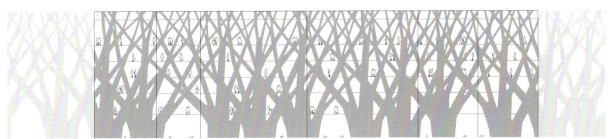

Wall pattern

Windows flush with wall

49

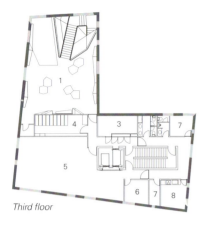
Third floor

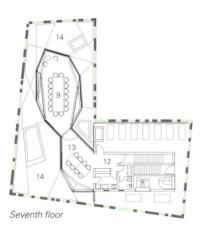
Seventh floor

Second floor

Sixth floor

First floor S=1:500

Fifth floor

Basement

Fourth floor

Entrance

Section S=1:400

1 SHOP
2 OFFICE ENTRANCE
3 MACHINE ROOM
4 STOCKROOM
5 OFFICE
6 STORAGE
7 LOCKER ROOM
8 LUNCH SPACE
9 MEETING ROOM
10 SHOWROOM
11 PARTY ROOM
12 HALL
13 DINING ROOM
14 ROOF GARDEN

Party room on sixth floor *Penthouse on seventh floor. View toward meeting room from dining room*

Second floor

View from landing at first floor: second floor above and basement below

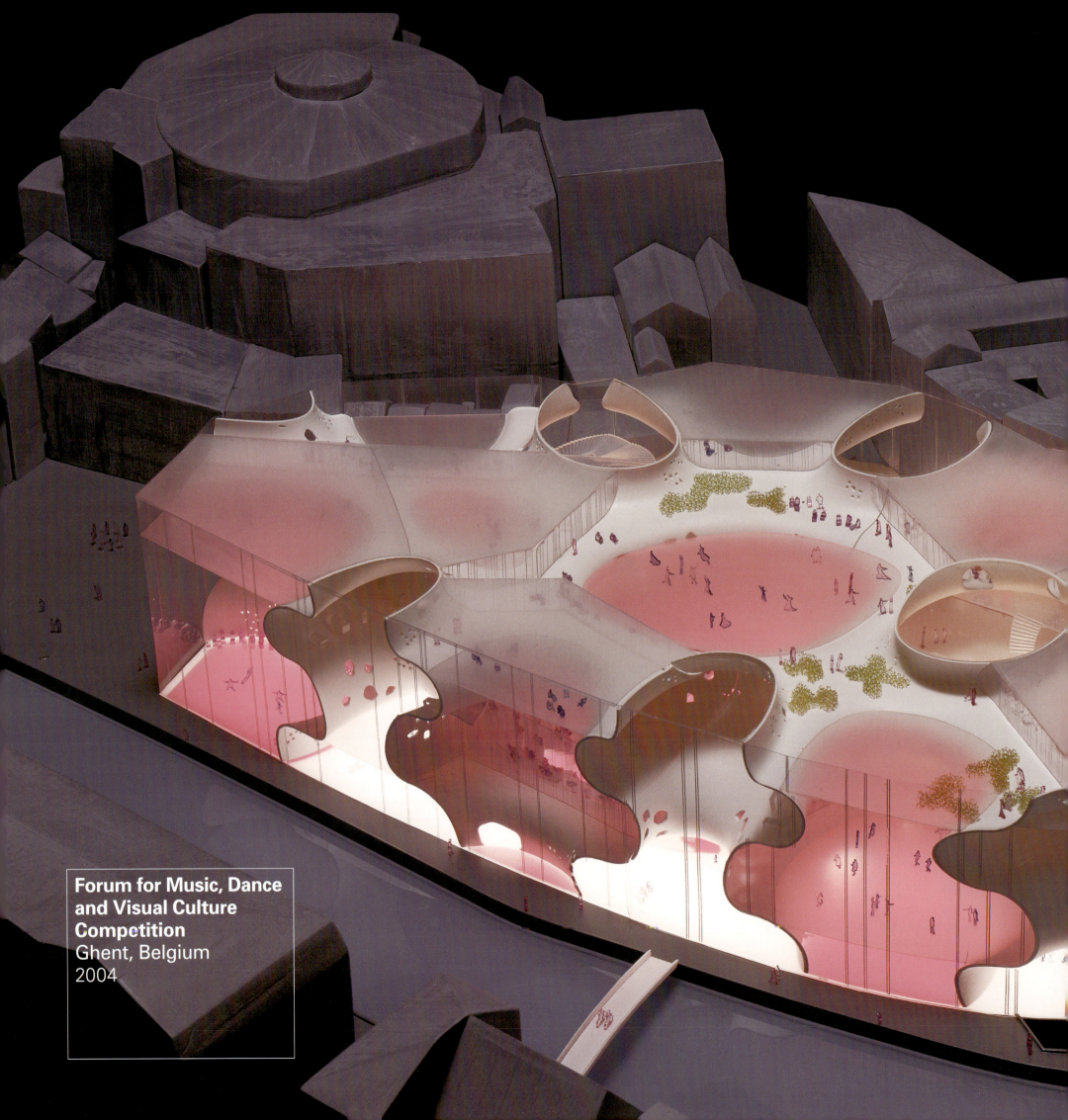

Forum for Music, Dance and Visual Culture Competition
Ghent, Belgium
2004

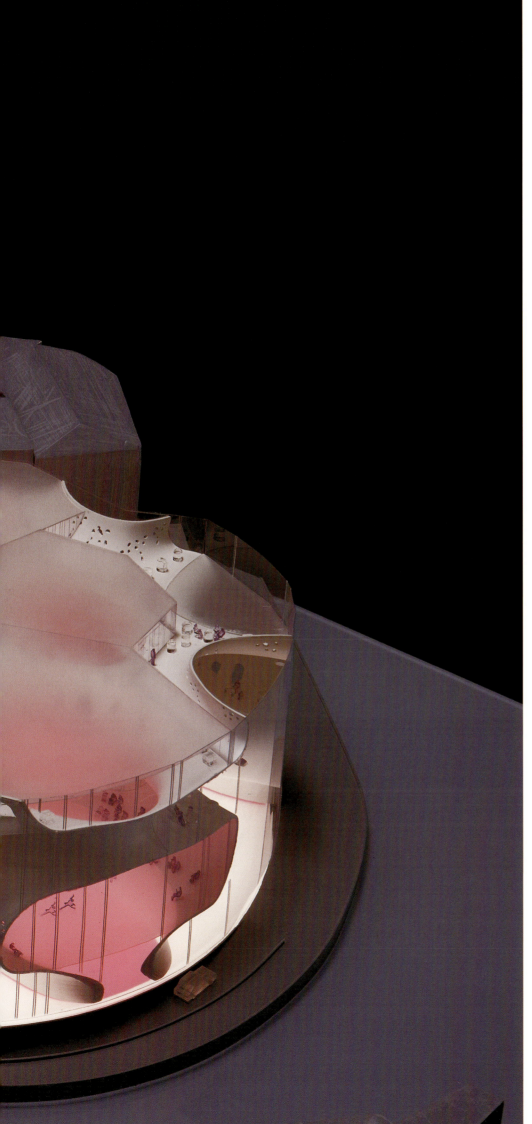

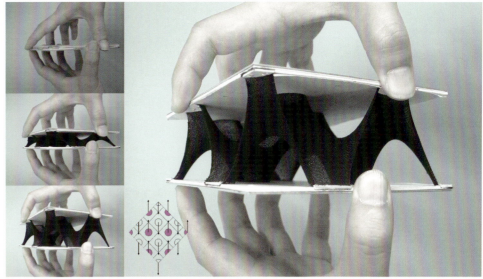

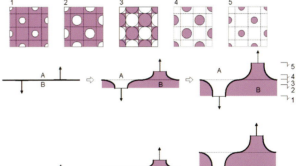

Basic system
Starting from one surface, dividing it into A & B zones, the A zones are pulled down, the B zones are pulled up. The surface is stretched between these two movements. They create continuos spaces, existing next to each other, but divided from each other by this one same surface.

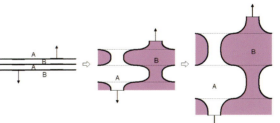

Combined system
This system can be expanded in the third dimension by adding layers of alternationg A and B spaces, resulting in an intertwined three-dimensional tube system. Connections between A and B caves can be made by cutting hole into the thin dividing skins in between them.

While the old city of Ghent in Belgium has the depth and layers of history in its envelope, the activities of people are spilled over into the public spaces of the street. People are freely performing something and playing music in plaza, intricate alleys, or the stair steps of the buildings. We thought of bringing the potential energy of people found throughout these urban spaces into the proposal of this building that provides a place for expressing cultures in music, dance and visual art forms, by connecting this architecture to the city scape rather than confronting.

The required programs of a concert hall with the capacity of 1,800 seats, rehearsal studios for dancers and orchestras, and the rooms for event such as workshops are incorporated into a three-dimensional, city street-like network, instead of providing generic spaces and programs of a typical concert hall. We came up to a method of giving the order to those complex, yet successive cave-like spaces with a simple but clearly configured system; first we prepared a basic configuration in a layer with two alternate circular zones defined in A and B within a uniformly configured grid; second, we prepared an alternative configuration with the same circular zones, while zone A and B is shifted vertically in one grid unit; then those zones in different layers are connected by membranes, producing two unique spaces separated by three-dimensional curved surface. For those two spaces, one is named as 'Sound Cave' as the space is filled with sounds of performers by contain an auditorium and work shops within it. The other is called 'Urban Cave' to become a foyer space, which connects to the city environment and invites the visitors spontaneously from the city street. Both spaces will constantly affect and influence each other.

The vertically penetrating 'Ana = hole/ hollow' in the volume of *Sendai Mediatheque* is now achieving the opportunity to continue in either vertical or horizontal orientation without loosing the relative relationship among them, forming a network with full of variety. We discovered a principle theory of configuring a space with organic quality, where the notion of 'inside and outside' is coexisting within a space. In other words, it is a new essential order of an architecture beyond the notion of space based on Cartéien Grid and Coordinate. This proposal was not accepted in the competition, but we continued to develop in the project, *National Taichung Theater (pp.268-279)*.

53

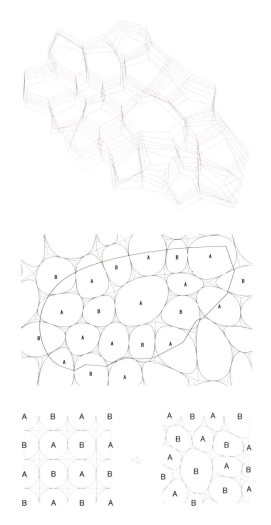

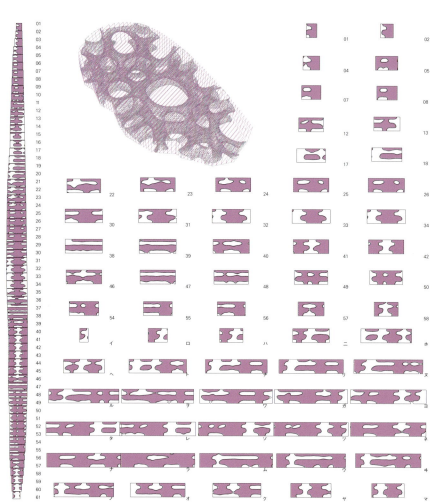

Geology of Sound Cave

Geometry
Starting from a basic geometric pattern, the system gets further distarted according to the functional requirements of sizes of space. In this way the orthogonal grid system can be transposed to a much freer geometry dividing the A and B area, inducing more complex and dynamic spaces.

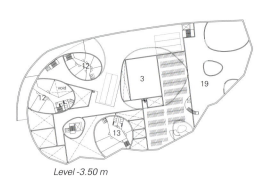

Level -3.50 m

Level -6.00 m S=1:1800

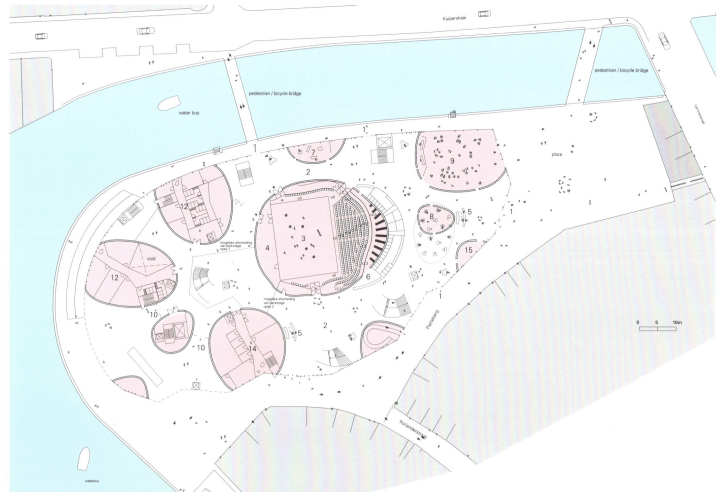

Level +0.00 m S=1:1000

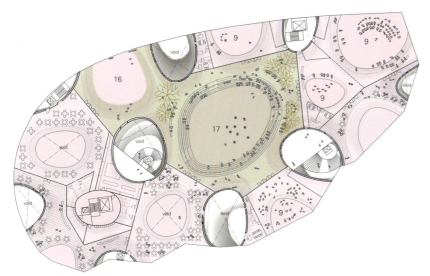

Level +19.00 m

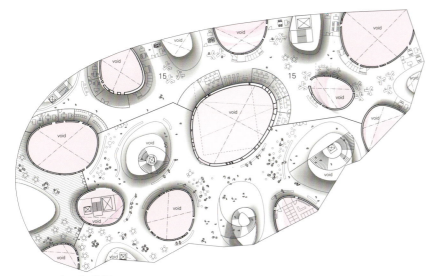

Level +13.00 m

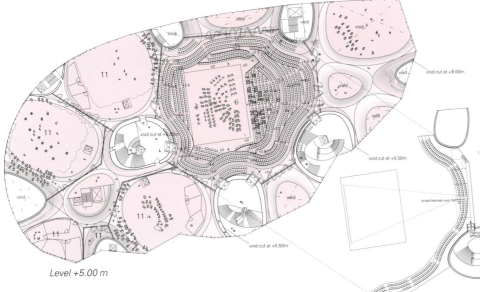

Level +5.00 m

South elevation S=1:1000

1 PUBLIC ENTRANCE	8 PUBLIC WORKSHOP	14 INSTRUMENT STORAGE
2 FOYER	9 ATELIER	AND PRACTICE ROOM
3 AUDITORIUM	10 ENTRANCE FOR ARTISTS	15 OFFICE
4 BACKSTAGE	(OPTIONAL PUBLIC ENTRANCE)	16 ROOF GARDEN
5 RECEPTION	11 REHEARSAL ROOM	17 OPEN-AIR STAGE
6 CLOAK	12 DRESSING ROOM	18 RESTAURANT
7 SHOP	13 ANTEROOM	19 TECHNICAL AREA

55

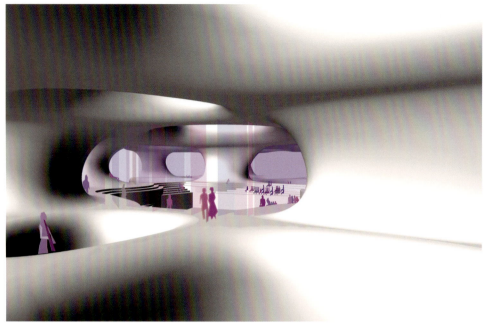
Sound Cave

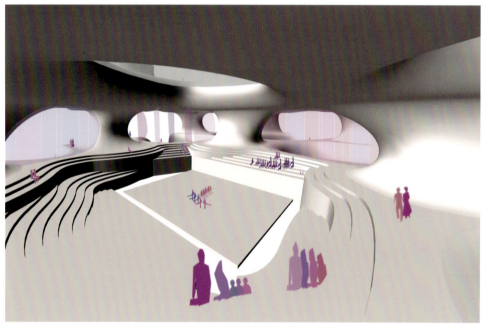
Auditorium

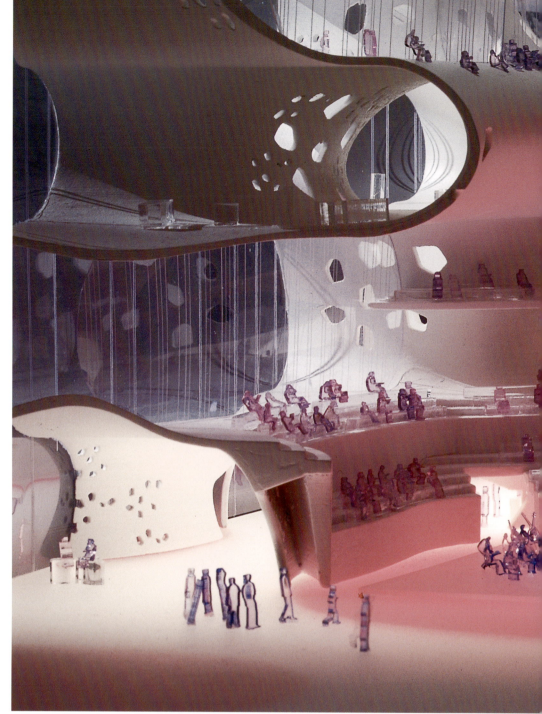

ゲント市文化フォーラム コンペティション応募案

ベルギーの古都ゲントは、歴史の重層性が残る街でありながら、人々の活動は外部空間に溢れ出している。街の広場や入り組む路地、階段などで自由に演奏やパフォーマンスをしていたりする。我々は、音楽、ダンス、視覚文化を表現する場を提案するコンペティションにおいて、建築が都市と対峙するのではなく連続することで、都市空間に潜在する人々のエネルギーを建築の内部に引き込みたいと考えた。

求められていた1,800席のコンサートホール、ダンスやオーケストラのためのリハーサルスタジオ、ワークショップなど諸室のための空間を、通常の形式化されたホールとしてではなく、立体的な街路のネットワークの中に組み入れようと試みた。我々は、どこまでも連続し複雑に入り組む洞窟的な空間を、単純で明快な構成のシステムに基づいて、秩序づける方法へと至る。均質なグリッド内に交互にA、B、二つの円形ゾーンを描いたものと、上下で1コマずらして描いたものを、膜で結び積層させることで、3次元曲面で隔てられた二つの空間ができる。ひとつは「サウンドケーブ」と呼ばれ、オーディトリアムやワークショップを含み、パフォーマーなどが集まる音で満たされる空間となる。もうひとつの「アーバンケーブ」は街と連続するホワイエとなり、来館者は街路から自然と招き入れられる。両空間は互いに絶え間なく影響し合う。

「せんだいメディアテーク」において、ヴォリュームを垂直に貫通していた「アナ」は、「ゲント市文化フォーラム」では相対関係をもちながら、水平にも垂直方向にも連続して絡み合い、変化に富むネットワークとなった。我々は、「ゲント」において、外部と内部が同時に存在する、生物的空間を生成する構成原理を見出したのである。言い換えれば、デカルト座標に基づいた空間概念を超えた新たな建築の秩序である。この提案はコンペティションでは採用されなかったが、「台中国家歌劇院」(pp.268-279)で引き継がれ展開される。

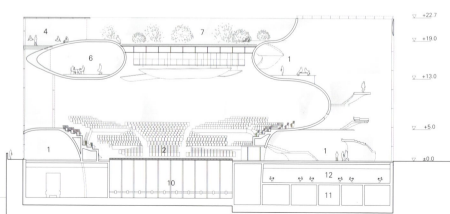
Cross section S=1:600

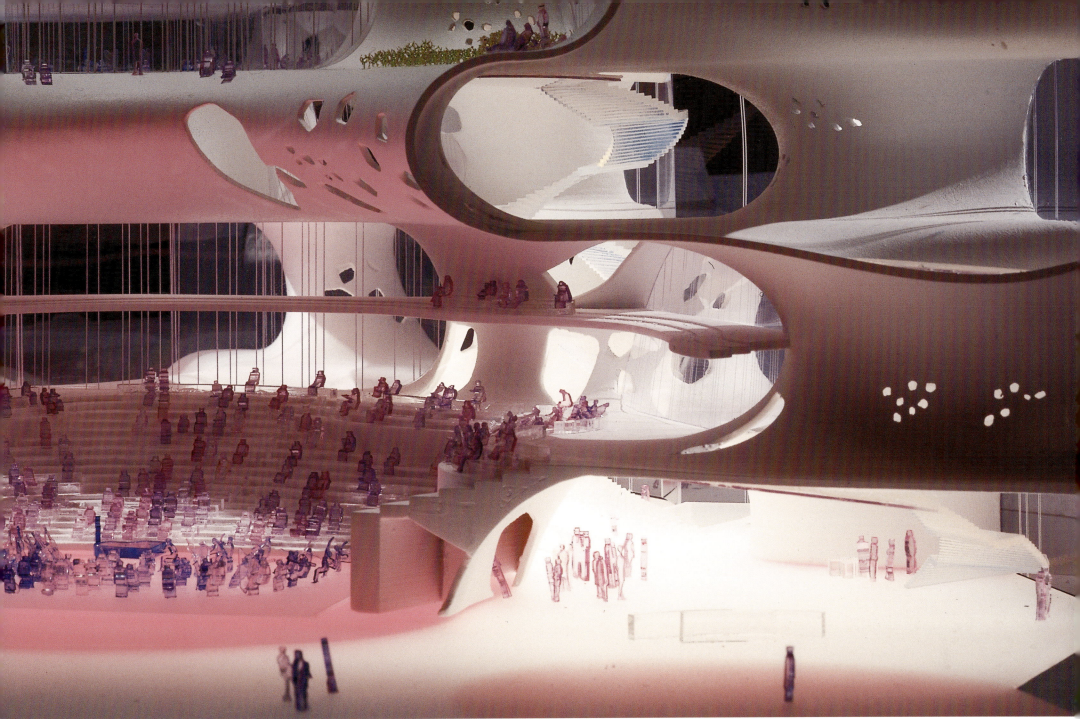

Auditorium

1 FOYER
2 STAGE
3 CLOAK
4 PUBLIC WORKSHOP
5 REHEARSAL ROOM
6 OFFICE
7 ROOF GARDEN
8 RESTAURANT
9 ACCOMMODATION AND LOCKER ROOM
10 SPACE FOR MOVING STAGE
11 TECHNICAL AREA
12 BICYCLE-PARKING
13 PARKING

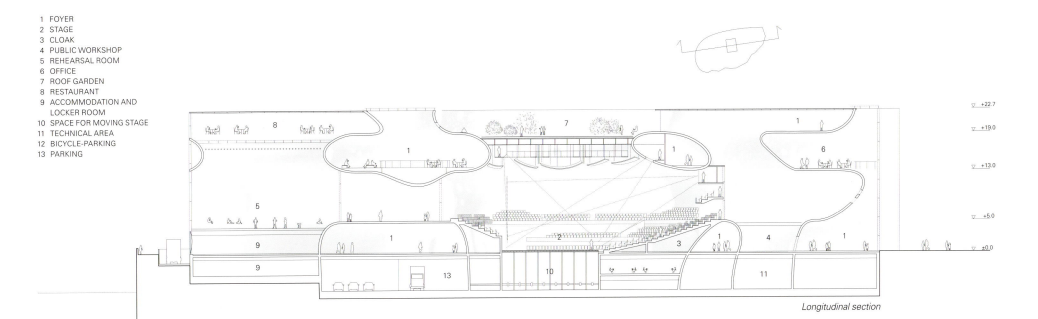

Longitudinal section

Gavia Park in Madrid
Madrid, Spain
2004–

The river bank vestige of Gavia River, located a few kilometer south of Madrid, was used to be a ground with surrounding greenery, filled with lives by the aid of the river water—but yet nowadays the water has dried up to bare the ground surface, appearing as a desolate field. However, water veins have survived under the surface of the ground, therefore it was decided to revive and reactivate the area utilizing the water veins, creating a sustainable new urban water park standing on an ecological point of view. The international competition was held in 2003, and it is how this project has started.

We thought of a method generating a topographic condition directly from the flow of the water, as we named the concept the 'watertrees'. Two types of watertrees are defined as the 'ridge watertree' and the 'valley watertree', and the topographic condition is generated as if like a fabric, sawing the ridge and valley conditions together. Each 'watertree' maintains its geometric form, while they grows up in fractal manner by increasing the pattern of a folding, to produce a place of cultivating various types of ecological systems as an environment full of variety. The water springs up from the ridge part, and leads to the bottom of the valley through the surface or the underground of the terrane, while the water is supplied by recycling the reclaimed water treated simply by the waste water disposal system located near. The water treatment is operated by pumping up the waste water to the center of the 'ridge watertree' and pour the water radially over the ground surface. The slowly flowing water is primarily treated by the ultraviolet rays of the sun light and the sedimentation of the sludge, while the water is further treated biologically by the plants and the microorganisms on the slopes. The original waste water is gradually treated to a clear, safe water by the time it reaches to the 'valley watertree'.

The series of water supporting system revitalizes the dried up Gavia riverside, and recreate a water park around it. While the 'watertree' is the purification system based on the cycle of nature, it also produces various horizontal landmarks on the ground in each independent geographical pattern. The bird's-eye view will reveal the scenery as if the trees are growing up from the dry earth ground.

Site plan S=1:20000

Revitalized Gavia River (right)

Planting Watertrees in the valley in order to plant trees

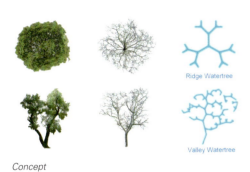

Concept

ガヴィア公園

マドリッドから南に数km離れた，ガヴィア河畔跡。かつて，水で潤い緑に包まれた生命に満ち溢れていた大地は，今では干上がった地肌が剥き出しになり荒涼とした風景が広がっている。しかし，地表面下には未だ途絶えることなく水脈が生き長らえており，これを蘇らせエコロジカルな視点に立った持続可能な新しい水の都市公園をつくり出したい。そこからこのプロジェクトは始まり，2003年に国際コンペティションが行われた。

我々は水の流れそのものから地形を生成させる方法として水の木（ウォーターツリー）を考えた。2種類のウォーターツリーは，それぞれ尾根のウォーターツリーと谷のウォーターツリーに分けられる。地形は，尾根と谷を縫い合わせるファブリックのように生成される。ウォーターツリーは共に幾何学的な形態を持ちながら，フラクタルに成長していくことで地形の襞を増殖させ，多様な生態系を育む場をつくり出し，変化に富んだ環境を生み出す。水は尾根から湧き出し，地表や地中を伝って谷へと導かれる。水源は，近くの下水処理施設で簡易処理された，中水レベルの水を再利用することで賄われる。これを尾根のウォーターツリーの中心にポンプアップし，放射状にゆっくりと水が流れることで太陽光による紫外線浄化と沈殿によって1次処理が行われる。さらに水は，斜面を通って植物や土の中の微生物によって生物浄化され，谷のウォーターツリーに到達する頃には十分に澄んだ安全性の高い水へと純化は進行する。

こうして一連の水の系が支える仕組みが，枯れたガヴィア河を蘇らせ，その周囲に親水公園をつくり出す。ウォーターツリーは自然のサイクルに基づいた浄化システムであると同時に，独立した幾何学的パターンによって水平のランドマークを随所に生み出し，その風景は空から眺めるとあたかも乾いた大地から芽生えた木々のように現れる。

この公園の計画は，建設半ばでスペインの経済危機に遭遇し，中断したままとなっている。

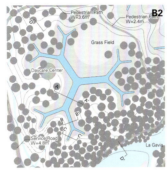

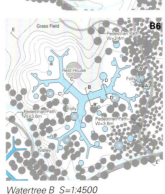

Watertree B S=1:4500

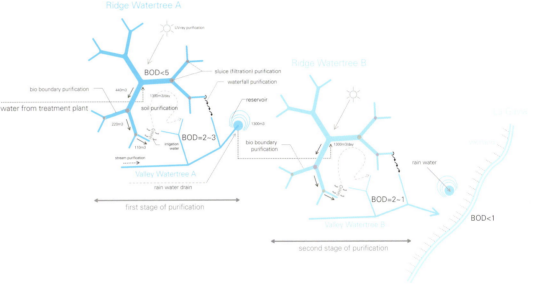

Diagram: landform creation

Diagram: water system

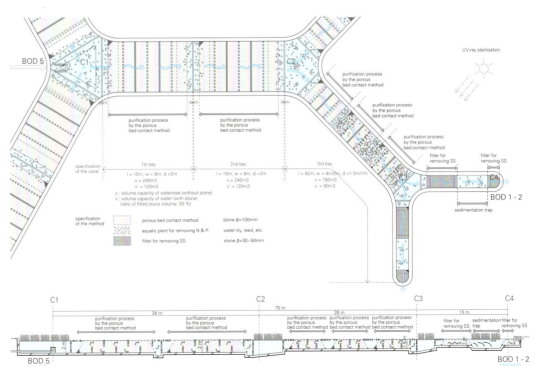

Ridge watertree S=1:600

59

**Island City Centrtal Park
"GRIN GRIN"**
Fukuoka, Japan
2002–05

Island City is an artificial island covering approximately 40 ha on the eastern side of Hakata Bay. To create a new place for nature on otherwise flat and empty land, the city of Fukuoka came up with a project to create a 1.53 ha park and a 1.7 km-long green belt, and in the fall of 2002 held a competition for the design of the park and its central facility. Our selected proposal included a plan to build mounds and craters of various sizes, and create a dynamically shaped landscape that encourages various activities among visitors.

GRIN GRIN is the Central Park's main facility, and the first building to be constructed on the island. Our proposal, which was found in the process of exploring a way to make a place in the landscape and blur the separation between the landscape/architecture or inside/outside, was to cover three separate interior spaces with a twisting, continuous shell.

The idea was rationalized through Mutsuro Sasaki's "Evolutionary Structural Optimization." A three-dimensional curved surface is converted to a set of points on a 2 m-grid. By gradually displacing each point, based on a certain mechanical premise, the 400 mm-thick free-form shell with maximum width of 40 m takes on a stable shape. The structural technique, designed to capture a certain moment within a free-flowing fluidity, coincided with our vision of creating an architecture that physicalizes an instance in the dynamic spiral.

Rather than relying on the modulor and pure geometry generated by connective joints of industrialization, we created a seamless, animated building and aimed for a dynamic architecture that is free from all formalities.

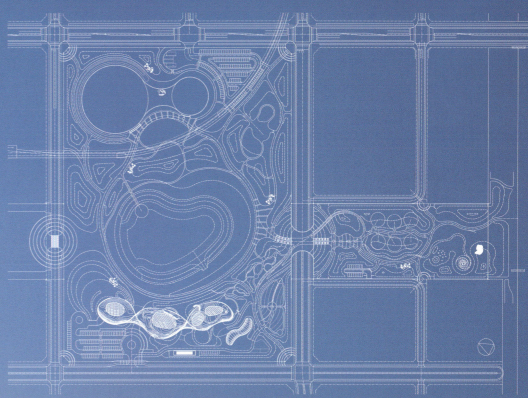

Site plan S=1:5000

アイランドシティ中央公園中核施設 ぐりんぐりん

博多湾東部に造成されたアイランドシティは，約40haに及ぶ広大な人工島である。福岡市は，何もない平坦な土地に新たな自然をつくりだすことを目的として，1.53haの中央公園と長さ1.7kmのグリーンベルトを計画し，2002年秋に公園と公園施設についてのコンペティションを開催した。そこで選ばれた我々の案は，様々な大きさのマウンドやクレーターをつくり，地形に変化を与えることで，人々のアクティビティを喚起しようというものであった。

「ぐりんぐりん」はその中央公園の中核施設，島最初の建築として計画されたものである。公園への提案を延長させ，地形をつくることで場所をつくり，ランドスケープと建築，建築の内外をあいまいにしていこうと模索する過程で発見された我々の提案は，三つの用途の異なる内部空間をねじれながら連続するシェルで覆うというものだった。

これは佐々木睦朗氏の提案する「進化論的構造最適化手法」を用いることで動的な合理性を得ることとなる。3次元の曲面を2mグリッドの点の集合へと置き換え，各点をある力学的根拠に基づき，段階を重ねながら少しずつ変位させることで，厚さ400mm，最大スパン40mの自由曲面シェルに，安定した形状が与えられたのである。この流動していく状況のある瞬間を選択する，という構造手法が，スパイラルという「動き」のある場面を建築化したいという我々のイメージと合致したのであった。

工業化に伴う目地，そこから発生するモデュロールや純粋幾何学に頼るのではなく，動きを感じさせるシームレスな建築を創造することで，ダイナミックで形式にとらわれない建築をつくろうとしたのである。

Overall view from east

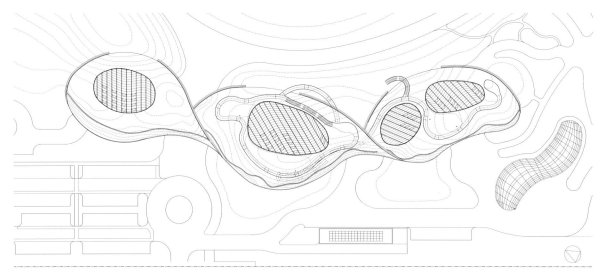
Roof

1 COUNSELING ROOM FOR GREEN
2 MEETING ROOM
3 NURSING ROOM
4 ADMINISTRATION ROOM
5 INSTRUMENT ROOM
6 WORKSHOP CORNER
7 INFORMATION CORNER AND
  ADMINISTRATION MEETING ROOM
8 VOLUNTEER STAFF ROOM
9 REST SPACE
10 PREPARATION ROOM

A NORTH BLOCK
B CENTER BLOCK
C SOUTH BLOCK

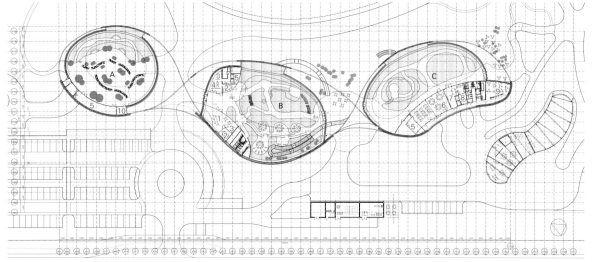
First floor S=1:1500

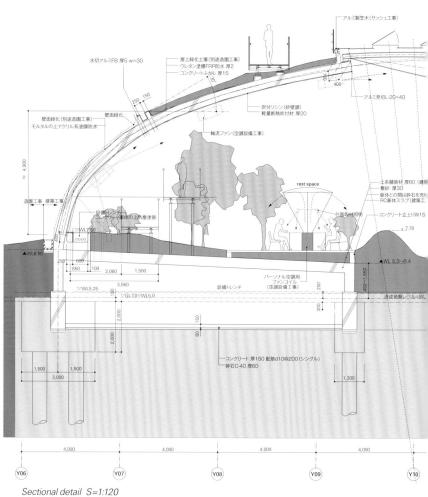
Sectional detail S=1:120

View toward center block (left) and north block (right) from north

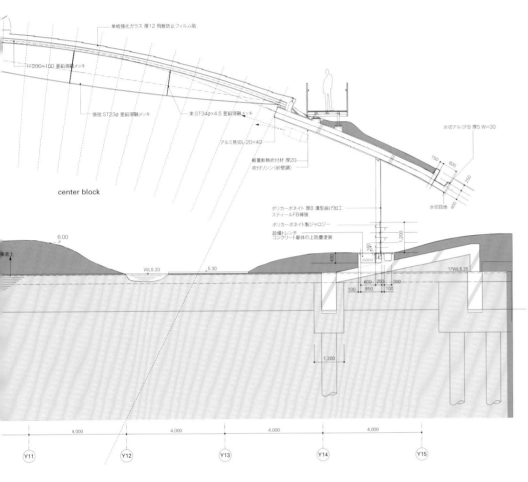

center block

Aerial view from north

Twisted structure between south block and central block

View toward central block from north block

Roof garden on central block

View toward north block from central block

Interior of south block

Dormitory for SUS Company Fukushima Branch
Sukagawa, Fukushima, Japan
2004–05

Overall view from east

1 APPROACH
2 ENTRANCE
3 GALLERY
4 CHANGING ROOM
5 SMALL PUBLIC BATH
6 CORRIDOR
7 LARGE PUBLIC BATH
8 MEETING ROOM
9 CAFETERIA
10 KITCHEN
11 STAFF LOCKER ROOM
12 LAUNDRY
13 STORAGE
14 BEDROOM
15 TRAINING ROOM
16 COMMON ROOM
17 LIBRARY
18 CONNECTING CORRIDOR
19 LIVING ROOM
20 GUEST ROOM
21 BATHROOM

Plan S=1:500

This dormitory building, designed for the employees of SUS Corporation who have transferred without family to work at the company's Fukushima branch, utilizes the company's own aluminum construction materials.

In order to alleviate aluminum's rigid and flat texture as much as possible, we arranged 15 gently curving walls made of extruded aluminum with two different curvatures throughout the site.

The curved walls enable the structure to support the lateral load with only one direction of the wall. Except for the main structure, which consists of 15 aluminum walls and a roof, we used timber materials in every part, including the fixtures. Our aim was to create a rich setting in which aluminum and timber materials coexist.

The dormitory houses nine residential rooms, guest rooms, and various public facilities. The residential rooms are arranged separately from each other, sandwiching various public spaces such as the cafeteria, library, training room and gallery space in order to enhance sound insulation. The spaces are semi-open air, and residents can open the north and south openings to take advantage of prevailing breezes.

Besides quality of living, another important aim of the design was to improve the workability of aluminum. The walls were produced in the company's own factory as prefabricated units made of multiple aluminum extrusions, which were then delivered and connected at the construction site. The roof is made using an extremely simple method in which an extruded connector is placed on top of the wall panel to join with the roof. The challenge was in controlling and adjusting the precision of the aluminum and the anchor bolts at the site. This problem was solved by welding the base plates attached to the wall to those on the foundations at the site.

Corridor

Overall view from south

Dining room

View toward dining room and corridor 03 from corridor 04

SUS福島工場社員寮

SUS福島事業所で働く，単身赴任者のためのアルミ構造の社員寮である。

硬質で平面的な印象を与えがちなアルミに，できるだけ柔らかく包み込むような表情を与えたいという意図で，2種類の異なる曲率のアルミ押出材から構成された，緩やかに湾曲する15列の壁を敷地全面に配置した。

湾曲した壁は構造的にも有利に働き，一方向の壁のみで水平力を負担することができている。主体構造である15列のアルミ壁と屋根以外は，建具も含めて木質系の素材を用いている。アルミと木のそれぞれの素材が共存することにより，今までにない豊かな空間をつくることが意図された。

この社員寮は，九つの居室とゲストルームや様々な共用部を備えている。居室同士は遮音の問題を考慮して隣接させず，間に共用部を挟み込む構成を採り，食堂や図書コーナー，トレーニングコーナー，ギャラリースペースなど居住者が共用で使える多様な場を設定している。気候の良い日に南北の建具を開放すれば，心地よい風が吹き込む，半屋外的なスペースである。

居住性だけでなく，アルミの施工性の向上も設計段階からの重要なテーマであった。壁は複数の押出材を工場でユニット化した上で，現場に搬入し，連結される。屋根は溝型の押出材を屋根勝ちの納まりで壁に載せ，壁パネルに接合されるという非常に簡便な建て方手順である。工夫を要したのは，アルミの精度の高さと，現場におけるアンカーボルトなどの精度の摺り合わせだった。この問題は，パネルの脚部において，基礎に固定されたベースプレートに，壁パネルに取り付けられたベースプレートを現場溶接で固定することでルーズを取り，解決した。

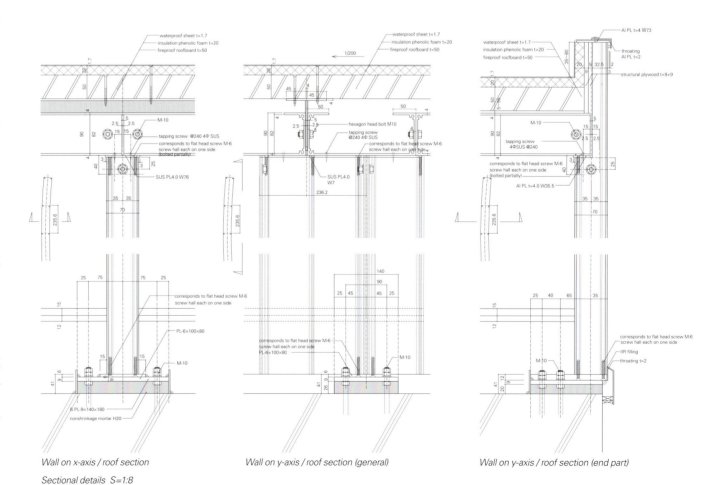

Wall on x-axis / roof section *Wall on y-axis / roof section (general)* *Wall on y-axis / roof section (end part)*

Sectional details S=1:8

Guest room 02

Gallery

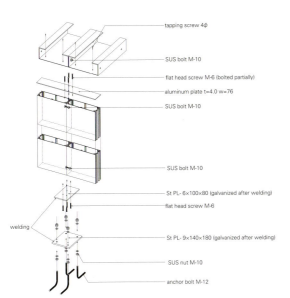
Axonometrics: joint part of roof and wall

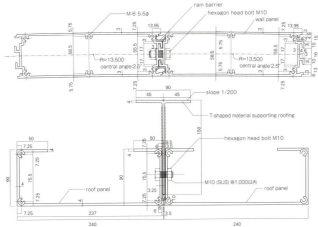
Sectional detail: joint part of roof and wall S=1:6

View toward library and dining room from corridor 05

MIKIMOTO Ginza 2
Chuo, Tokyo, Japan
2003–05

This is a commercial building located in the center of Ginza. The lower floors are composed of the MIKIMOTO boutique, while the higher floors are rented out to other tenants, including a restaurant. The site is on a corner lot with an area of 17 m x 14 m, the building height is 56.5 m including the hidden part of the penthouse. The volume carries a vivid expression that other commercial buildings lack, which is also the most important characteristic that we wanted to have. The challenge to create a new symbol among other commercial buildings is a feature that is common to TOD'S Omotesando Building (pp.48-51).

The vivid expression with certain tension was largely achieved by incorporating a new structure type as steel plate concrete structure. In between the steel plate panels that were unitized at the factory, the walls that are casted with high fluid concrete are 200 mm-thick. This seamless and abstract, tall elevation was possible by having this thin wall that unifies the structure and the surface of the building. In order to achieve a flat surface without any joints, we did not allow any redundancy up to a few-millimeters when welding the steel panels. As a result of pursuing this precision throughout the whole construction process, we were able to achieve a facade that carries a certain tension that cannot be found on curtain walls.

Another characteristic of this scheme is the irregular aperture pattern that consists of a combination of seven different types of triangles that can be repeated based on the length of the sides and angles. These triangles are not periodical, and can expand endlessly. The positions of the openings are not dependent on the slab lines, allowing us to achieve a facade that is not affected by the divisions of the floors, and give a dynamic energy flow to the architecture at the same time.

Without using decorative techniques, we were able to achieve an extremely difficult construction and create a new architecture with a strong symbolic character that will not be overlooked within other commercial facilities in the surrounding area.

Evening view from west

Fourth floor: multipurpose hall

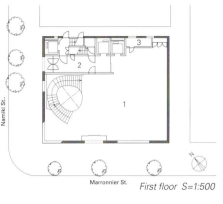

Typical floor

1 SHOP
2 TENANT ENTRANCE
3 OUTDOOR MECHANICAL SPACE
4 TENANT SHOP
5 LOCKER ROOM
6 STORAGE

Basement *Second floor*

Evening view from crossing of Namiki St. and Marronnier St.

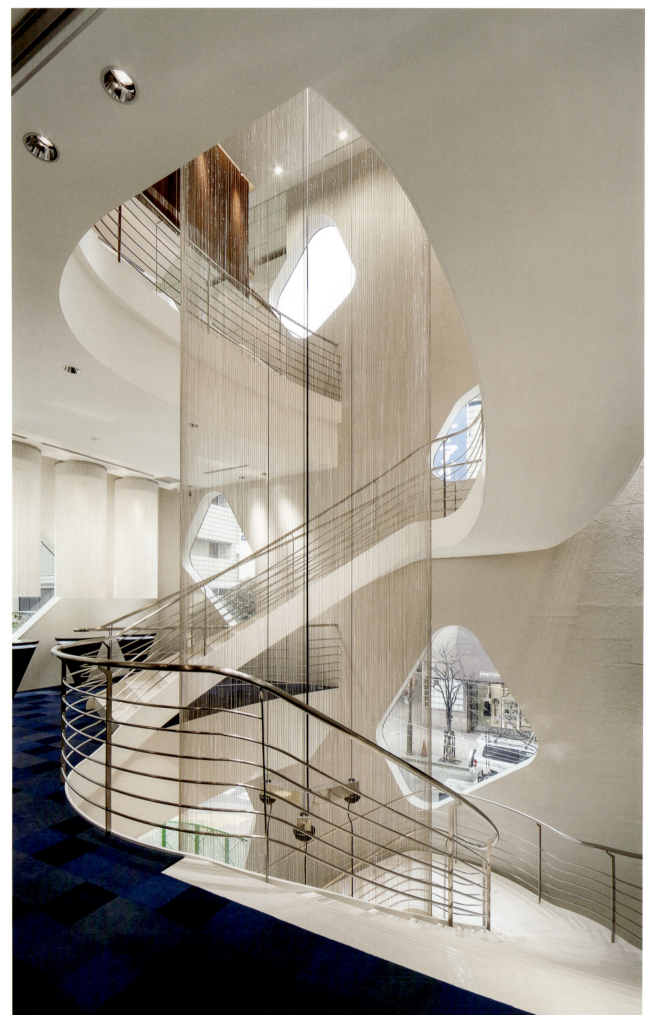

View toward staircase with void from second floor

Third floor: downward view of spiral staircase

1 SHOP	8 MULTIPURPOSE HALL
2 TENANT ENTRANCE	9 ROOF MECHANICAL
3 OUTDOOR	SPACE
MECHANICAL SPACE	10 OFFICE
4 TENANT SHOP	11 FIRE PRESERVATION
5 LOCKER ROOM	WATER TANK
6 STORAGE	12 PUMP
7 WATER TANK	

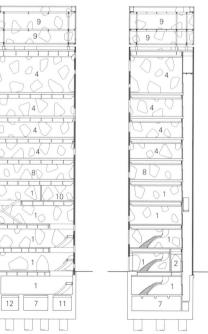

Sections S=1:800

Nineth floor: highest space

Upward view from Marronnier St.

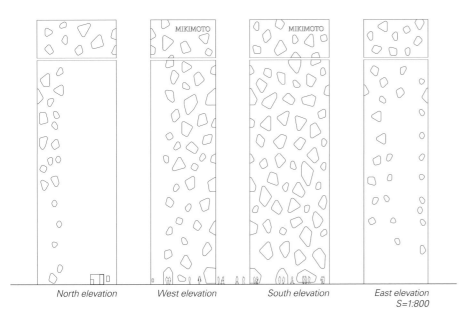

North elevation   *West elevation*   *South elevation*   *East elevation S=1:800*

MIKIMOTO Ginza 2

銀座の中心部に位置する，商業ビルの計画である。低層部は，MIKIMOTO boutique の店舗，上層部は飲食店などのテナント用賃貸フロアで構成されている。敷地は 17m×14m の角地にあり，塔屋の目隠し部分を含めると建物高さは 56.5m となる。このヴォリュームに他の商業ビルにはない強い表情を与えることが，我々にとっての主要なテーマとなった。それは，「TOD'S 表参道ビル」（pp.48-51）と共通する，商業施設における新しいシンボル性の創造という試みであった。

緊張感のある強い表情は，「鋼板コンクリート構造」と名付けられた新しい構造体に因るところが大きい。工場でユニット化された鋼板パネルの間に，高流動コンクリートを流し込んだ壁の厚みは 200mm である。この薄い壁により，構造と表層は一体化され，シームレスで抽象度の高い立面が可能となった。目地のないフラットな表層を得るため，パネル化された鋼板の溶接作業には，ミリ単位の精度が求められた。すべての過程で一貫して求めた精度の追求の結果は，カーテンウォールには見られない緊張感のあるファサードとなって表れている。

この建築のもうひとつの特徴となっている不定形な開口部のパターンは，反復可能な長さの辺と角度を持つ 7 種類の三角形の組み合わせによって決められている。これらの三角形は，周期性を持つことなく，どこまでも拡張することができる。孔の配置は，スラブラインとは無関係に決められており，層に影響されないファサードの面としての存在感を際立たせ，且つ，そこにダイナミックな力の流れを感じさせる。

デコラティブな手法によらず，周辺の商業施設の中に埋もれてしまわない強いシンボル性の創造という建築的課題は，特に，難易度の極めて高い施工を伴って実現に至った。

73

'Meiso no Mori' Municipal Funeral Hall
Kakamigahara, Gifu, Japan
2004–06

The site is in a corner of a quiet funeral park with lush woodlands in the south and a small pond in the north. Confronted with this environment, we proposed a magnanimous curved roof that feels like it is floating. The roof could be deciphered as clouds floating in the sky, mountain ridges, or a bird gliding down with its wings spread; each person can develop their own image of the building when they look at it. While blending into the landscape, we aimed to create a space where people can find peace and tranquility.

Around 20-30 people move slowly along a flow line at the crematory. The shape of the roof was designed as one united space, almost like as if it is cradling the slow flowing movement of the people. The magnanimous shape of the roof made possible appropriate ceiling heights according to the requirements of the program and connecting them continuously. It gives an impression that the roof is floating by softly lighting the whole ceiling from the lower parts. The attendants slowly proceed as if they are led by the light. The free-curved shell structure made of reinforced concrete was developed by Mutsuro Sasaki's method for "evolutionary structural optimization", which allowed us to follow a process that automatically evolves into a shape with good stress conditions. This evolution is the process where we attempt to find the ideal curved structure that is form resistant through mechanical modifications to the initial conditions to minimize the stress from bending. This magnanimous shape was achieved as a result of several dozens of simulations.

In harmony with the scenery of woodlands, the roof reflects on the lake and allows the architecture blend into nature. By making an architecture that conveys the spiritual nature of the boundary between life and death, we tried to get closer to principle of nature and organic materials, and not architecture as a geometry.

Northwest view

Roof: finished with white urethane-based coating film waterproofing

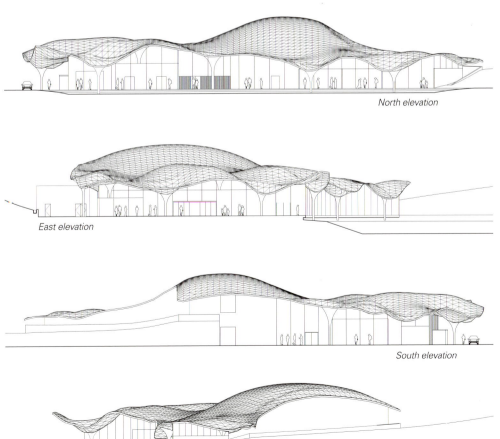

North elevation

East elevation

South elevation

West elevation S=1:600

North eaves and pond: view from east

North eaves and pond: view from west

瞑想の森 市営斎場

敷地は，南側に緑豊かな里山が連なり，北側に溜め池の水面が広がる静かな墓地公園の一角にある。そのような環境に対し我々は，浮遊感のあるおおらかな曲面屋根を提案した。この屋根は，空を流れる雲や，背後の山の稜線，舞い降りて羽を広げた鳥など，それぞれ見る人なりにイメージを拡げることができる。景観に溶け込みながら，安らかさや静けさを感じさせる空間を目指した。

火葬場は，20～30人の人々が，ゆっくりと定められた動線に従って動く。屋根形状は，そのようなゆったりとした人の動きを包み込むように，一体的な空間として考えられた。おおらかな屋根形状は，プログラムの要求に従って適当な天井高を与え，それを連続的に結んでいくことでできた。内部空間は，曲面天井全体を下方からの照明により柔らかく照らすことによって，屋根面が浮かんでいるような印象を与える。参列者たちは，この光に導かれるように，ゆっくり進んでいく。屋根を構成する鉄筋コンクリートによる自由曲面シェル構造は，佐々木睦朗氏の「進化論的構造最適化手法」によって，自動的に応力状態のよい形態に「進化」していく過程を踏んだ。進化とは，設定した初期条件に若干の力学的修正を加えていくことで，曲げ応力が極力少なく，かつ歪みエネルギーと変形が極小となるような形態抵抗型の曲面構造体を探していくプロセスのことである。数十回に及ぶシミュレーションの結果，おおらかな屋根形状が得られた。

山並みに調和する屋根は池に映り込み，建築が自然に溶け込む。生と死の境目にある精神性を感じられるような建築をつくることで，建築を単なる幾何学ではなく，自然のシステムや有機的な物質の持つ原理に近づけようとした。

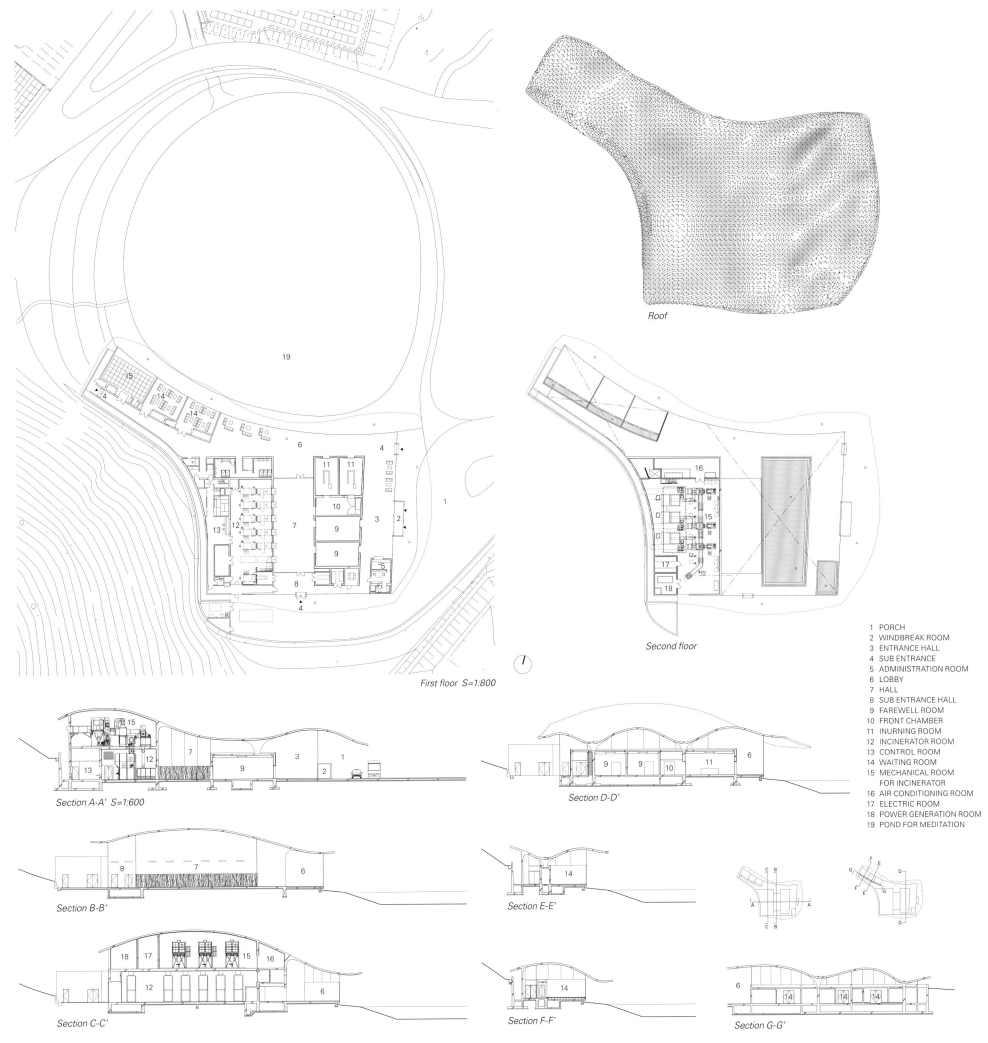

Lobby

Hall in front of cremation furnace

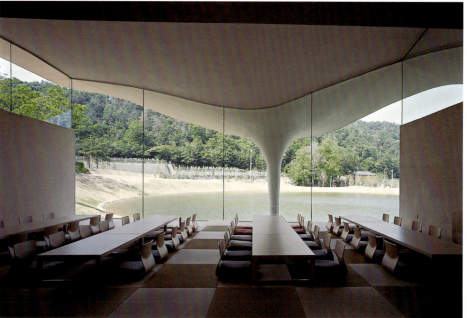
Waiting room in west corner

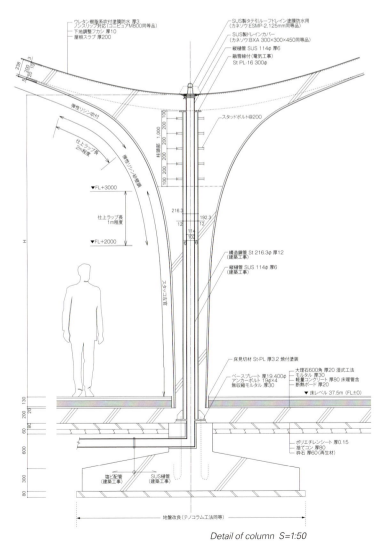

Detail of column S=1:50

Downward view toward lobby and pond from rooftop

VivoCity
Singapore
2003–06

Aerial view from inside cable car going to Sentosa Island on southwest

While Singapore is a small country with a population of approximately 5.5 million people, it has a leading economic system and promises a rich consumer life as one of the main centers in Asia. On the other hand, they also try to draw out potential on architectural design as much as they can, where commercial values rise as the consumer society continues to develop. *VivoCity* is a large-scale shopping center that was planned on the basis of this background.

Since the shopping center is expected to attract both local and foreign customers, we challenged to create a new symbol in the area. Standing in between the sea and mountains, the site is directly connected to nature, which is unusual for shopping centers. We thought that the dynamism of using nature as a symbol might be able draw out the unique potential of the place, which might help it to flourish and prosper.

We incorporated the two natural elements of waves and plants as symbols into the design of the shopping center. Waves signify movement, which is visualized through the roof that covers the overall building and run down as walls at the sides. On top of creating an image of waves, the compelling landscape that displays a large undulation also creates a flow of people, and helps to boost the atmosphere. On the other hand, there is a rooftop garden and courtyard brimming with plants under the waves. It is rare to actively put effort in designing outdoor spaces in Singapore because of its oppressively hot and humid climate, but it could inspire people to become more aware of the raw energy of nature by refining the outdoor space.

Through the symbols of these two natural elements, it is expected that people would recall their animal instincts to react to nature. Even 10 years after the opening of *VivoCity*, it is still full of energy and vitality.

East elevation

North plaza and main entrance

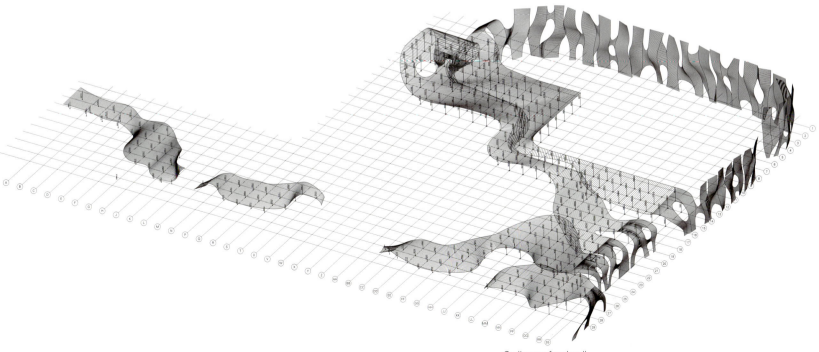

Outline: roof and wall

83

1 NORTH SQUARE
2 ANCHOR SHOP
3 EVENT SPACE
4 TENANT SHOP
5 HYPER MARKET
6 RESTAURANT
7 HARBOR FRONT CENTER
   (SHOPPING MALL + OFFICE)
8 FERRY TERMINAL
9 CINEMA COMPLEX
10 COURTYARD
11 POND
12 FITNESS CLUB
13 FOOD COURT
14 OUTDOOR THEATER
15 PMS STATION (MONORAIL)
16 PARKING
17 MRT STATION (SUBWAY)

Third floor

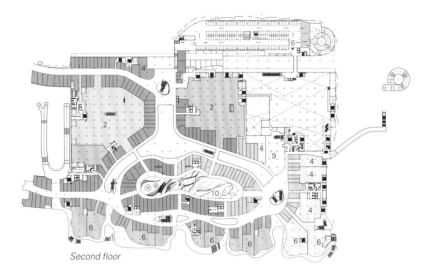

Second floor

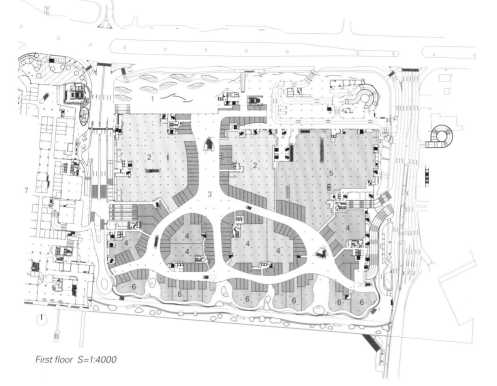

First floor S=1:4000

Main entrance

▽ *Escalator in north area*

First floor: event space

Third floor: rooftop garden

85

VivoCity

シンガポールは人口約550万の小国でありながら先鋭的な経済体制を打ち出し、アジアの中心のひとつとして人々の豊かな消費生活を保証している。また、建築デザインについてもポテンシャルを最大限に引き上げ、商業価値を高めながら消費社会をひたすら拡張し続けている。「VivoCity」は、そのような背景のもとに計画された、大規模ショッピングセンターである。

ここで我々は、シンガポール国内外から多くの集客を見込むため、「新しいシンボル」をつくり出すことを試みた。海と山に挟まれ、自然と直結した立地は、ショッピングセンターとしては珍しい。つまり、自然のダイナミズムをシンボル化することで、その場所特有のポテンシャルを引き出し、賑わいに繋げていけるのではないかと考えたのである。

「波」と「植物」という二つの自然のエレメントをシンボル化し、ショッピングセンターに持ち込む。動きを内包した「波」は視覚化された屋根として建築全体を覆い、端部では壁として流れ落ちる。大きなうねりを見せるその力強い風景は、波をイメージさせると同時に人々の流れをつくり出し、気分を高揚させるものとなる。そしてその波の下には、植物で満たされた屋上庭園や中庭が広がっている。高温多湿のシンガポールにとって屋外空間を積極的につくることは稀であるが、敢えてそこに外部を持ち込むことによって、生な自然の力強さを意識させようとしたのである。

こうして二つの自然のエレメントがシンボル化されることによって、忘れかけていた人々の動物的本能を蘇らせることを期待した。「VivoCity」はオープン後10年を経てもなお、活気と賑わいで満ち溢れている。

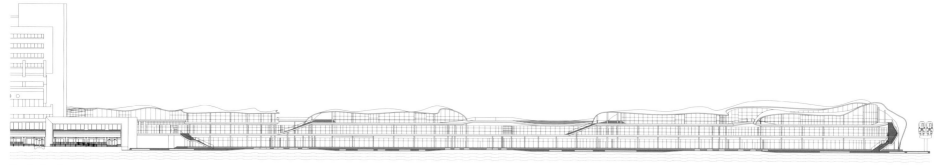

South elevation

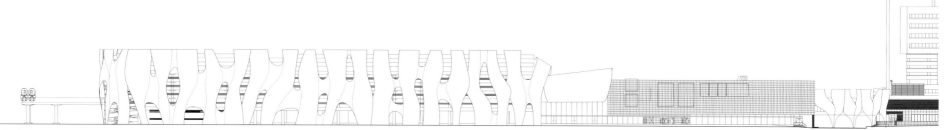

North elevation

Overall view from southeast

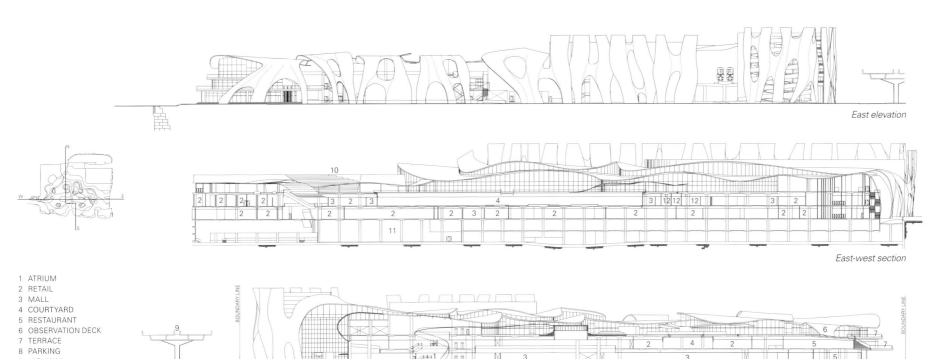

East elevation

East-west section

1 ATRIUM
2 RETAIL
3 MALL
4 COURTYARD
5 RESTAURANT
6 OBSERVATION DECK
7 TERRACE
8 PARKING
9 HIGHWAY
10 OUTDOOR THEATER
11 MECHANICAL ROOM
12 F&B (FOOD & BEVERRAGE)

North-south section

Hôpital Cognacq-Jay
Paris, France
2000–06

Court: view from southeast

The project involves the rebuilding of *Cognacq-Jay*, a private hospital having a history of 100 years. The site is located in the 15th district in Paris near *Eiffel Tower*, within a residential quarter characterized by the presence of many hospitals. Many of them stand independently on their own, among the surrounding residential blocks. The existing *Cognacq-Jay* is not an exception, presenting itself in an autonomous T-shaped plan. A group of small buildings and blank patches of garden are scattered about the site.

The program has required an increase of beds from the present 72 to 168, a parking space for 128 cars, brand-new rehabilitation facilities and a section for children suffering from various handicaps. Amelioration in the quality of medical services is anticipated, including improvement of the hospice section. Each of these rooms had been strictly defined in advance. A mere combination of these would simply make the required volume monstrous, and organization of volume has proved to be difficult in the extreme.

We have aligned the wall surface lines with the two streets on north and south, then placed three hospital-ward buildings inside, and maximized the patios (green areas) emerging between the wards. The linear block along the street accommodates, facing the street, spacious gallery-type nursing rooms, and facing the garden, private rooms arranged like apartment houses, with corridors in the middle. As the wall surface lines facing the garden are maximized, most of these private rooms are provided with views and natural lighting. Privacy inside the block, including the garden, is assured by closing the building with regard to the streets. On the first basement level are gathered all the service functions, offering a strong linkage between the two blocks in north and south. This floor is in need of sunshine and ventilation to make up satisfactory environment for the staff, and is ready to deform the garden for the sake of it. We believe that it would play a key role in bringing the entire hospital together in a functional manner.

View from Rue Blomet:
Milky white opaque glass sandwiches
light transmissive insulation with straw-like section

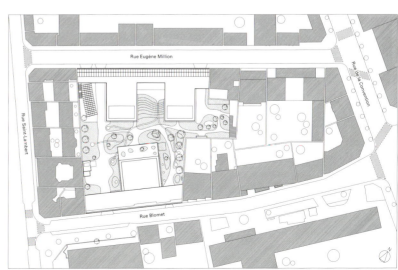

Tiered landscape faced rehabilitation room on basement

Site plan S=1:2000

89

コニャック・ジェイ病院

敷地はパリ市内15区にあり，既に100年の歴史を有する私立病院「コニャック・ジェイ」の建て替え計画である。エッフェル塔にも近いこの地区は住宅地域であるが，付近には病院が多い。それらの多くは街区ブロックの中にあってもブロックから自立して建つ傾向がある。既存の「コニャック・ジェイ」も周辺ブロックに対して独立したT字型プランをもち，敷地内には独立した小さな建物群や，余白の庭が分散している。

規模の要求としては，現状の72床を168床へ，128台分のパーキングや新規のリハビリセンター，ハンディキャップの子供のセクションなどがあり，ホスピス部門だけでなくホスピタル部門の充実も含めた，医療サービスの質的拡大が行われる。その諸室は厳密に定められ，要求ヴォリュームを単純に組み上げると，実に大規模で，ヴォリュームの配置は困難を極めた。

まず，南北の2本の街路に対して壁面線を合わせた街区ブロックを形成し，病棟を内側に3棟張り出させる。そして，それらの間に形成される中庭=グリーンエリアを最大化する。街路に沿ったリニアな棟には，街路に面した広い片廊下の看護諸室が置かれ，内に張り出した部分に中廊下の個室の病室を集合住宅のように置く。庭に対する壁面線も最大となり，ほとんどの個室に対して眺望と採光が可能となる。街区に対して一端閉じることで，この庭を含んだブロック内側のプライバシーを確保させる。地下1階はサービス機能が集中し，南北二つの棟を強く連結している。このフロアは，裏方というよりもスタッフの環境充足のためには，庭を変形してでも日当たりや通風を取り入れることが必要であり，病院全体を機能的に統合する重要な役割を果たすと考えられる。

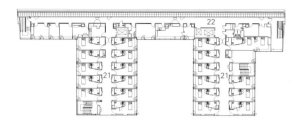

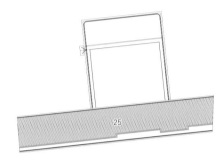

Fifth floor

Ground floor S=1:1000

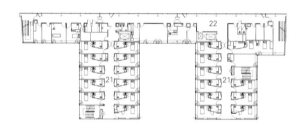

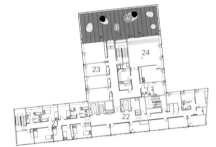

Third floor

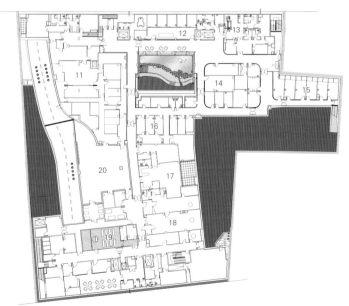

Basement

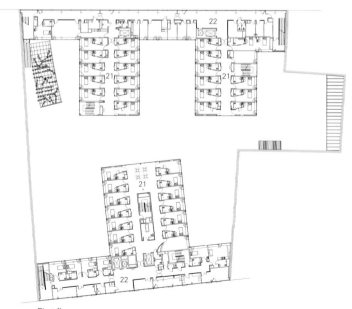

First floor

1	RESTAURANT	10	OXGEN TANK
2	RECEPTION	11	KITCHEN
3	TERRACE	12	ATHLETIC ROOM
4	ADMINISTRATION AREA	13	RADIATION ROOM
5	RECEPTION (PRIVATE CARE WARD)	14	EXERCISE THERAPY ROOM AND REHABILITATION ROOM
6	RECEPTION (DISABLED CHILD CARE WARD)	15	PHYSICAL THERAPY ROOM
7	MULTIPURPOSE ROOM	16	CONSULTING ROOM
8	PILOTI	17	LINEN ROOM
9	GREENHOUSE	18	PHARMACY
		19	MORTUARY AND CHAPEL
20	LOADING/UNLOADING DOCK		
21	WARD		
22	ADMINISTRATION BUILDING		
23	CLASSROOM		
24	CAFETERIA		
25	MECHANICAL ROOM		
26	SLOPE		
27	PARKING		
28	POND		

View toward court from reception facing Rue Eugène Millon

North elevation (Rue Eugène Millon)

South elevation (Rue Blomet) S=1:800

Corridor facing Rue Eugène Millon: transparent glass is attached at respective height of sight line for wheelchair users and pedestrians

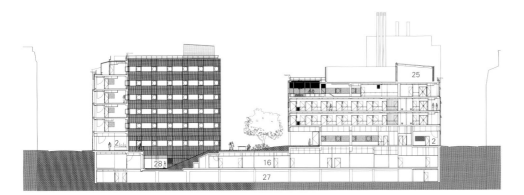

Sections S=1:800

Piloti: northwest view

Tama Art University Library (Hachioji campus)
Hachioji, Tokyo, Japan
2004–07

At the beginning of the project, Tama Art University asked us to create a library building to stand in front of the new main entrance and serve as the school's symbol, as well as provide a place for socializing between students from different departments.

We proposed a structure made of arches: a series of columns that join rigidly to the horizontal slab at the ceiling, but narrow like a stiletto where they touch the floor. By eliminating obstructive elements such as reinforcement braces and shear wall, we aimed to generate activity on the sloping floor, and create an environment that overlooks the surrounding greenery.

The columns are arranged as intersections of a grid made of gently curved lines, which continue in a smooth rhythm from one point to another like the tracks of a bouncing ball. By continuously combining the columns with the load bearing wall, we hoped for various types of spaces to emerge like a forest with ambiguous boundaries between its subdivided parts.

With the suggestion by Mutsuro Sasaki, the building was structured using iron plates wrapped in concrete. By employing a seismic device, we were able to achieve a planar shape in which all arches, ranging in width from 1.8 to 14.5 m, have a uniform thickness of 200 mm, and fall towards the foot of the columns to create rectangular intersections of 200 mm x 400 mm. This is how, unlike the familiar measurements found in common concrete structures, we arrived at an architectural experience light and likely to feel tense.

The tensions within the interior colonnade are apparent in the elevation as well. By installing a flush glass window in each arch-shaped opening which was the result of connecting the columns, the impressive facade was to become the campus symbol have appeared. Furthermore, the quintessential arch pattern resonates with the classic libraries of the West as a place for accumulation of knowledge.

By developing a rhythmic and continuous structure over a curving grid, and expressing it through a certain amount of abstraction, we aimed to create a building that simultaneously contains the natural richness of caves and forests, and the quiet atmosphere of the library.

View from northeast

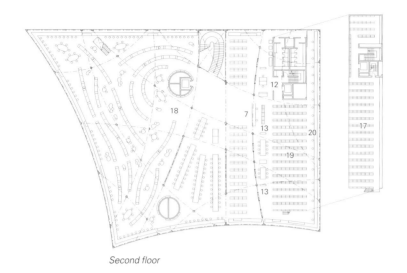
Second floor

First floor S=1:800

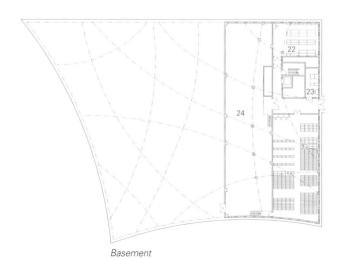
Basement

1 NORTH ENTRANCE
2 CAFETERIA
3 THEATER AREA
4 ARCADE GALLERY
5 SOUTH ENTRANCE
6 LIBRARY ENTRANCE
7 RECEPTION COUNTER
8 LOCKER BOOTH
9 MAGAZINE/AUDIOVISUAL AREA
10 LOUNGE
11 AUDIOVISUAL BOOTH
12 OFFICE
13 LABORATORY
14 MEETING ROOM
15 DIRECTOR'S ROOM
16 OFFICE ENTRANCE
17 CATWALK OF CLOSED-STACKS
18 READING AREA OF OPEN-STACKS
19 READING AREA OF CLOSED-STACKS
20 PERSONAL READING ROOM
21 COMPACT STACKS
22 PRESERVED BOOK STACKS
23 SERVER ROOM
24 MECHANICAL

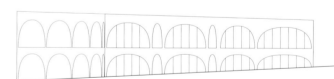
West elevation

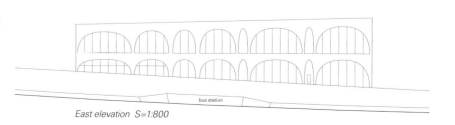
East elevation S=1:800

View from street on east

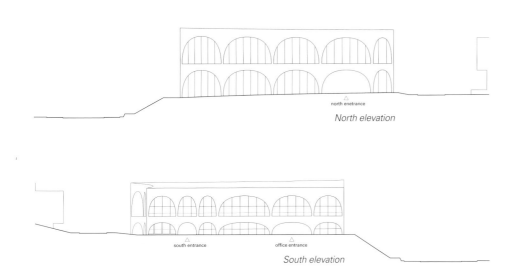

多摩美術大学図書館（八王子キャンパス）

プロジェクト開始時に大学より望まれたのは、新しく移設される正門の正面に大学の顔となるような建物をつくること。そして、新しい建物が異なる学科同士の交流の場となることであった。

これに対して我々は、天井面でスラブと剛に接続するが、下部ではピンヒールのように細くくびれた柱を並べた、アーチの連続体からなる構造体を提案した。ブレースや耐震壁等の視線をさえぎる要素がなくなり、スロープ上に展開されるであろう多くの活動や、周囲の緑豊かな風景を一望できる環境が生み出せるのではないかと考えた。

これらの柱は緩やかに曲線を描くグリッドの交点として配置され、隣から隣へと、弾むボールの軌跡のように、なめらかにリズムを持ってつながれている。柱と板状躯体を連続的に組み合わせることで、曖昧な連続や分節を持つ森のように、様々な場所が現れるのを期待した。

佐々木睦朗氏の提案により、この構造体は鉄板をコンクリートで包んだものとして構想され、さらに免震装置を併用することで、1.8m〜14.5mという全く異なるスパンが全て、厚さ200mm、柱の足元で200mm×400mmの長方形が交差する平面形にまで絞られた。見慣れたコンクリート構造の寸法体験とは異なる、軽やかであり、且つ、背筋が引き締まるような建築体験は、こうして導かれた。

緊張感を持った内部の柱列は、そのまま立面にも表れている。柱を繋いだ結果、形づくられたアーチ型の開口に、ガラスを躯体と同面で嵌め込むことで、キャンパスの顔となる強く印象的なファサードがつくり出された。また、アーチというアーキタイプは、知の集積する場としての西欧の古典的な図書館をどこかで思い出させる。

湾曲したグリッド上に展開されるリズムを伴い連続した構造体を、ある抽象性を持って表現することで、洞窟や森といった自然の持つ豊かさと、図書館という知の集積する場所ならではの緊張感が、同時に存在した建築をつくろうとしたのである。

95

First floor: magazine/audiovisual area

△▽ Reading area and open-stacks on second floor

Reading tables along windows

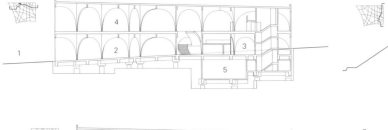
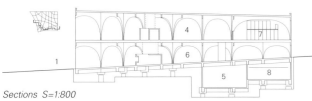
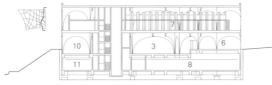
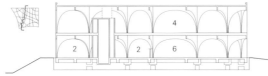

1. "SCULPTURAL FOREST"
2. MAGAZINE/AUDIOVISUAL AREA
3. OFFICE
4. READING AREA OF CLOSED-STACKS
5. MECHANICAL
6. ARCADE GALLERY
7. READING AREA OF OPEN-STACKS
8. COMPACT STACKS
9. DIRECTOR'S ROOM
10. PRESERVED BOOK STACKS

Sections S=1:800

Arcade gallery on slightly sloped floor according to site's inclination

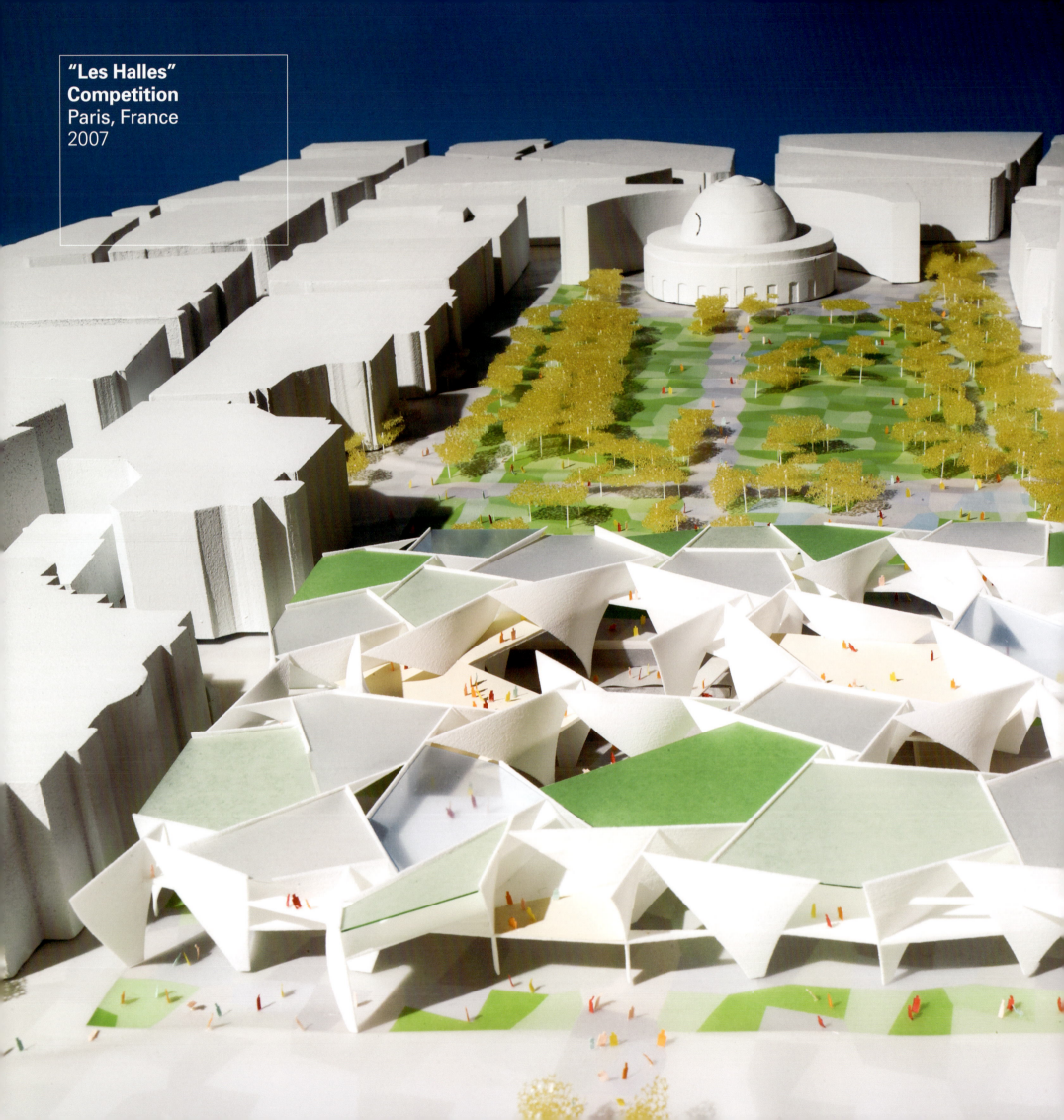

Plaza on top of north wing

Dance room

Dance room

Level +8.0: south terrace

Level +0.0: health promotion area

Auditorium

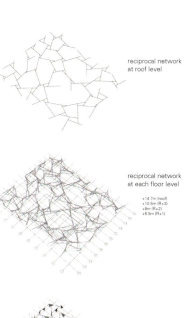

Diagram

Les Halles, a former central public market of Paris, was filled with a dynamic atmosphere that houses the biggest junction of the subway lines in Paris, *the Forum des Halles*, which is the 60,000 m² commercial building in three stories underground, the Regional express railway connecting the both riverbank of Paris in the underground, and the public park open to the residents. However, on the contrary to its dynamic potential of the area, the biggest issue of *Les Halles* was the lack of communications among those various functionalities and facilities, and the dilapidation of the park was particularly in a terrible condition. To activate the park as the public gathering space of the residents, it was intended to bring up the potential of the underground facilities to the park ground by creating a new gate of Paris—with a plaza space that allows the access to the underground facilities and a combined public programs such as a music school, a library, a spa facility housed under a low-rising roof.

In this project, we tried to reflect the changing movements themselves as the architectural expression, depicting the conditions of how the underground energy springs up to the ground and how the energy fluidly flows on the ground. As a result to actualize our concept, we suggested the structural walls named 'sails' and their 'Reciprocal Network'. The 'sails' stand up on the existing perpendicular grid of the underground structure system. The 'sails' opens up their hands as they rotate and ascend, connect each other at the top, and spread out in lattice pattern. The rules of the movements are defined by algorithm pattern; the concrete walls in 400 mm thickness all rotate in the same orientation while the rotation angles are set in 30 and 60 degrees as standard, which will achieve the maximum span in 30 m at the height of 14.7 m. Then, the open plaza with an open view on the ground level will rise as it also shift to the fluid space, gradually articulated by the walls as rotating elements to also form a unified image of the space with series of sails floating in the wind. An architecture is generated as if the trees gradually grow into a forest. The process of mulitiplication, and the environment itself that taken in the external conditions into the space will become the architecture, while this conceptual image is recognized as a whole when the series of fragmented spatial experiences are articulated. In this proposal, it is clearly visualized the process of how the uniformly systemized underground grid is transformed into a completely different geometric space via the algorithm patterns.

Our proposal was not accepted, and it was unrealized .

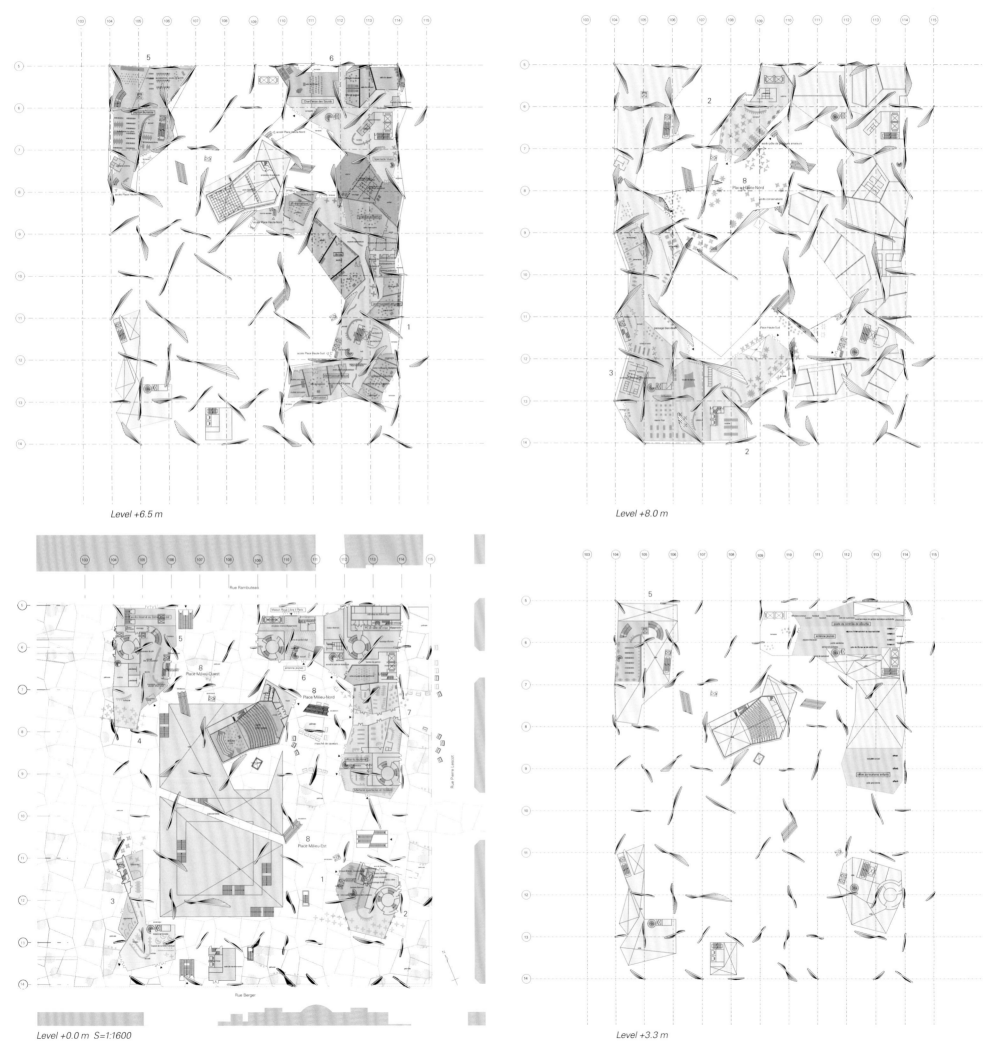

Level +6.5 m

Level +8.0 m

Level +0.0 m S=1:1600

Level +3.3 m

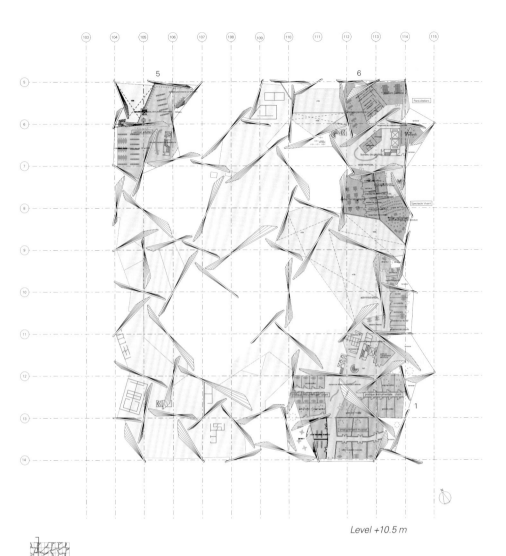

1 CONSERVATORY
2 21ST CENTURY CAFE
3 WELLNESS SPACE
4 LITERARY CAFE
5 LIBRARY
6 WORKSHOP CENTER
7 VILLAGE OF FLAVORS
8 PLAZA

Level +10.5 m

Court

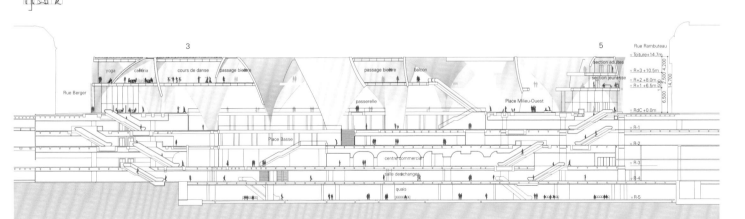

North-south section

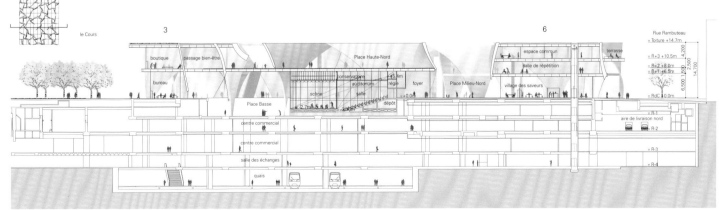

Section through auditorium S=1:1000

レ・アール国際設計競技応募案

かつてのパリの中央市場レ・アール跡地は，パリ最大の地下鉄のジャンクションと，約6万平米の地下3階建て商業施設「フォーラム・デ・アール」，パリ両岸を地下で結ぶ高速鉄道，市民に開放された公園とが複合するダイナミズムに満ちていた。当時，レ・アールの抱えていた最大の問題は，そのダイナミックなポテンシャルに反して，様々な機能間のコミュニケーションが枯渇している点であり，とりわけ，公園の荒廃ぶりは目を覆うばかりであった。公園を市民の公共の場として活性化し，地下のポテンシャルを地上まで浮上させるべく，地下へのアクセスを誘導する広場と，音楽学校や図書館・スパなどの複合した公共プログラムを低層の屋根で覆い，パリの新たな玄関をつくり出す計画が求められた。

我々はここに地下のエネルギーが湧き出し，これが地上で多様に流動する空間に変遷していく動きそのものを，建築的表現にしようと試みた。それを成立させるために我々が提案したのは「セイル（帆）」と呼ばれる構造壁とそれらの相補的ネットワーク（Reciprocal Network）である。「セイル」は地下構造の直交する既存グリッドの上に立ち上がり，回転上昇しながらその手を広げ，頂部で連結しながら網の目状に拡散していく。運動のルールはアルゴリズムに基づき決定される。厚さ400mmのコンクリート壁はすべて同じ向きに回転し，回転角が30度と60度に標準化された結果，高さ14.7mで最大スパン30mを達成する。こうして，地上では見通しの効く広場空間が，回転体としての壁によってゆるやかに分節された流動的な空間へ，徐々に移行しながら上昇し，同時に風にたなびく帆の集まりのような全体像をつくり上げる。木々が育まれ森へと成長していくように，建築が生成される。増殖のプロセス，そして外部をも取り込んだ環境自体が建築となり，このイメージは断片的な空間体験の総体として認識される。地下の完璧なグリッドシステムが，アルゴリズムを介して全く異なる幾何学空間へと変換されていく。そのプロセスが，ここでは明確に視覚化されている。

我々の提案は受け入れられず，実現に至らなかった。

Extention for "The Fair of Barcelona Gran Via Venue"
Barcelona, Spain
2003–

This is an expansion Extension for "The Fair of Barcelona Gran Via Venue". The site is at the west side of the hill of Montjuic located in between the airport and the city area, whose context shifts from the urban to seaside condition. Through the competition, new proposals for various facilities were developed, for building four exhibition halls, the central axis transferring space to connect those exhibition halls, an auditorium complex housing those conference halls in various scales and the office spaces of the Trade Fair Association, and Twin Towers and commercial complex for containing a hotel and office spaces. This expansion project of 250,000 m² is expected to produce one of the leading trade fair facilities in Europe.

The theme in this project was based on the concept of "fluidity", and what it can produce within an urban environment. The proposed pavilions are rectangle shaped box spaces with various functionalities, and there is the transferring space called 'central axis' that penetrates those boxes to unify and link each facility. The swaying and winding 'central axis' provides human scale locations by allowing visitors to come out to the terrace spaces distributed along with the axis, providing visual accessibility to the surrounding exterior sceneries.

At its end and starting points, there are entrance halls spreading as if like puddles of water. The wall surfaces with openings are named as "organic walls" for its plastic quality, while those wall surfaces symbolize the "fluid body" to give the sense of dynamic energy,

Aerial view from southwest

becoming the face of the entire facilities.
We tried to bring in flavors and joys by creating "fluid spaces" within the urban space produced for functionalities. Modernism movement tried to apply the layer of homogeneity to abstract the human actions and behaviors, but we tried to fulfill the unpredictable, latent desire of human beings by the notion of "fluidity". That is the attempt of discovering "new abstraction" based on our five senses.

Site plan S=1:8000

Overall view from east of Pavilion 8

Overall view from south of Pavilion 8

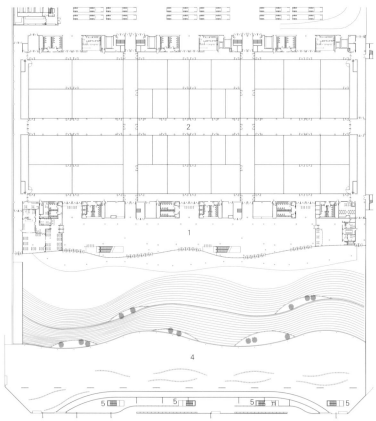

+2.5 m level: Pavilion 8   S=1:2000

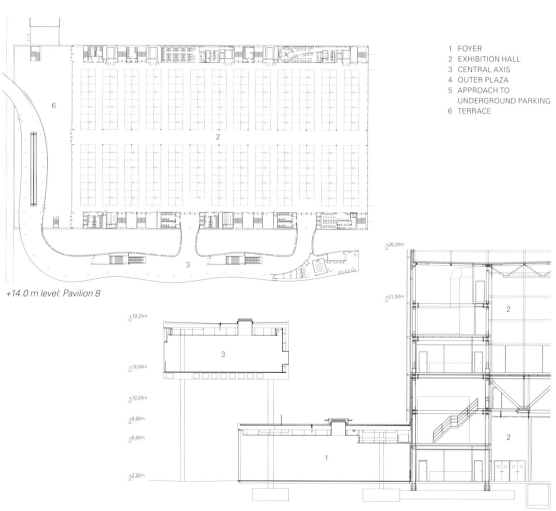

+14.0 m level: Pavilion 8

1 FOYER
2 EXHIBITION HALL
3 CENTRAL AXIS
4 OUTER PLAZA
5 APPROACH TO UNDERGROUND PARKING
6 TERRACE

Section: Pavilion 8   S=1:400

Central axis of Pavilion 8 on south

Relation between central axis and west terrace in Pavilion 8

Central axis of Pavilion 8

Entrance Hall (left) and Pavilion 1 (right)

View of Entrance Hall from southwest

GL +14.0 m of Entrance Hall: view toward "organic walls" from corridor

GL +7.0 m of Entrance Hall: south reception counter and "organic walls"

バルセロナ見本市・グランビア会場 拡張計画

バルセロナ見本市協会のモンジュイック2展示会場拡張計画である。敷地は空港と市街の中間地点，モンジュイックの丘の西側にある都市部から臨海部へと移り変わる地域である。コンペティションを経て，新たに4棟の展示場，それらを結ぶ交通空間としてのセントラル・アクシス，大中小様々な規模を持った会議室と見本市協会のオフィスの入るオーディトリアム・コンプレックス，そしてホテルとオフィスからなるツインタワー及び商業施設といった様々な施設群が計画され，25万m²に及ぶ拡張によってヨーロッパ屈指の見本市会場にしようとする計画である。

ここでは，都市空間における「流動性」がテーマとなった。目的空間であるパヴィリオン（展示場）はファンクショナルな矩形のボックス状空間であり，それらを統合するものとして貫通しながら連結しているのが移動空間である「セントラル・アクシス」である。ゆらゆらとうねりながら続く「セントラル・アクシス」は，屋外の風景を眺め，一部テラスに出られるようにすることで，ヒューマンスケールな場所となる。

その終点，あるいは始点として，水溜りのように広がったエントランスホールがある。エントランスホールの壁面は，「有機壁」と名付けられた。「有機壁」は「流動体」のイメージをシンボライズし，施設の顔として会場全体に躍動感を与えている。

「流動的な空間」をつくることによって，機能性を重視した都市空間に，うるおいや楽しさを持ち込もうとした。モダニズムは人間の行動を，均質性というベールをかけて抽象化したが，我々は予測不可能で潜在している人間の欲望を，「流動性」によって満たそうとした。それは五感を用いた「新しい抽象さ」を追求する試みである。

GL +14.0 m: Entrance Hall

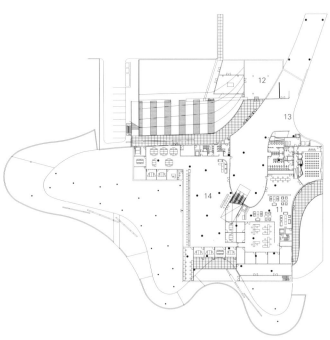

GL +2.0 m: Entrance Hall S=1:1500

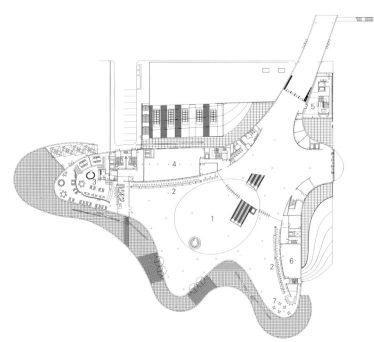

GL +7.0 m: Entrance Hall

1　ENTRANCE HALL
2　RECEPTION COUNTER
3　RESTAURANT
4　KITCHEN
5　LOBBY OF HELIPORT
6　CLOAK
7　CAFE/BAR
8　RESTAURANT FOR VIP
9　BUFFET
10　VIP ROOM
11　PRESS ROOM
12　MECHANICAL
13　APPROACH TO METRO
14　CUSTOMER INTERACTION SERVICE

West elevation: Entrance Hall and Pavilion 1 S=1:1500

GL +7.0 m: Entrance Hall

GL +7.0 m: Entrance Hall

GL +14.0 m: view toward Entrance Hall from central axis

ZA-KOENJI
Public Theatre
Suginami, Tokyo, Japan
2005–08

The part of Koenji where elevated rail lines of JR and the Beltway No.7 are crossing is a condensed area with various types of buildings such as houses, an elementary school, and the retail stores.

To design a theater within such condition, we thought of giving a boldness particular to this site, by clearly providing a dividing line between the realm of the theater play performed inside of the building and the rambling, chaotic daily lives of the city. We tried to represent a symbolical quality of the building as a 'theater house', by applying curtains produced in steel plate and concrete to the building above the ground level, in order to close down the building against the surrounding urban conditions.

While the building had a cubic form with a flat roof above the ground level in the competition phase, we reconsidered the design throughout the actual design implementation phase to give a bold symbolic quality to the building as a theater. The roof located at the center of the theater is lifted up to produce a peak representing the highest point of the theater, which would create a centrality and introversive character to the building, reflecting and symbolizing the image of the 'theater house' in previous days. To realize this roof in the shape of a catenary curved surface hollowed by the gravity, we studied to produce an expandable plan of a paraboloid surface—since the curve has a uniform curvature, it is considered the production and treatment of the steel plates into curved surface would be easier. In other words, we repeated the operation of hollowing out a geometric shape from a cubic volume, such as a cylindrical pipe that becomes a flat surface when it is exploded. As a result, the roof was configured by seven cylindrical pipes and circular cones above the hall at the center of the building. Those geometric intersection lines are curved to the unpredictable directions as if like a ridge line produced by the breaking of large 'waves' against each other; consequently the dynamically waving roof is produced only by those seven surfaces in different curvature ratio. The roof is the continuous surface of steel plates in the thickness of 150 mm, while the walls are in 225 mm. Now the building surfaces not only symbolize the building as a 'theater house', but also become the element representing a metaphor of a 'wave', with a dynamic notion of nature in motion.

We are hoping to create a 'new symbol' within today's urban environment, by transcoding and abstracting the 'architectural' membrane of a 'theater house' produced by the thin, materialistic steel enclosure into a series of 'waves' as the 'elements found in nature'.

◁ *View from train (JR Chuo-line). Waving roof is composed with seven surfaces in different curvature ratio*

Evening view of roof with curved surface

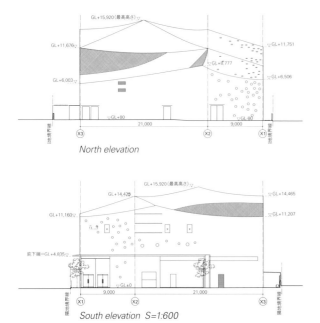
North elevation

South elevation S=1:600

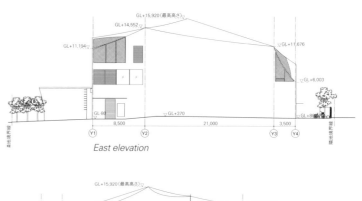
East elevation

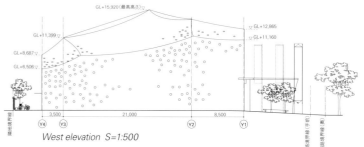
West elevation S=1:500

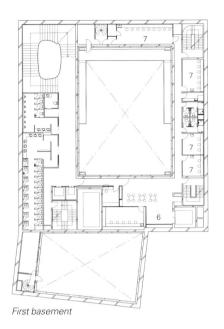

First basement

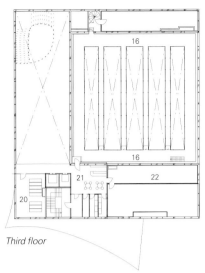

Third floor

View from street on south

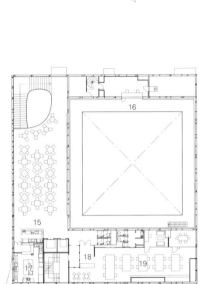

Second floor

Second basement

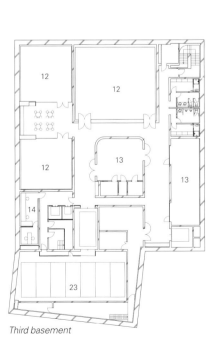

Third basement

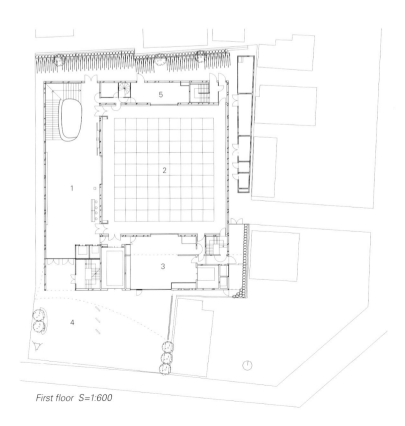

First floor S=1:600

1 MAIN LOBBY
2 MAIN AUDITORIUM (ZA-KOENJI 1)
3 LOADING AREA
4 PLAZA
5 STORAGE
6 LOUNGE OF MAIN AUDITORIUM
7 BACKSTAGE
8 CIVIC LOBBY
9 CIVIC HALL (ZA-KOENJI 2)
10 AWA-ODORI HALL
11 LOUNGE OF CIVIC HALL
12 TRAINING ROOM
13 WORKPLACE
14 ACOUSTICAL CONTROL ROOM
15 CAFE
16 GALLERY
17 KITCHEN
18 RECEPTION
19 OFFICE
20 ARCHIVE
21 REST ROOM FOR STAFFS
22 MECHANICAL
23 PARKING

座・高円寺

JR線の高架と環状7号線の交差する高円寺の一角は，住居，小学校，商店など様々な建物が密集するエリアである。

我々はここに劇場を設計するにあたり，建築内部で行われている芝居のもつ世界と，混沌としたとりとめのない日常との境界を明確に引くことで，場所に特別な強さを与えようと考えた。そこで，地上に現れる部分を鉄板とコンクリートからなる幕によって覆い，周辺の都市的状況に対してあえて閉じ，「芝居小屋」としての象徴性を表現しようとした。

コンペティション段階では地上部にフラットルーフを持つキュービックな形状であったが，実施設計段階で劇場中心部の屋根を吊り上げ，その最も高い点を頂点とすることで，かつての芝居小屋を象徴するかのような中心性と内向性を生み，建築に劇場としての強いシンボル性を与えようと考えた。この重力によってくぼんだカテナリー曲面のような屋根を実現するために，展開可能な2次曲面を考えた。これらは一定の曲率なので，鉄板の曲面加工をする際に容易と考えたためである。例えば円柱のように，展開すると平面になる幾何学形態を用い，キューブからえぐり取るようにする。これを繰り返し，最終的にはホールを中心として，屋根を七つの円柱，円錐で構成した。それらの幾何学による交線は大きな「波」同士がぶつかる時に生じる稜線のように予測不可能な方向へ曲がる。こうして，たった七つの曲率の面だけでダイナミックに波打つような屋根が生まれた。屋根は厚さ150mm，壁は厚さ225mmで連続する鉄板の面となる。その結果，「芝居小屋」としての象徴性のみならず，「波」という自然のもつ運動のダイナミズムがメタファーとして浮かび上がったのである。

薄く物質感のある鉄によって場を覆い込むことで発生した建築の境界面を，「芝居小屋」から「波」という自然へと置き換え抽象化することにより，現代都市における「新しいシンボル」となることを期待している。

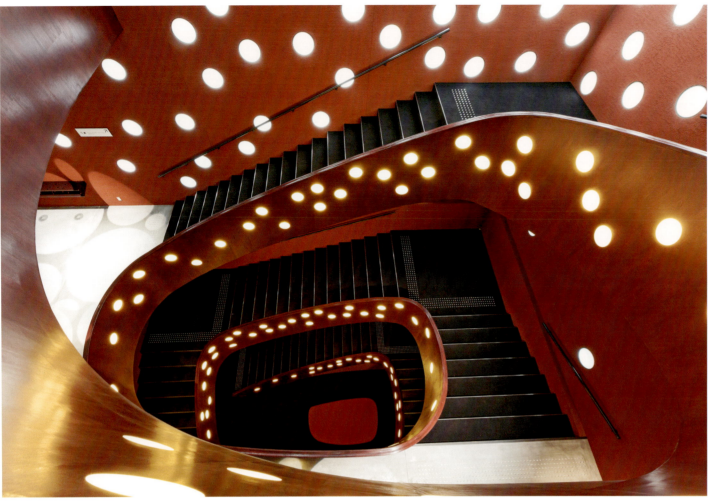
Downward view of staircase

Staircase at end of main lobby

Second floor: cafe behind staircase

*Staircase on second basement:
bench at civic lobby designed by Kazuko Fujie*

Civic lobby on second floor: furniture designed by Kazuko Fujie

Civic lobby on second basement: bench designed by Kazuko Fujie

Civic hall on second basement (250-300 seats, fixed raked seating)

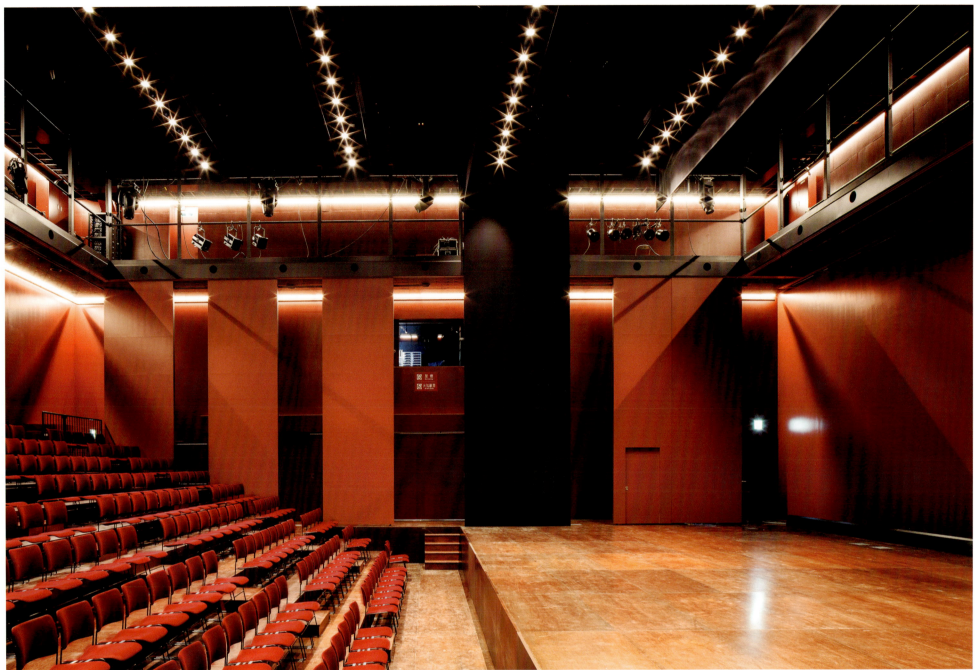

Main auditorium on ground floor (flexible flat space, 230 seats)

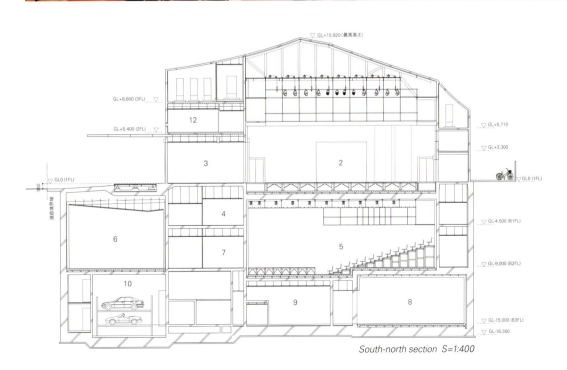

South-north section S=1:400

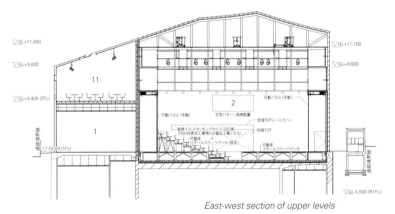

East-west section of upper levels

1	MAIN LOBBY	7	LOUNGE OF CIVIC HALL
2	MAIN AUDITORIUM (ZA-KOENJI 1)	8	TRAINING ROOM
3	LOADING AREA	9	WORKPLACE
4	LOUNGE OF MAIN AUDITORIUM	10	PARKING
5	CIVIC HALL (ZA-KOENJI 2)	11	CAFE
6	AWA-ODORI HALL	12	OFFICE

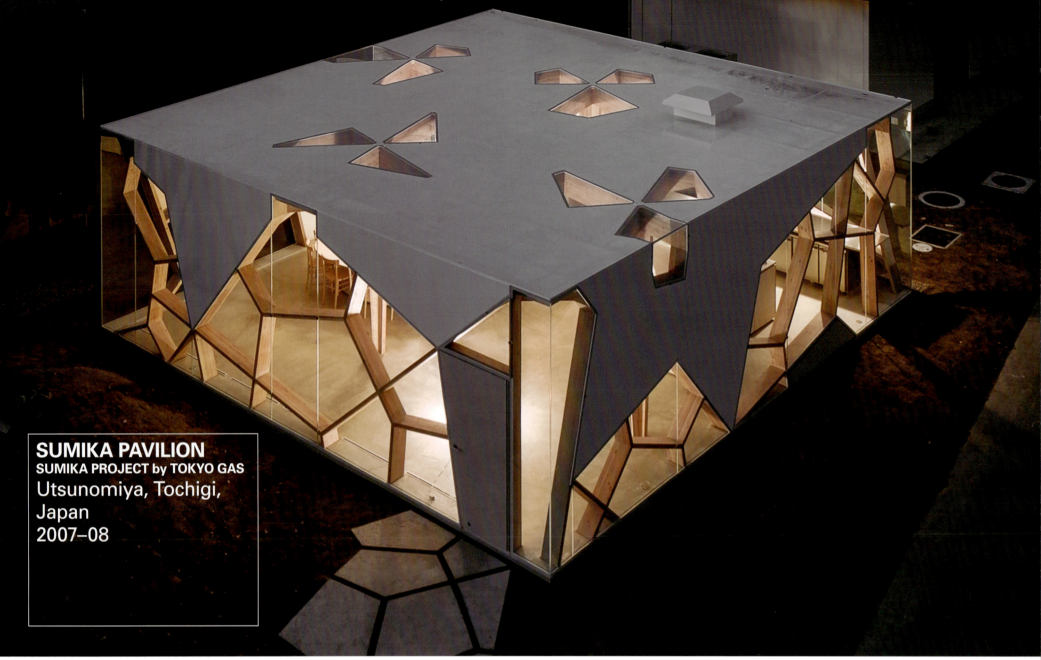

SUMIKA PAVILION
SUMIKA PROJECT by TOKYO GAS
Utsunomiya, Tochigi, Japan
2007–08

Downward view from southeast

Four architects designed each model house in Utsunomiya City to promote 'the life with flames' campaign, which has been suggested by Tokyo Gas. This project is to design an information center for the visitors of those four model houses to show the theme of this project. This is also intended to be used as a presentation space for the local residents to experience the Gas Life through the participation in cooking classes.

Our initial concept was a space where trees provide various spatial conditions under their shades, allowing to place kitchens and tables for people to cook and dine. In this particular project, we tried to create such space by networking the unit patterns produced by extending branches from the stem. The original model was a unit pattern that those branches are extending out in six different directions from the stem. Then, the tip of each branch separates again in six directions to provide a minimum unit pattern, repeated to form networks. The angle and the length of each diverging unit pattern are parametrically modified and updated through the repetitive operations performed by the structural engineer Mr. Masato Araya, and the model starts to form an inconsistent yet infinitely sequencing framework network, which is later constructed in laminated wood. The system of this framework in repetitive patterns produced by the successive little alteration of parameters is intended to achieve more stable condition when 'the number of repetitive operation' = generation is increased. From the branch network patterns limitlessly extending out in our tests, we selected four suitable tree patterns to be actualized as an architecture—like the outdoor lunch to curtain and enclose the shade of trees to create a dining space.

Finding a comfortable self space under the shade of tree is an ordinary experience. The realization of a simple space to provide such simple experience is what we expected from this project.

This pavilion was taken apart in 2015, and will be rebuilt into a park in Rikuzentakata in the near future.

SUMIKA パヴィリオン／
SUMIKA PROJECT by TOKYO GAS

東京ガスがアピールしている「火のある暮らし」を具体的に提案すべく，宇都宮市内で4戸のモデルハウスが4人の建築家によってデザインされた。本計画は，モデルハウスの見学者にプロジェクト全体の趣旨を説明するためのインフォメーション・センターであり，地域の人たちに対しては，クッキング・スクールなどへの参加を通して，ガス・ライフを体験してもらうことができるプレゼンテーション・スペースでもある。

我々が最初にイメージしたのは，樹々の間に生まれる様々な場所に，テーブルやキッチンが置かれ，食事ができるような空間であった。ここではそのような空間を，木のように幹から枝をのばした単位パターンをネットワーク化していくことで，実現しようと試みた。幹から6方向に枝をのばした木のようなモデルがまず想定された。さらに，そこから各枝の先端を6分岐させたものが，反復されるパターンの最小単位となる。構造エンジニア新谷眞人氏の提案によって，各単位パターンにおける枝の角度と長さは，繰り返される際にパラメトリックに変更・更新され，不均一だが，無限に連続する集成材による架構ネットワークを形成する。パターンの単位が少しずつ変化しながら繰り返されるこの架構のしくみは，繰り返しの世代数を増やすことによって，より安定した状態に近づいていくよう意図されている。最後に，木陰を帳幕で囲って領域化するように，どこまでも広がる枝のネットワーク・パターンから，目的に見合った4本の木が選びとられ建築化された。

木陰の下に，居心地の良い自分の場所をみつけるという行動は，誰もがしたことがあるプリミティブな経験である。そのようなプリミティブな経験を生む，プリミティブな空間を実現すること。それが本計画に我々が期待したことである。

このパヴィリオンは2015年に解体され，近く陸前高田市の公園内に再建される予定である。

Interior

1 APPROACH
2 ROOM
3 ISLAND KITCHEN
4 COUNTER KITCHEN
5 WC
6 OUTDOOR MECHANICAL SPACE
7 WATER HEATER
8 POND (EXISTING)
9 CHERRY TREE (EXISTING)

A FRP+FIREPROOFING TOPCOAT
B GLASS
C OPENING
D CONCRETE FOUNDATION
E LAMINATED WOOD 60×240 (OUTSIDE)
F MPG
G AIR SUPPLY OPENING
H AIR EXHAUST OPENING
I DRAINER
J VENTILATING TOWER
K COLUMN (LAMINATED WOOD)
L LAMINATED WOODEN STRUCTURE
M WALL AND CEILING
N OPENING
O WALL FOR HANGING TELEVISION
P HANGING SEALING
Q GAS ALARM
R MAIN SWITCH
S VENTILATING CEILING

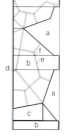
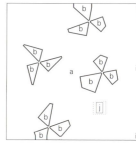
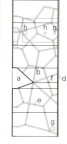
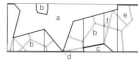

Expansion plan (exterior)

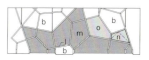
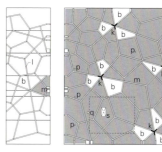

Expansion plan (interior) S=1:250

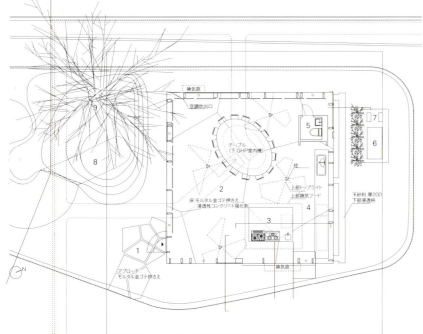

Plan S=1:200

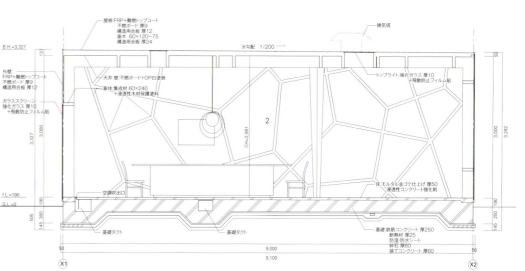

Sectional detail S=1:80

Overall view from northeast

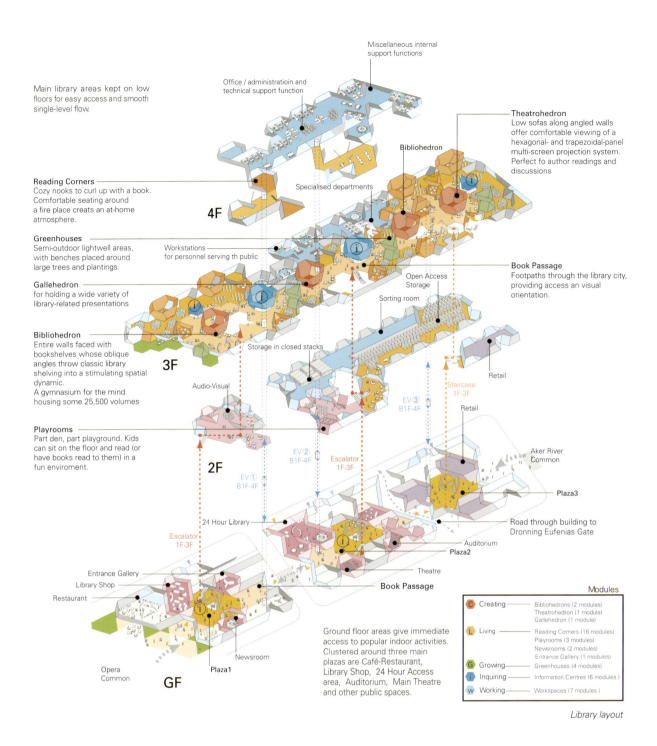

Library layout

In Oslo, a city situated in the inner part of the fjord shaped by glacial erosion, large-scale redevelopment of the harbor area has made progress in recent years. At the end of 2008, an international invited competition to design a cultural facility at the core of this redevelopment was held, in regard to the relocation of the old town's main public library which had become too small. The complex was required to accommodate the new main library with a floor area of 18,000 m² and a collection of 800,000 books, as well as 40,000 m² of flexible office and residential spaces.

Considering circulation from various directions, including the station plaza and the residential area planned to the east of the site, the library was positioned in the lower floors, and the office and housing in the upper floors. Our aim was to create a city-like space in which the complex is bound together organically.

Thus we proposed a concept of the "library city". The idea captures the library, which is used by many on a daily basis, as an extension of the living room or study at home, and employs human-scale components to constitute a whole. In order to realize this concept, we used a geometry in which polyhedrons fill up the space. Unlike a simple sphere or cube, the three kinds of semi-regular polyhedrons were able to fill the space densely, whilst maintaining flat floors. At the same time, they allowed us to explore new architectural possibilities that could not have been sought with the conventional orthogonal grid, such as a new relationship between interior and exterior, or being able to handle plan and section equivalently.

Although the overall appearance created by the geometry of the three polyhedrons is fractal and complex like crystals, the entire structure is constituted by constructive elements of only two different lengths: 4.4 m and 8.8 m. Making use of this, we were able to propose an extremely simple and clear logic of the construction, along with an economically efficient structural system. In this system, three tubular structures which we call "spine", each with a different configuration of stacked polyhedrons, are arranged on site, after which steel members of the two lengths are mounted.

Small enclosed spaces like a house, continuous spaces like a street or open spaces like a plaza could be created freely using the polyhedron modules, which allowed the library to become a "city" in itself.

North elevation

South elevation S=1:400

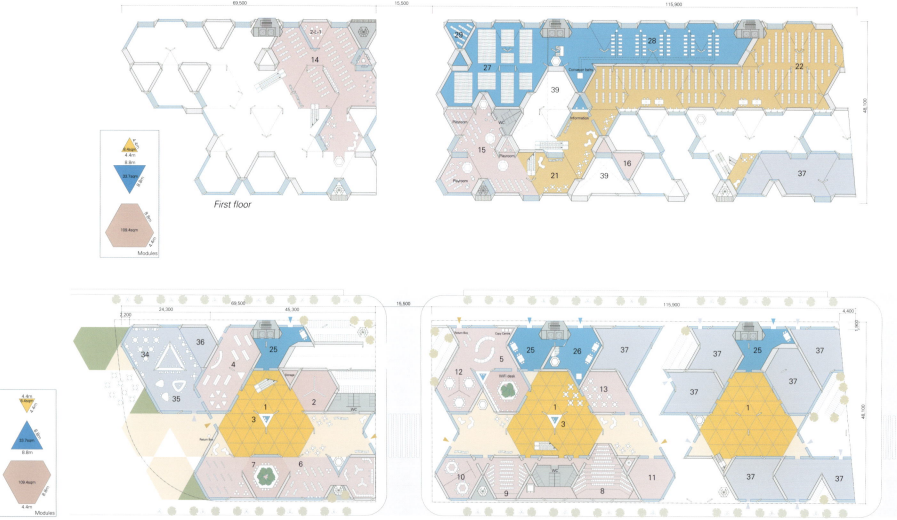

First floor

Ground floor S=1:1000

East elevation

Entrance

West elevation

1 PLAZA	15 KID'S AREA	28 SORTING ROOM
2 ENTRANCE GALLERY	16 AUDITORIUM OPERATION	29 CLIMATE-CONTROLLED ROOM
3 INFORMATION	17 BOOK PASSAGE	30 WORKSTATIONS FOR PERSONAL
4 LIBRARY SHOP	18 BIBLIOHEDRON	SERVING THE PUBLIC
5 24-HOUR LIBRARY	19 GALLEHEDRON	31 SPECIALISED DEPARTMENTS
6 MAGAZINE & NEWSPAPER	20 THEATROHEDRON	32 ADMINISTRATION OFFICE / TECHNICAL SUPPORT
7 NEWSROOM	21 LOUNGE	33 OFFICE / INTERNAL SUPPORT
8 AUDITORIUM	22 OPEN ACCESS STORAGE	34 RESTAURANT
9 THEATER	23 CARREL	35 CAFE & DELI
10 CONFERENCE	24 STUDY	36 PANTRY
11 STUDIO	25 OFFICE LOBBY	37 RETAIL
12 MEETING SPACE	26 LIBRARY OFFICE ENTRANCE	38 TERRACE
13 CAFE BAR	27 STORAGE IN CLOSED SACKS	39 VOID
14 AUDIO-VISUAL		

オスロ市ダイクマン中央図書館
コンペティション応募案

氷河の浸食により生まれたフィヨルド地形の湾奥に位置するオスロ市では，近年港湾エリアの大規模な再開発が進んでいる。その核を成す文化施設として，2008年末，手狭となった旧市街の中央図書館を移転する国際指名コンペティションが行われた。床面積 18,000m²，蔵書数 80万冊の市中央図書館に加え，床面積 40,000m²のフレキシブルな利用が可能なオフィス，ハウジングを含む複合施設とすることが求められた。

駅前広場や敷地東側に計画中の住宅エリアなど様々な方向からの人の流れを考慮し，図書館を低層部に，オフィスやハウジングを上層部に配置し，施設全体が有機的に結ばれる都市的な空間を目指した。

そこで我々が掲げたのが，「本のまち」というコンセプトである。日常的に多くの人々が利用する図書館を住宅の居間や書斎の延長として捉え，ヒューマンスケールの単位を集積させて全体を構成しようという考え方である。このコンセプトを実現するために，我々は多面体で空間を充填する幾何学を採用した。単純な球やキューブと異なり，3種類の半正多面体を密実に充填することで，フラットな床をキープしながらも，従来の直交グリッド空間では得られない，新しい内・外の関係や平面と断面を等価に扱えるといった建築の新たな可能性を模索した。

3種類の多面体が持つ幾何学は，全体の表情としては結晶体のようにフラクタルで複雑な様相を呈するが，4.4mと 8.8mの線分の組み合わせのみで，全体を組み上げることを可能とする。この特性から，多面体の積層パターンが異なる3種類の「スパイン」と名付けられたチューブ状の構造体を敷地に配置し，上記2種類の長さに対応する鋼材を架け渡していく，施工の合理性や経済性に優れた，極めてシンプルかつ明快な構造システムの提案が可能となった。

壁で囲まれた家のような小さな空間や，道のように連続する空間，あるいは広場のような広がりのある空間を多面体モデルによって自在に構成することができ，「まち」そのもののような図書館が生まれた。

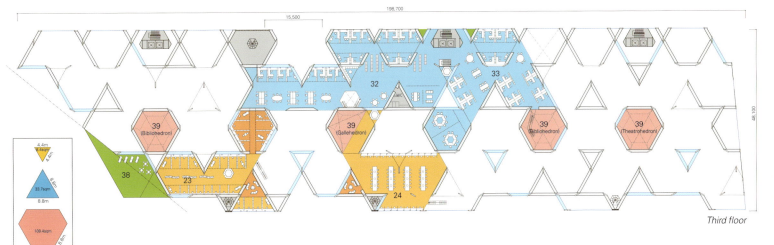
Third floor

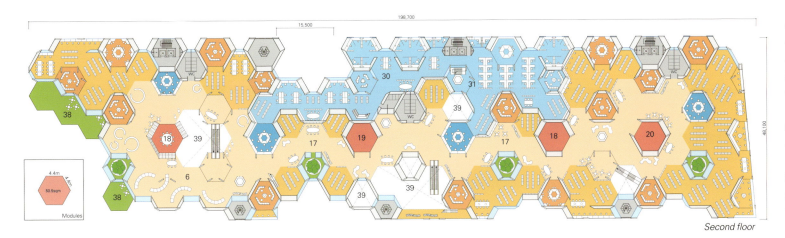
Second floor

1 OFFICE	8 BOOK PASSAGE	15 THEATROHEDRON
2 LIBRARY	9 AUDIO-VISUAL	16 READING CORNER
3 STUDIO	10 PLAYROOM	17 OPEN STACKS
4 TERRACE	11 BIBLIOHEDRON	18 RETAIL
5 COURTYARD	12 CARRELS	19 PLAZA
6 ENTRANCE	13 GALLEHEDRON	20 MACHINE ROOOM
7 INFORMATION	14 LOUNGE	21 PARKING

Truncated octahedral open-stacks

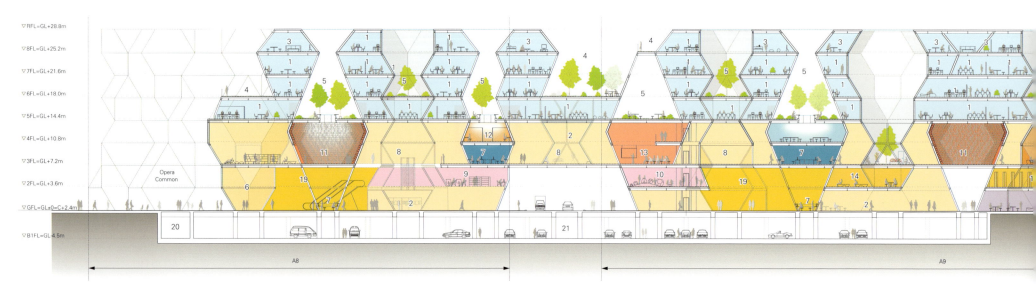

Section S=1:600

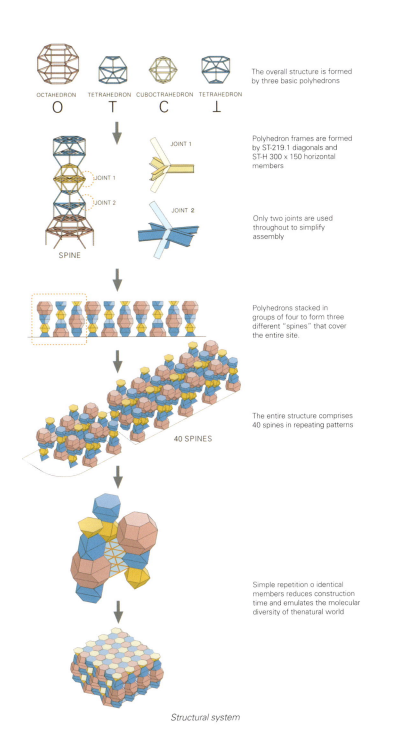

The overall structure is formed by three basic polyhedrons

Polyhedron frames are formed by ST-219.1 diagonals and ST-H 300 x 150 horizontal members

Only two joints are used throughout to simplify assembly

Polyhedrons stacked in groups of four to form three different "spines" that cover the entire site.

The entire structure comprises 40 spines in repeating patterns

Simple repetition o identical members reduces construction time and emulates the molecular diversity of thenatural world

Structural system

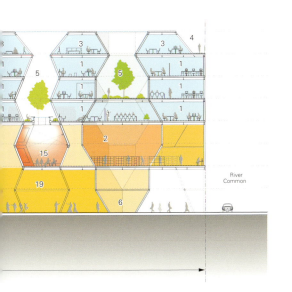

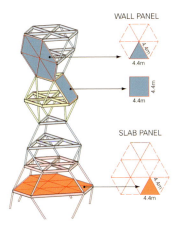

All modules are constituted of semi-regular polyhedron, 4.4 m on each side. And each of them is self-supported only by frames structurally

Terrace

View toward harbor from terrace

Library

127

BAMPFM
University of California, Berkeley
Art Museum and Pacific Film Archive
California, U.S.A.
2009

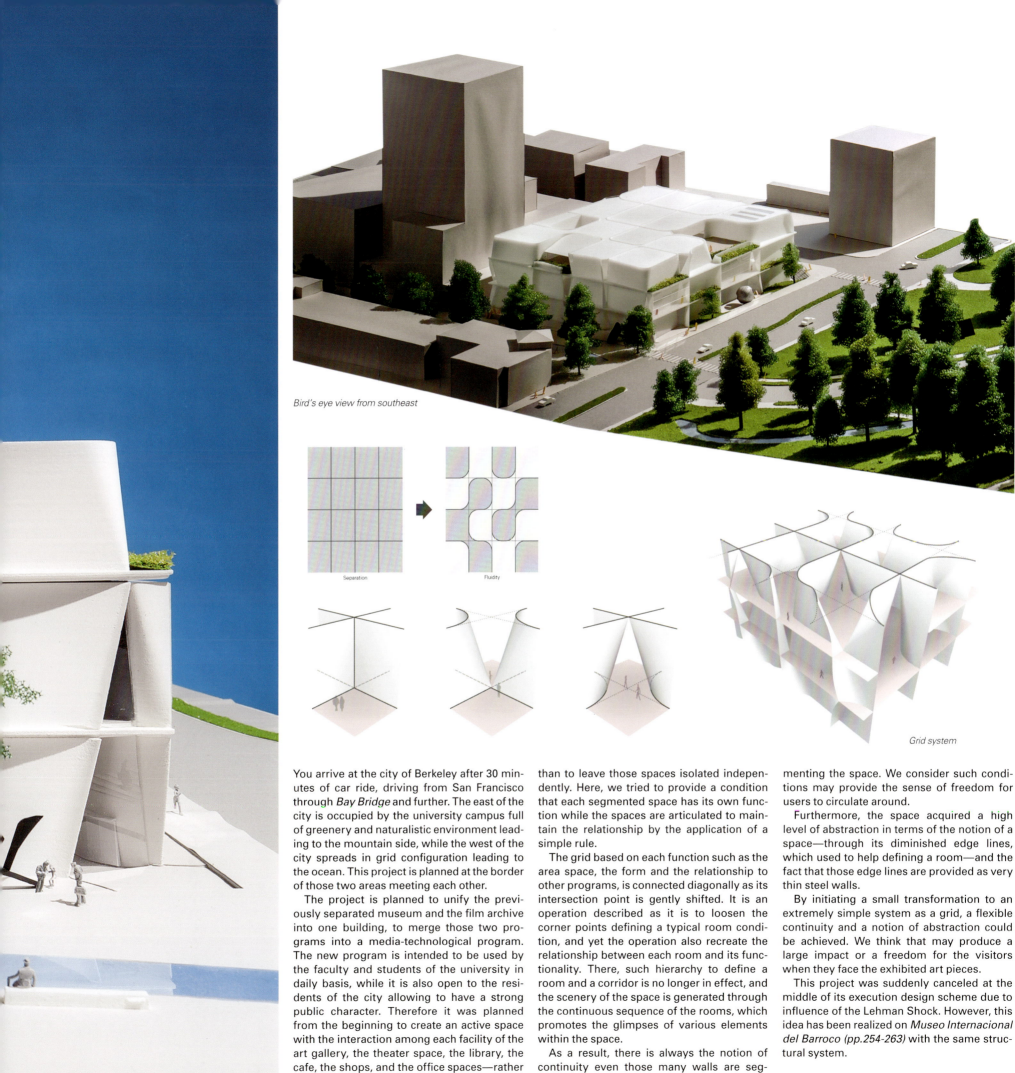

Bird's eye view from southeast

Grid system

You arrive at the city of Berkeley after 30 minutes of car ride, driving from San Francisco through *Bay Bridge* and further. The east of the city is occupied by the university campus full of greenery and naturalistic environment leading to the mountain side, while the west of the city spreads in grid configuration leading to the ocean. This project is planned at the border of those two areas meeting each other.

The project is planned to unify the previously separated museum and the film archive into one building, to merge those two programs into a media-technological program. The new program is intended to be used by the faculty and students of the university in daily basis, while it is also open to the residents of the city allowing to have a strong public character. Therefore it was planned from the beginning to create an active space with the interaction among each facility of the art gallery, the theater space, the library, the cafe, the shops, and the office spaces—rather than to leave those spaces isolated independently. Here, we tried to provide a condition that each segmented space has its own function while the spaces are articulated to maintain the relationship by the application of a simple rule.

The grid based on each function such as the area space, the form and the relationship to other programs, is connected diagonally as its intersection point is gently shifted. It is an operation described as it is to loosen the corner points defining a typical room condition, and yet the operation also recreate the relationship between each room and its functionality. There, such hierarchy to define a room and a corridor is no longer in effect, and the scenery of the space is generated through the continuous sequence of the rooms, which promotes the glimpses of various elements within the space.

As a result, there is always the notion of continuity even those many walls are segmenting the space. We consider such conditions may provide the sense of freedom for users to circulate around.

Furthermore, the space acquired a high level of abstraction in terms of the notion of a space—through its diminished edge lines, which used to help defining a room—and the fact that those edge lines are provided as very thin steel walls.

By initiating a small transformation to an extremely simple system as a grid, a flexible continuity and a notion of abstraction could be achieved. We think that may produce a large impact or a freedom for the visitors when they face the exhibited art pieces.

This project was suddenly canceled at the middle of its execution design scheme due to influence of the Lehman Shock. However, this idea has been realized on *Museo Internacional del Barroco (pp.254-263)* with the same structural system.

Third floor

Second floor

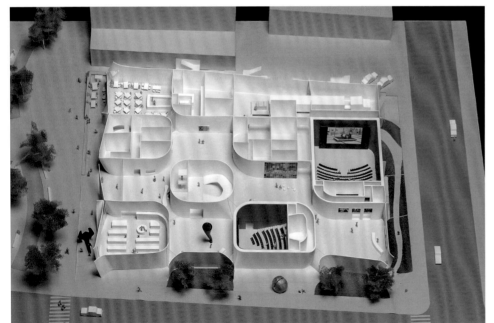
First floor

First floor: public gallery

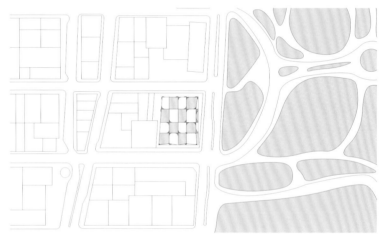
Site plan S=1:5000

カリフォルニア大学 バークレー美術館／パシフィック・フィルム・アーカイブ計画案

サンフランシスコからベイブリッジを渡り，車で30分ほど走るとバークレー市はある。東には山へと続く豊かな自然を持った大学キャンパスが広がり，西には海へと続くグリッド状に構成された市街地が広がる。その二つが向き合う境界に，このプロジェクトは計画された。

従来独立していた美術館とフィルムアーカイブをひとつの建築に統合し，メディアテーク的な融合を図ろうという企画である。また大学の教職員，学生たちが日常的に利用すると同時に，市民の人々にも開放された公共性の強いプログラムから成っている。したがってアートギャラリー，シアター，ライブラリー，カフェ，ショップ，オフィスなど様々な機能が自立して存在するのでなく，相互に関係し合って活気のある空間を生み出すことが当初から意図された。ここで我々は，分節された各々の空間がある単純なルールによって関係を持ちながら，うまく棲み分けられている状態をつくり出すよう試みたのである。

各機能の広さや形状，関係に応じて描かれたグリッドは，その交点がやわらかく曲げられ対角につながっていく。それは部屋を規定する角をひとつ一つほどいていくような作業で，同時に部屋相互のつながりを生み出すものとなる。そこに，もはや部屋と廊下といった空間のヒエラルキーは無く，切れることのない部屋の連続として様々なものが見え隠れしながら風景を展開していく。

こうして多くの壁が空間を分節しながらも，そこには常に連続性が存在し，それが訪れる人に自由な感覚をもたらしてくれるのではないだろうか。

また，部屋を規定する稜線の消失と，それがスティールの非常に薄い壁でつくられることによって，空間に高い抽象性も生まれている。

極めて単純なグリッドというシステムに少しの変形を加えることによって，自由な連続性と抽象性をつくり出す。それが，アートを観る感覚に，大きな揺さぶりと自由をもたらすと考えている。

このプロジェクトは，実施設計の半ばでリーマンショックの影響を受けて，突如中止された。しかし，同様の構造システムを用いた「バロック・インターナショナル ミュージアム・プエブラ」（pp.254-263）として実現された。

Third floor: gallery

Third floor: event space

First floor S=1:800

Second floor

Third floor

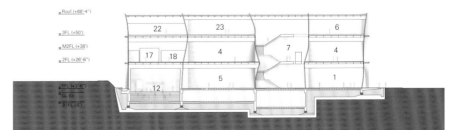
Section S=1:1000

1 MAIN ENTRANCE	8 CAFE/RESTAURANT	15 ART & FILM LIBRARY	22 OFFICE
2 SUB ENTRANCE	9 KITCHEN	16 FILM LIBRARY	23 BOARDROOM/
3 OFFICE &	10 RETAIL	STORAGE	EVENT ROOM
ACADEMIC ENTRANCE	11 THEATER LOBBY &	17 SCREENING ROOM	24 BOARDROOM TERRACE
4 GALLERY	GALLERY	18 MEDIA SEMINAR ROOM	25 ASIAN GARDEN
5 PUBLIC GALLERY	12 THEATER L	19 REST AREA	
6 ASIAN GALLERY	13 THEATER M	20 STUDY CENTER	
7 GALLERY LOBBY	14 LOADING DOCK	21 ART STORAGE	

131

White O
Marbella, Chile
2004–09

In Marbella located 160 km northwest of Santiago, the capital of Chile, a resort has been developed where weekend houses are scattered in a golf course. The site is in this *Marbella Resort* and located downhill toward the northeast. You can see the golf course below, and a range of mountains in the far east. Weekend houses designed by leading Chilean architects, such as Mathias Klotz and Christian de Groote, are built in a row around the area. To unify the designs of the resort, white external walls, horizontal roofs and vertical walls were requested.

While the site for this house is on the sloping site, the main floor is horizontally located on the west, at the far, high ground. People visiting this house passes though under the bedrooms, located on the east, and go up the slope, arriving at the entrance.

Except for garages and rooms for the maids in the basement, main rooms are located on the main floor which circulates surrounding the courtyard. Scenery was taken into consideration so that you can look down at the golf course on the east from the living room, dining space and each bedroom.

The facade with pilotis and the flat roof indicates a rational composition as in initial houses designed by Le Corbusier. Fluidity of a space which spirals tour around from the drive, forms a contrast with the facade.

This house was named *White O* after *White U* built in Tokyo 33 years ago. *White U* is closed to the exterior as if it were underground. On the other hand, a circuit of *White O* floats freely as if it were on air.

Overall view from northeast

View from rooftop

Overall view from north: bedrooms (left) and living/dining room (right)

133

White O

南米チリの首都サンティアゴから160km北西に位置するマルベーリャでは、ゴルフコースの中に別荘が点在するリゾート開発が進んでいる。敷地はこのマルベーリャ・リゾートの一角にあり、北東に向かって緩やかに下る斜面の途中に位置する。眼下にはゴルフコースが広がり、遥か東方に山々の連なりを望む。周辺には、マティアス・クロッツ、クリスチャン・デ・グルーテ等、チリの著名建築家による別荘が建ち並んでいる。全体のデザイン統一のため、白い外観、水平な屋根と垂直な壁が求められた。

傾斜した敷地に対し、メインフロアは西側のかなり高いレベルに水平に設定された。したがって、ここを訪れる人々は、東側に置かれたベッドルームの下を通過してスロープを上り、エントランスに到達する。

下階のガレージやメイドルームを除けば、主要な諸室はすべて、中庭を囲い込みながらサーキュレートするメインフロアに置かれている。リビングやダイニングスペース、各ベッドルームはすべて東側のゴルフコースを見下ろせるよう眺望に配慮された。

フラットルーフにピロティを持つファサードは、ル・コルビュジエの初期住宅のように理性的な構成を示しているが、アプローチから内部を周遊しながらスパイラルを描く空間の流動性は、ファサードと強いコントラストを形成する。

40年前に東京につくられた「White U」に因んでこの住宅は「White O」と命名された。「White U」が地下を周遊するかのように外界に対して閉ざされているのに対し、「White O」は空中を周遊するかのように開放的に宙に浮かぶ。

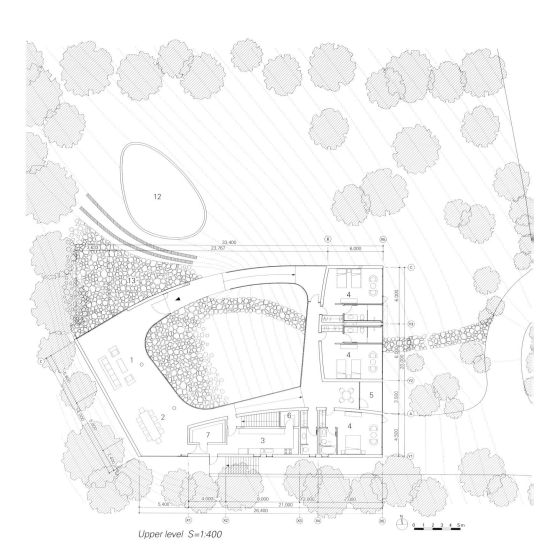

Upper level S=1:400

1 LIVING ROOM
2 DINING ROOM
3 KITCHEN
4 BEDROOM
5 TERRACE
6 PANTRY
7 WINE CELLAR
8 MECHANICAL
9 CLOSET
10 LAUNDRY
11 PARKING
12 POOL
13 BARBECUE TERRACE

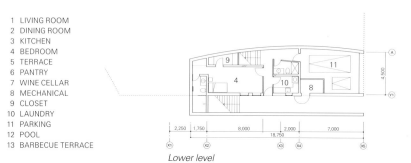

Lower level

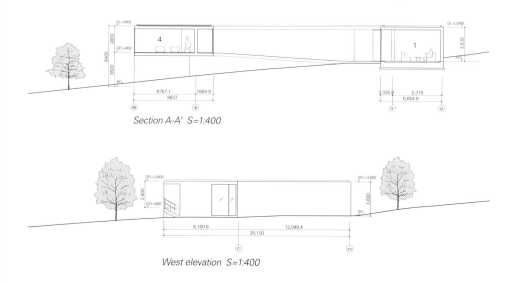

Section A-A' S=1:400

West elevation S=1:400

Ramp to entrance on east

View toward living/dining room from entrance on east

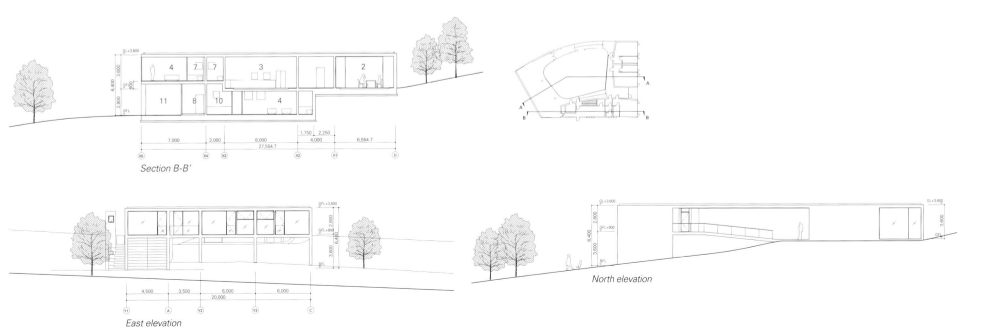

Section B-B'

East elevation

North elevation

Evening view from north: bedrooms (left) and living/dining room (right)

Ramp and corridor: bedrooms on right

Bedroom

Living/dining room

View toward living/dining room through court

Facade Renovation "Suites Avenue Aparthotel"
Barcelona, Spain
2003–09

Many buildings created by the hand of Antonio Gaud stand in Barcelona and now those have become the symbols to build up the identity of the local residents, with the great presence to be loved by anybody. This project of converting an existing office building to a hotel was developed within such atmosphere. We are commissioned to design the building facade and the staircase hall.

The existing building is facing to the Passeig de Gracia, the main street of the area, and there stands the Gaudí's *Casa Milá* with its unique waving facade on diagonally opposite side across the street. This organic impression represented by *Casa Milá* aroused great sympathy from our team as we also considered it is where the essential concept lies to enliven people. Then we groped for the way of a facade, which carries the organic quality as found in *Casa Milá*'s while at the same time it also goes along with the scale of the city. As a result we suggested a 'wave' that involves the notion of movements illustrated by the steel plate in 8 mm thickness.

The 'waves' are produced in numbers as they appear to be flowing across on facade. If each wave is close together, they form a wall to enclose the building, while the separate waves will create a large opening to provide a surrounding view. Originally those waves were designed in large scale, but the scale has gradually changed to smaller size in consideration to the visibility issue. In addition, the existing office building has the same configuration with the surrounding building that the front facade of the seven-story building is divided into four sections to allocate the rooms. The waves are produced based on this 7 x 4 grid in order to make the sense of a linkage of this facade to the scale of the city.

Therefore, the forms of the waves were instinctively determined but at the same time they are following a certain order. We consider that this design approach allowed to give the notion of organic movement while the facade also harmonizes with the scale of the city—to become one of the new faces of the city to illustrate the uniqueness of Barcelona.

And yet, this project consequently became the starting point of our direction in design to link a 'movement' with an 'order'.

View from Passeig de Gracia ▷

View toward "Casa Milá" through facade

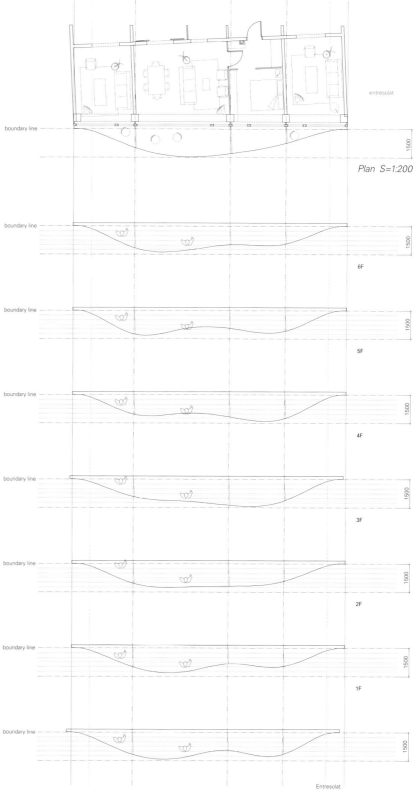
Plan S=1:200

Facade line S=1:200

スイーツアベニュー・アパートホテル
ファサードリノベーション

バルセロナに幾つも建つガウディの建築は、市民のアイデンティティをつくり上げるシンボルとなっており、誰からも愛されている大きな存在である。そのような街で、既存のオフィスビルをホテルに改修する計画が進められた。我々に依頼されたのは、その建物のファサードと階段室のデザインである。

既存の建物は目抜き通りとなるガルシア通りに面し、はす向かいには波打つファサードが特徴的なアントニオ・ガウディ設計の「カサ・ミラ」(1910年)が建っている。ここで我々は、「カサ・ミラ」の持つ有機的なイメージに大きな共感を覚えていた。そこに人々を活気づける本質があると、我々も考えていたからである。そこで、「カサ・ミラ」のような有機性を持ちつつも街のスケールに調和する、ファサードのあり方を模索した。そして、我々が提案したのは、厚さ8mmの鉄板で描かれる動きを内包した「波」である。

「波」は横に流れるかのように何本も描かれ、波同士が近付けばそれは壁として建物を覆い、波同士が離れれば景色を見渡す大きな開口となる。元々、大きな波としてデザインしていたが、視認性の問題を考慮して現在の細かい波へと変更されていった。また、既存のオフィスビルは周辺の建物と同じ構成を採っており、7階建ての前面は間口が四つに分けられ、部屋が並んでいる。「波」は、この7×4のグリッドを下敷きとして描かれることによって、街のスケールに繋がる印象を生み出しているのである。

こうして波の形状は、感覚的に決められながらもある基準に沿って描かれている。そうすることによって、有機的な動きを持ちつつ街のスケールに調和したファサードとなり、バルセロナの街の特長を形づくる新たな顔のひとつと成り得たのではないかと考えている。

そしてこのプロジェクトは、後に「動き」と「ルール」を結びつける志向の契機となった。

Kaohsiung National Stadium
Kaohsiung, Taiwan, R.O.C.
2006–09

Kaohsiung City, located south of the Tropic of Cancer, is blessed with the wealth of the nature and the climate among other Taiwan cities, allowing the active and lively lifestyles of the residents. This project located at the south of Kaohsiung City, will be the main stadium of the World Game held in 2009. The stadium houses 40,000 seats, (55,000 seats when it includes the temporal additional seating) and the project has been progressed since the international competition in 2005, with three main concepts of providing an 'open stadium', an urban park, and a 'spiral sequential form'.

On the contrary to the conventional closed stadium, the spectator seating of *Kaohsiung National Stadium* is open to the frontage road. This allows to provide a circulation to bring in visitors from MRT station located south-east of the site, defined as the first concept, the 'open stadium'.

This open stadium can provide the daily use of the athletic field and the plaza space in front of the entrance area as one combined field even when there is no event. The visitors for taking a walk on Sunday can experience a completely new type of park leading to this athletic field. This is the second concept, the 'urban park'.

The roof over the spectator seating area opened up to the frontage road has 32 streaks of pipes called 'Oscillate Hoop' with the outside diameter in 318.5 ø, forming continuous spirals as part of the structure system. These 'Oscillate Hoops' following the flowing wavy roof shape then become the spiral sequential forms extending from the athletic field to the entrance plaza. It is intended that those spiral sequential forms will bring in event visitors to the spectator seating area by uplifting their emotion.

Kaohsiung National Stadium, based on those three concepts, represent the dynamic expressions filled with the unstable but fluid movements found in the energetic gestures of the human body.

Overall view from south.
Seating is open to front road unlike ordinary circular stadium

Southwest end of "Spiral Continuum"

高雄国家体育場

北回帰線よりも南に位置する高雄市は，台湾の中でもとりわけ豊かな自然，風土に恵まれ，人々の生活は活気に満ち溢れている。高雄市北部に位置するこのスタジアムは，2009年に開催されたワールドゲームズの主会場となった。40,000席（仮設増設席を加えると55,000席）を収容するこのスタジアムは，2005年の国際コンペティション以来，オープン・スタジアム，アーバン・パーク，スパイラル連続体の三つのコンセプトを掲げてプロジェクトが進行した。

従来の閉鎖的なスタジアムとは異なり，このスタジアムは前面の中海路へ向けて観客席が開かれている。それによって敷地南東のMRT駅からの来場者を迎え入れるような動線計画が実現し，第一のオープン・スタジアムのコンセプトとなっている。

オープン・スタジアムは，イベントのない日常時でも，エントランス前の広場と，競技フィールドを一体化して利用することも可能である。日曜日に散歩に訪れる人々は，競技フィールドと連続した全く新しい形の公園を体験することができる。これが二つめのアーバン・パークのコンセプトである。

前面道路に向かって開かれる観客席に架けられた屋根には，32条の「オシレート・フープ」と呼ばれる外径318.5φの鋼管が，構造体の一部としてスパイラルを描きながら連続している。流動的にうねる屋根形状に沿うオシレート・フープは，競技フィールドからエントランス広場へと連なるスパイラル連続体となる。イベントに訪れる人々の高揚感を高めながら観客席へ迎え入れる，スパイラル連続体にはそのような効果が意図されている。

これら三つのコンセプトに基づくスタジアムは，躍動する身体のように，不安定ではあるが流動性に満ちたダイナミズムが表現されている。

View from north

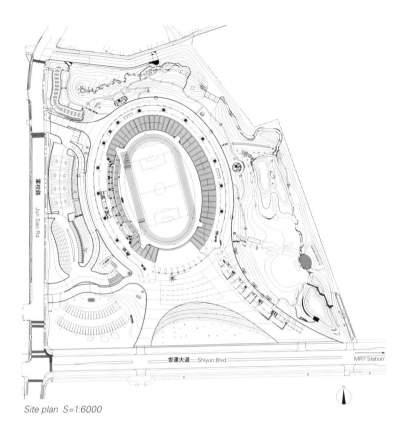

Site plan S=1:6000

Stand on first floor: view toward series of "Saddle"

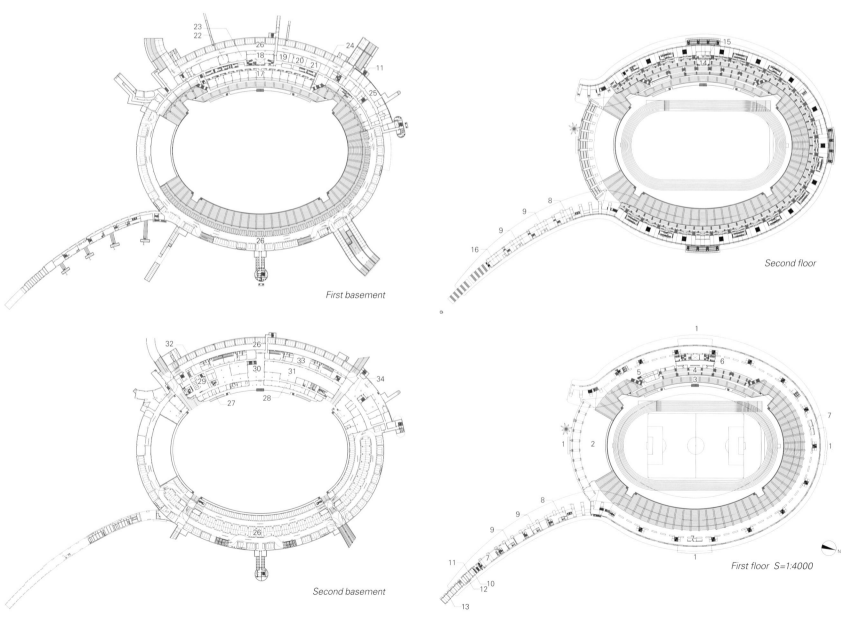

First basement

Second floor

Second basement

First floor S=1:4000

1 ENTRANCE	14 PODIUM	26 CAR PARKING SPACE
2 LAWN SEATS	15 GUARD'S ROOM	27 ANNOUNCE BOOTH
3 LOWER SEATS	16 "GREEN ARCHITECTURE"	28 ADMINISTRATIVE ROOM
4 RESERVED SEATS FOR GUESTS	LECTURE ROOM	29 BRIEFING ROOM
5 MONITORING ROOM	17 VIP ROOM	30 ATHLETES LOBBY
6 CLOAK ROOM	18 VIP LOBBY	31 WARMING-UP ROOM
7 SHOP	19 VIP PREPARATION ROOM	32 MULTI PURPOSE REST ROOM
8 SPORTS BAR	20 PANTRY	33 ATHLETES REST ROOM
9 RESTAURANT	21 KITCHEN	34 LOADING AREA
10 WHEEL CHAIR AND PRAM PARK	22 MEDIA ROOM	35 MAINTENANCE ROUTE
11 OFFICE	23 MEDIA WORK ROOM	36 LED DISPLAY
12 INFORMATION	24 STAFF ROOM	
13 TICKET COUNTER	25 MEETING ROOM	

Concorse on second floor

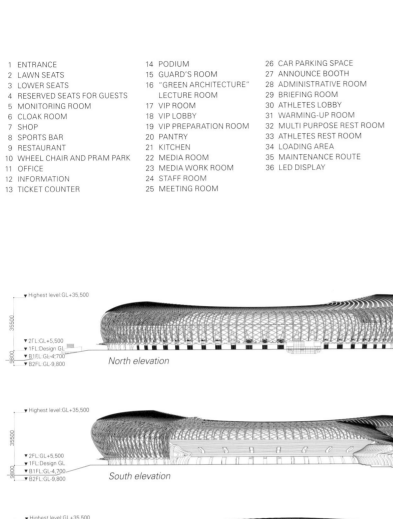

North elevation

South elevation

West elevation

East elevation S=1:2500

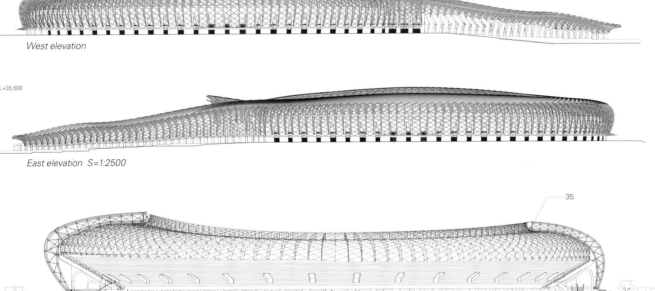

East-west cross section

North-south longitudinal section S=1:1500

Looking southeast from north stand

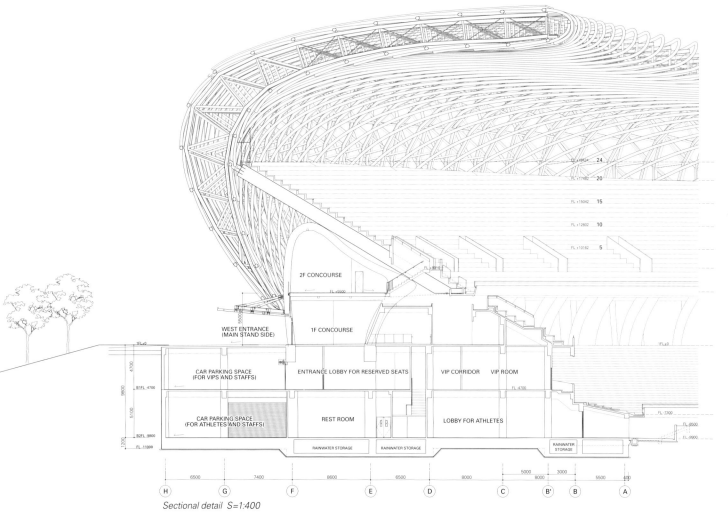
Sectional detail S=1:400

Downward view of field from north stand

South view from fourth floor of Block 9

Club house floating above pool

Concept diagram

Singapore, a city state built within the tropical forest, receive an overwhelming life force of the nature to energize the lives of the residents. Especially the high-class condominiums is where the pioneering experimental models are suggested for new ways of lifestyle, presented with the abundance of quality in materials and designs, and the unique and original design identities.

Belle Vue Residences are created by directly reflecting the vitality of the nature to the formation system of a building. In other words, the condition of a growing tree whose spaces are sequenced and spread out, is overlaid on a building floor plan. This operation largely reflects the restricting conditions of the site, that it is located on a hill close to the presidential residence and the area is designated as the special scenic zone to limit the height of the buildings to low—therefore the buildings had to be distributed in extremely high density condition with small building intervals.

We attempted to solve this severe restrictions through architectural operation by using the visibility shifting condition created by the floor plan branching out like a tree. A tree grows up in fractal manner by branching out from its thick stem to twigs and leaves, looking for a daylight. Based on this growth of a tree as an essential idea, nine houses as trees—with the elevator shafts as stems, and the floor plans spreading out as if the twigs and leaves—grow as they sometimes take adequate distance from each other to efficiently bring in the daylight, natural wind, or the scenery, or sometimes connect with others. In the end, they stood up as four wings of residential buildings in five story high, surrounding a courtyard with a large water surface. Those 176 residences achieved free and diversely changing floor plans, and each brings in the green courtyard space to every single corner of the building as each residence interweaves with the folding shape of the building. In addition, the large surface area of the facade allowed to provide windows facing to various directions. Furthermore, this branching system also enabled to fulfill the request for efficient planning by eliminating the corridor space, as it allows a direct access to each residence from the core.

By conceptualizing architecture through the notion of the nature that forms in fractal manner, and by setting up an intimate conditions with the nature, we produced a new value to create richer and more diverse relationships. In other words, it is a new suggestion of raising questions derived from our thought of producing a living environment as if the forest—against the 20th century concept of producing a stable but artificial environment through repetitive or uniform application of a concept, often led to the isolation from the surrounding nature. As we human beings are the part of the nature, it is one of the large significant points of this project to explore the possibility of an architecture also to be united with the nature.

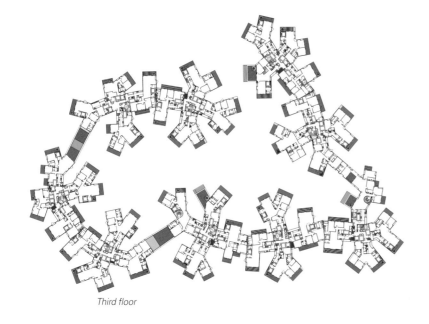
Third floor

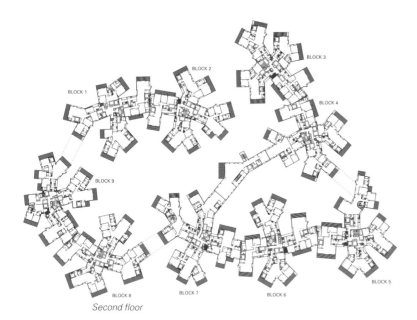
Second floor

First floor S=1:1800

Type-A

Type-B

Type-C

Type-D

Type-E

Type-F

Unit plan S=1:200

1 LIVING ROOM
2 DINING ROOM
3 KITCHEN
4 MASTER BEDROOM
5 BEDROOM
6 BATHROOM

Unit on fourth floor of Block 9

View toward sunkun garden from exterior corridor beside club house

Connection of club house with Block 7

ベルビュー・レジデンシズ

熱帯雨林の中にできた都市国家シンガポールは、その圧倒的自然の生命力に後押しされ、人々の暮らしもエネルギーに満ち溢れている。とりわけハイクラスなコンドミニアムは、そこに質的な豊かさと独自のアイデンティティによって、新しいライフスタイルの先駆的モデルを提案する場となっている。

「ベルビュー・レジデンシズ」は、自然の活力をそのまま建物が生成する仕組みに投影し、あたかも木が成長するように、空間が連続し広がる様を建築プランに重ね合わせることで生まれた。この背景には、敷地が大統領官邸にほど近い高台にあり、建築高さが低く制限される特別景観地区に指定されているため、非常に高密で隣棟間隔が小さな配置にならざるをえなかった要因が大きい。

我々は枝分かれする木のような平面がもたらす視線のずれを利用して、その厳しい条件を建築的に解決することを試みた。木は太い幹から光を求めて分岐した枝がさらに小枝へと派生し葉を茂らせ、フラクタルに成長していく。これと同様の原理に基づいて、エレベータ・シャフトを幹に見立て、枝葉が伸びるようにフロアが展開する9本の木の家が、日差しや風・眺望を有効に取り込むために互いに適度な距離をとったり、時には連結したりして成長し、全体として5階建て4棟の住宅が大きな水面をたたえた中庭を囲むような形で建ち上がった。こうして176戸に及ぶ住戸は自由で多様に変化する平面形を持ち、襞状の建物形状と絡み合うように隅々にまで緑の中庭を引き込む。また、この襞がつくり出す大きな立面によって、様々な方向に窓が開けられた。この枝分かれシステムは、コアから直接アクセス可能な廊下を持たない、極めて効率の高いプランニングの要請も同時に満たすことを可能とした。

フラクタルに自己生成する自然の原理を手がかりに建築を発想し、自然と極めて親密な状態を築くことによって、より豊かで多様な関係を生み出す新たな価値を導き出した。これは森がつくられていくように住環境をつくるという想いが、反復や均質化・外界との断絶によって安定した人工環境をつくり上げてきた20世紀的思考に対する新たな問題提起であるとも言える。人間が自然の一部であるように、建築もまた自然と一体になりえる可能性を探求することが、このプロジェクトに込められたひとつの大きな意義である。

TORRES PORTA FIRA
Barcelona, Spain
2004–10

Torres Porta Fira (left), Entrance Hall (center), and Pavilion 1 (right)

It is one of the series of expansion plans started in 2002, for Barcelona trade fair convention center called *Montjuic 2*. This particular project is the complex building including the office space, a hotel, a spa facility, and conference halls. The site is in the city of L'Hospitalet de Llobregat, located between the airport and the center of Barcelona. Because of its location, we intended to provide a role to the building as a gate to the whole complex of this convention center, by providing twin towers facing the west entrance hall of the convention center across the plaza.

The two towers are configured as an hotel wing in an organic volume with a simple circular core, and as an office wing in simple rectangular volume with an organic core. We considered the dynamic contrast in volume between those two towers would produce a boldness to be the symbol of the town.

The volume of the organic form is defined by the locus of a curve rotating as it rises up. The shape of the plan of this curve is controlled by six points on the curve, while those points are clustered in half and batch processed for scaling to produce the impression of the volume rising up smoothly with oscillation. The rising curve with rotation gradually expands larger as it reaches to higher floor levels, while its rotation angle also gradually increases. By this operation, the higher floor levels concentrated with the suit rooms will achieve the view toward the surrounding city scape.

The core of the office wing with a rectilinear silhouette is also generated by the locus of a curve rising up with rotational movement. This core is sectioned by the rectangular surface of the glass to reveal its section shape.

Those two towers are in the complemental relationship for each other, as they transform the expression of a static architecture into the expression of the kinematic volume that is twisted and rotated within the notion of time.

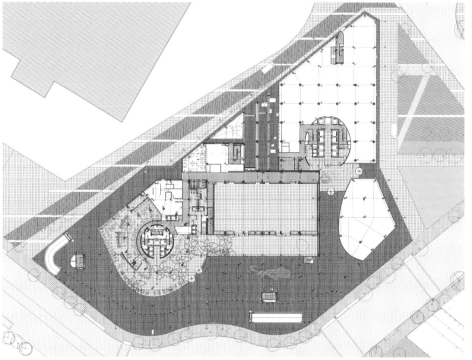

Site plan S=1:1000

Overall view from southeast: hotel wing (left) and office wing (right)

トーレス ポルタ フィラ

「モンジュイック2」と呼ばれる2002年に始まった一連のバルセロナ見本市会場の拡張計画のひとつであり，オフィス，ホテル，スパ，カンファレンスホールなどからなる複合施設である。敷地は，オスピタレット市に位置し，空港とバルセロナ市中心部との間に立地することから，見本市会場全体にとってゲートの役割を果たすよう，見本市会場の西側エントランスホールと広場を挟んで向かい合うツインタワーとして計画された。

2本のタワーは，それぞれ有機的な形の中に円形のシンプルなコアを有するホテル棟，矩形のシンプルなヴォリュームの中に有機的なコアが入ったオフィス棟からなる。この二つのダイナミックな対比が，街のシンボルとなりうる強さを生むと考えた。

有機的なヴォリュームは，回転しながら上昇するカーブの軌跡によって決定されている。カーブの平面形状は，六つのコントロール・ポイントによって制御されており，その半分をクラスター化し一括してスケーリングすることで，滑らかに揺らめきながら立ち上がる印象を生み出している。回転しながら上昇するカーブは，高層階に近づくほど緩やかに広がりながら，その回転する角度を増していく。スイート・ルームが集中する上層階は，街を一望する眺めをより多く確保することができる。

直線的なシルエットのオフィス棟のコアも，同様に回転しながら上昇するカーブの軌跡によって生み出されている。コアは，ガラスの矩形面によってカットされた断面形を示すことになる。

これら二つのタワーは，ともに静的な建築の表現を時間とともにねじれ回転する運動体の表現に変換しつつ，相互に補完し合う関係にある。

Typical floor of office wing: view toward hotel wing through window

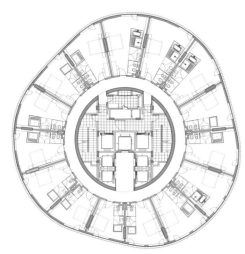
13th floor: hotel wing S=1:500

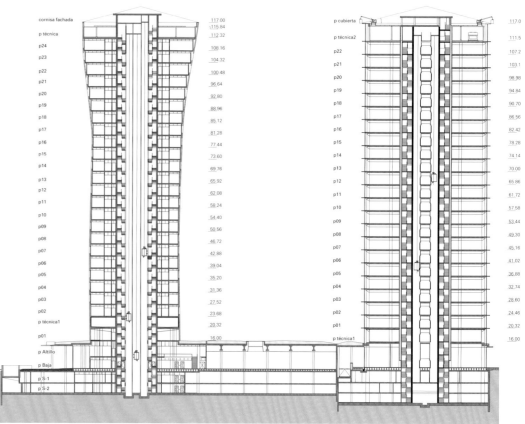

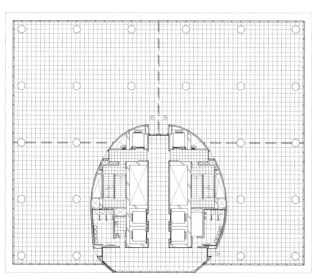
Typival plan: office wing S=1:500

Entrance of office wing

Section S=1:1200

Lobby of hotel wing

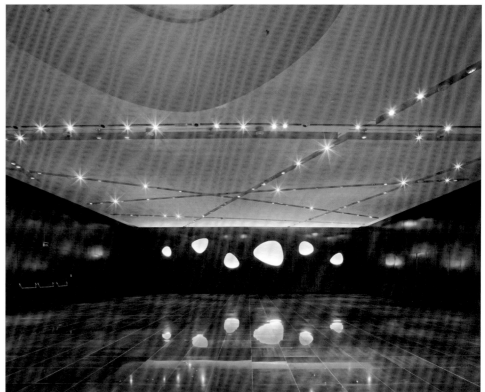

Foyer of hotel wing

Entrance hall and reception of hotel wing

Restaurant on ground level of hotel wing

Toyo Ito Museum of Architecture
Imabari, Ehime, Japan
2008–11

Overall view from east of Steel Hut

South view: Silver Hut (left) and Steel Hut (right)

Located on the southwest side of Omishima, an island that floats in the Seto Inland Sea, Ito's very own museum is built facing the sea on a steep slope next to *mikan* (mandarin oranges) fields. The site is especially impressive for its sunset that sets over the sea.

The museum is composed of two buildings—Steel Hut that houses the main exhibition and Silver Hut that acts as an archive and workshop space for different activities.

Steel Hut is located on top of a hill at the ridge of the site. On a topography that is full of undulations, we purposely decided to adapt a geometric plan that is independent of the topography.

The geometry came from ideas we proposed for the competition for *Oslo City Central Library (pp.122-127)* that ran in parallel with this project; by filling up the space with four different types of polyhedrons, we were able to achieve a 3-dimensional space with a flat floor and walls that are not perpendicular.

The polyhedron interior space without clear distinctions between the roof, walls and floor of the Steel Hut are all completed as an exhibition room on its own, while the spatial character of being cradled within it is being highlighted. Even though each exhibition room has the same plan, the ways that the spaces extend out are completely different, enabling people to feel like they are walking across different universes even within a small space.

Furthermore, the linear silhouette of the polyhedron sits distinctively within the surrounding nature, and echoes in harmony with the calm horizon of the Seto Inland Sea.

On the other hand, Silver Hut is located on the valley of the site that also has a beautiful view. It is a recreation of Ito's old residence in Tokyo that follows the original structure, but moreover, it became a more primitive architecture by minimizing the indoor spaces and expanding the courtyard by adjusting the columns and the roof.

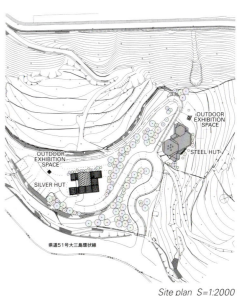

Site plan S=1:2000

157

1 ENTRANCE HALL
2 ROOM
3 SALON
4 STORAGE
5 UTILITY / WC
6 VOID
7 TERRACE

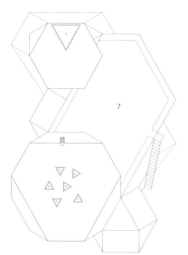

Roof: Steel Hut

Overall view from west of Steel Hut

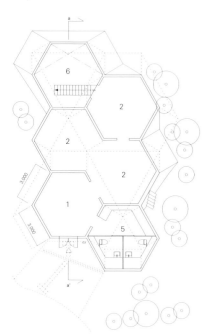

Second floor: Steel Hut

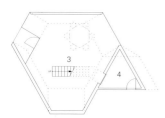

First floor: Steel Hut S=1:300

Section: Steel Hut S=1:300

West elevation: Steel Hut S=1:300

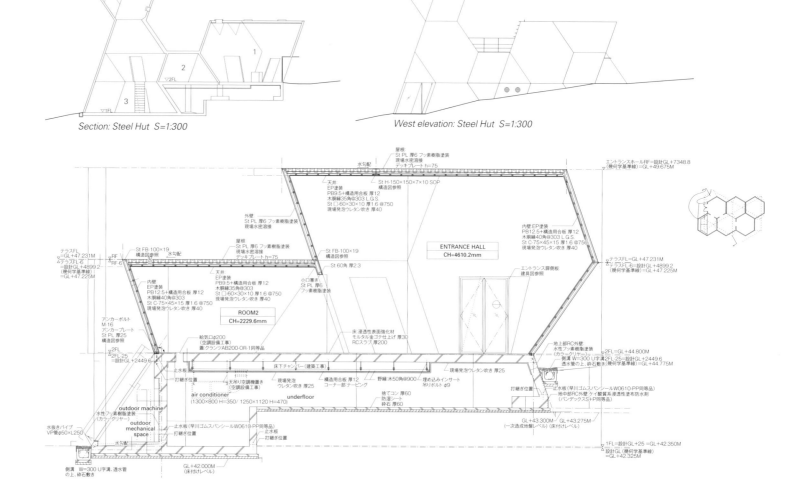

Sectional detail: Steel Hut S=1:100

Overall view of Silver Hut from east

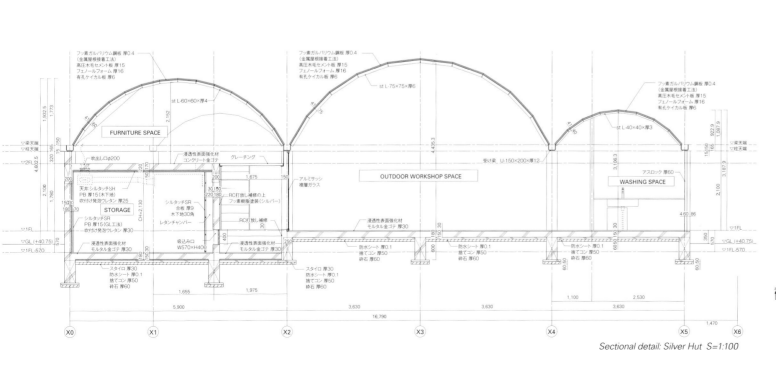

Sectional detail: Silver Hut S=1:100

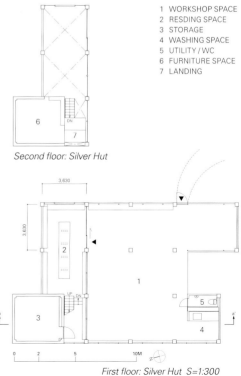

1 WORKSHOP SPACE
2 RESDING SPACE
3 STORAGE
4 WASHING SPACE
5 UTILITY / WC
6 FURNITURE SPACE
7 LANDING

Second floor: Silver Hut

First floor: Silver Hut S=1:300

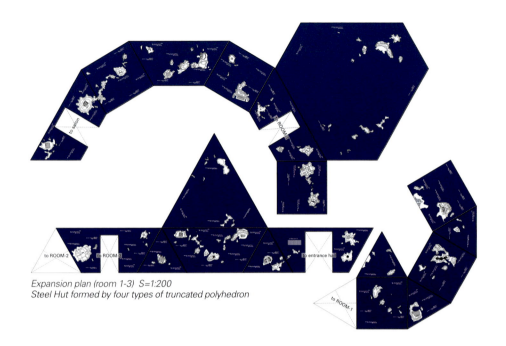

Expansion plan (room 1-3) S=1:200
Steel Hut formed by four types of truncated polyhedron

Room 1 of Steel Hut: Entrance hall (left), room 2 (center) and room 3 (right)

今治市伊東豊雄建築ミュージアム

瀬戸内海に浮かぶ大三島の南西部，海を臨むみかん畑の急斜面に建つ，伊東自身のミュージアムである。とりわけ，海に沈む夕陽が印象的な敷地である。

ミュージアムは，展示をメインとする「スティールハット」と，アーカイブ機能と合わせてワークショップなどの活動の場となる「シルバーハット」の2棟で構成される。

「スティールハット」は，敷地の尾根にあたる高台に位置する。起伏に富んだ自然地形に対して，我々はあえて地形とは無関係の自立した幾何学を持ち込むことにした。この幾何学は同時期に進行していた「オスロ市ダイクマン中央図書館 コンペティション応募案」(pp.122-127)で提案したアイデアであり，4種類の多面体を隙間無く充填することで，フラットな床をつくりながらも，直交ではない新たな3次元グリッド空間が立ち現れるものである。

「スティールハット」において，屋根・壁・床の区別のない多面体の内部はひとつ一つが完結した展示室となり，個々の多面体のもつ包み込むような空間性がより際立っている。各展示室は同じ平面を持ちながらも，それぞれに空間の広がりがまったく異なり，小さいながらも異なる宇宙を渡り歩くような感覚を得られる。

また，この多面体がかたちづくる直線的なシルエットは自然の中に起立し，穏やかな瀬戸内海の水平線と呼応するかのようである。

一方，「シルバーハット」は敷地の谷間の見晴らしの良い場所に位置する。東京にあった伊東の旧自邸を再生したもので，当時のストラクチャーを踏襲しながら，屋内化するスペースを最低限とすることで，柱と屋根によって規定される「中庭」が拡張され，より原始的な建築となった。

Salon of Steel Hut

Outdoor workshop space of Silver Hut (court of old Silver Hut): view toward Osakikamijima on west

Furniture space of Silver Hut (children's space of old Silver Hut): furniture designed by Teruaki Ohashi

View toward reading space from outdoor workshop space of Silver Hut

Reading space of Silver Hut (kitchen of old Silver Hut)

House H
Hokkaido, Japan
2009–11

The project is a weekend house that is situated on a slope that overlooks Lake Toya in Hokkaido.

The interior space is created with five curved walls inside of the simple 12 m square concrete box. The 12 cm-thick walls are structure that surround spotting mats like stepping stones and a bathroom.

Each mat is similar to a tatami mat raised 40 cm above earth-floor-like concrete floor and used both as sofa and bed. Each could be separated with curtains and during the daytime it becomes lighting tube filled with natural light falling from above. There will be various kinds of space between the tubes.

For the client, who grew up in Hokkaido and now lives in Tokyo, this place is as if his hometown. Deriving from a wish to plant vegetables, cook food and throw parties with many friends as much as possible, the house was planned. After retirement he wishes to live here and revitalize the village together with neighbors, who carry on farming. Although the space is small, the dream extending from the place is big.

Overall view from southeast

洞爺湖H邸

北海道洞爺湖を見下ろす傾斜地に建つ週末住居である。

12m四方の単純なコンクリートボックスの内部は、5枚の湾曲する壁面によって空間が形成されている。これらの壁は、飛び石のように点在するマット部、及び浴室部を囲い込む12cm厚の構造体である。

各マットは土間のようなコンクリート床から40cm持ち上げられた置き畳のような存在で、ソファ兼ベッドでもある。それぞれカーテンによって遮蔽することができ、昼間は上部からの自然光に満たされた光のチューブとなる。これらチューブの間には、様々な場所がつくられることになるだろう。

北海道育ちで現在は東京に住むクライアントにとって、ここは故郷のような土地である。時間の許す限り、野菜を栽培し、多くの友人たちと食事をつくってパーティを催したいという想いから、この住居を企画した。老後はここに住み、農業を営む近隣の人々と村起こしをしたいとも考えているようである。単純で素朴な小さな空間であるが、ここから拡がる夢は大きい。

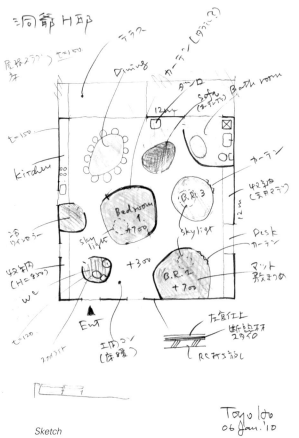
Sketch

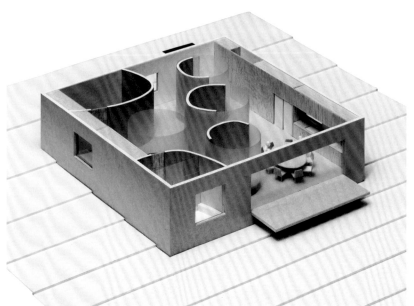
Model

Five curved walls inside of the simple 12 meters square (under construction)

Living/dining room

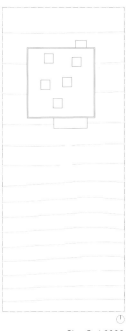
Site S=1:2000

Plan S=1:200

1 ENTRANCE
2 LIVING ROOM
3 DINING ROOM
4 KITCHEN
5 BED ROOM
6 BATHROOM
7 TERRACE

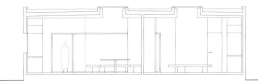
East-west section S=1:200

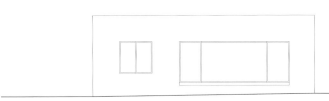
South elevation

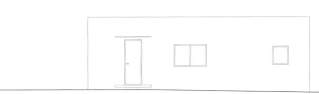
North elevation

East elevation

West elevation S=1:200

Ken Iwata
Mother and Child
Museum, Imabari City
Imabari, Ehime, Japan
2009–11

Downward view from east

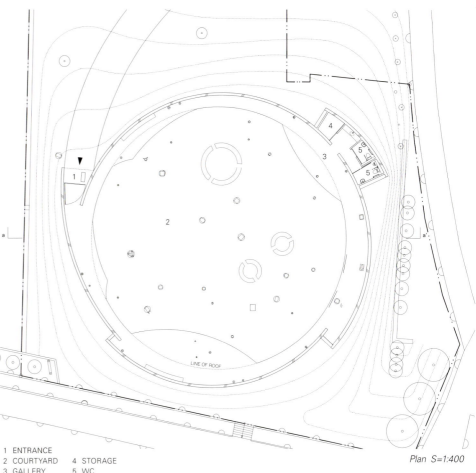

1 ENTRANCE
2 COURTYARD
3 GALLERY
4 STORAGE
5 WC

Plan S=1:400

The museum stands on the southern edge of Omishima, a small island lying off the city of Imabari, Ehime Prefecture. It is designed to house artworks created by the sculptor Ken Iwata.

With the *Ohyamazumi Shrine* at its heart, Omishima has long been regarded as a sacred island and a spiritual center for the local people. Sculptor Ken Iwata was drafted into the Japanese air force while attending the Tokyo School of Fine Arts towards the end of World War II. Peace was declared only moments before he was due to fly out as a *kamikaze* pilot. After the war, Iwata taught art at the Keio Yochisha Elementary School while producing artwork on the theme of "mother and child" at his atelier studio in Kawaguchi, Saitama Prefecture. When Iwata visited Omishima in 2009, he immediately sensed the richness of the land, and decided to build and donate a museum on a beachfront site within the schoolyard of a former elementary school.

Of the 44 permanently installed works, the majority are figurative bronze sculptures. At first, we studied various ideas such as attaching the front yard to the exhibition building, and attempting to only design the landscape and placing the majority of the artwork outside. Ultimately, we decided to pursue the idea of an exhibition space surrounded by a circular concrete wall in a manner similar to *manmaku* (the curtains hung during special events in Japan).

Five arc-shaped walls, each 2.7 m in height, are arranged slightly offset from each other to create an enclosure of approximately 30 m in diameter. The upper parts of the wall have eaves that project inward in widths of 1.2 to 2.5 m. The eaves protect two marble sculptures from rain and sunlight, as well as providing resting spaces for visitors. The open-air central area is laid with grass, with sculptures of various sizes installed at different heights and directions throughout the courtyard and beneath the eaves. We were especially focused on maintaining the balance between the placement of the sculptures and the height of the walls. Visitors slip through the openings between the circular walls and enter the exhibition space, where they experience the ever-changing view of the sculptures and the surrounding scenery. The open sky, tiered orange groves, and tiled roof of the former school building-turned hotel peek overhead, while the sculptures are rhythmically arranged at different heights and angles in relation to the backdrop. Entering further inside, visitors discover that the sounds of birds and waves are amplified by the curved walls. Although the museum essentially consists of a single wall, it creates a different world that is simultaneously outdoors and internal.

At the opening ceremony in the summer of 2011, the museum's theme music was performed by Akira and Mariko Senju, who were Ken Iwata's students at the Keio Yochisha Elementary School. It was as though the museum itself became an instrument, with the sound of cicadas and birds layering on top of the music. During 2015, traditional Japanese music concerts were held in the open courtyard, further cultivating deeper aspects of the museum. In the five years since its opening, the museum has continued to instill in visitors Ken Iwata's deep passion for his works on the theme of "mother and child".

Court/exhibiton space

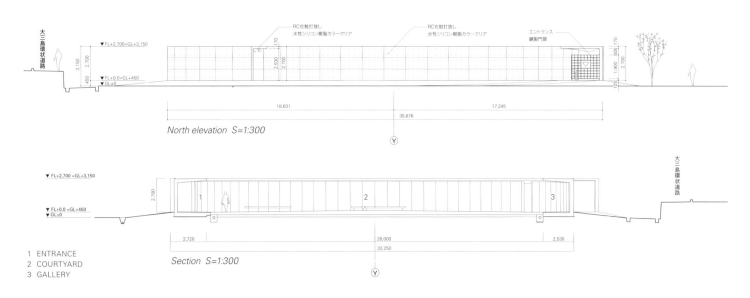

North elevation S=1:300

Section S=1:300

1 ENTRANCE
2 COURTYARD
3 GALLERY

今治市岩田健母と子のミュージアム
愛媛県今治市大三島の南端に佇む，彫刻家岩田健氏のミュージアムである。

　大山祇神社を中心に据えた大三島は，神の宿る島として昔から人々の精神の拠り所とされてきた。岩田氏は東京美術学校在学中に，特攻隊として飛び立つ直前に終戦を迎えた経験をもつ彫刻家である。終戦後は，慶應義塾幼稚舎の美術教師をしながら，埼玉県川口のアトリエにて「母と子の優しさ」をテーマに制作活動に取り組んでいた。2009年，大三島を訪れた岩田氏は土地の魅力を瞬時に感じとり，浜辺に面した元小学校校庭の敷地に自身のミュージアムを建設し今治市に寄贈することを決断した。

　常設展示される作品は44体，ほとんどが具象的な塑彫のブロンズ像である。展示室の建物と前庭を併設する案や，大部分の作品を屋外に置き庭園のみをつくる案などをスタディしたが，最終的に嵌幕のようなコンクリートの壁を円環状にまわすことで彫刻を囲む鑑賞空間をつくることにした。

　5枚に分けられた高さ2.7mの円弧状の壁が，互いに少しずつずれて重なりながら直径約30mの空間を構成する。壁の上部には1.2～2.5m程内側に迫り出した庇

をかけ、雨や日射しから2体の大理石作品を保護すると共に、人々が休憩をとれるスペースを設えた。中央部分は青々とした芝生が広がり、芝の上や庇の下に大小の彫刻が様々な方向や高さに配置される。特に注力したのは、壁の高さと彫刻の置き方である。訪れた人は円弧の壁をすべり抜けるように展示空間に入ると、彫刻と景色がくるくると移り変わる空間を体験する。広く抜ける空や段々のみかん畑、現在は宿泊施設の元校舎の瓦屋根が空間上方に覗き、その背景に呼応するように高さや方向の異なる彫刻がリズミカルに配置されている。歩みを進めると、曲面の壁沿いに音がまわりこみ、鳥の声や波の音がより鮮明に聞こえることにも気づく。壁1枚で隔てただけの単純な建築だが、屋外でありながら内部的な別世界が生み出された。

2011年夏のオープニングでは、慶應幼稚舎の教え子であった千住明氏と真理子氏によってミュージアムのテーマ曲が披露され、蝉や鳥の声と折り重なってミュージアム全体が楽器のように感じられた。2015年は、雅楽のコンサートが開催され新たな魅力を引き出している。開館して5年、岩田氏が母と子の作品に込めた思いは、訪れた多くの人々の心に響き広がっている。

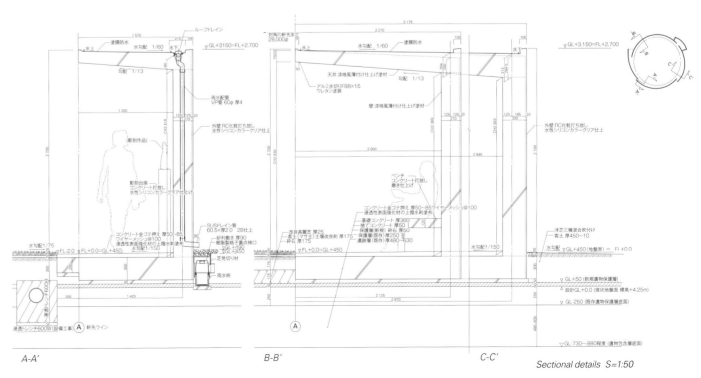

Sectional details S=1:50

Yaoko Kawagoe Museum
(Yuji Misu Memorial Hall)
Kawagoe, Saitama, Japan
2009–11

Overall view from southwest

Known locally as "Little Edo," the city of Kawagoe in Saitama Prefecture retains an old-town ambience of the Edo Period, allowing visitors to enjoy a stroll down streets lined with historic *kurazukuri* (warehouse-style) buildings. The client for this project, a company that owns a chain of supermarkets throughout Saitama, is headquartered in Kawagoe. The client had long been collecting artworks by the late artist Yuji Misu. In celebration of its 120-year anniversary, the company planned a cultural project to build this museum and share its collection of artworks with the local community.

Rather than building a "white cube" that strives strictly for uniformity, we thought that for a museum dedicated to a single artist, exhibition spaces reflecting the artwork's impressions and style transitions would be more appropriate. Through the process of researching the works and history of the artist Yuji Misu, who had produced many representational oil paintings, we decided to pursue an echoing relationship between the artworks and the quality of the space using light as a medium.

The building, 20 m-wide on all sides, is enclosed in an RC wall of 4 m-height. A cross-shaped RC wall that continues on a gentle curve from the museum approach divides this space into four sections: two exhibition rooms, entrance, and a lounge open to locals. By using different roof structures, materials, and wall colors in each room, we physicalized the uniquely shifting expressions of light throughout the building. The brilliant force of life

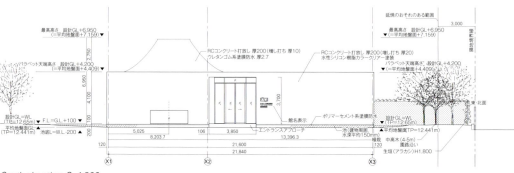

South elevation S=1:300

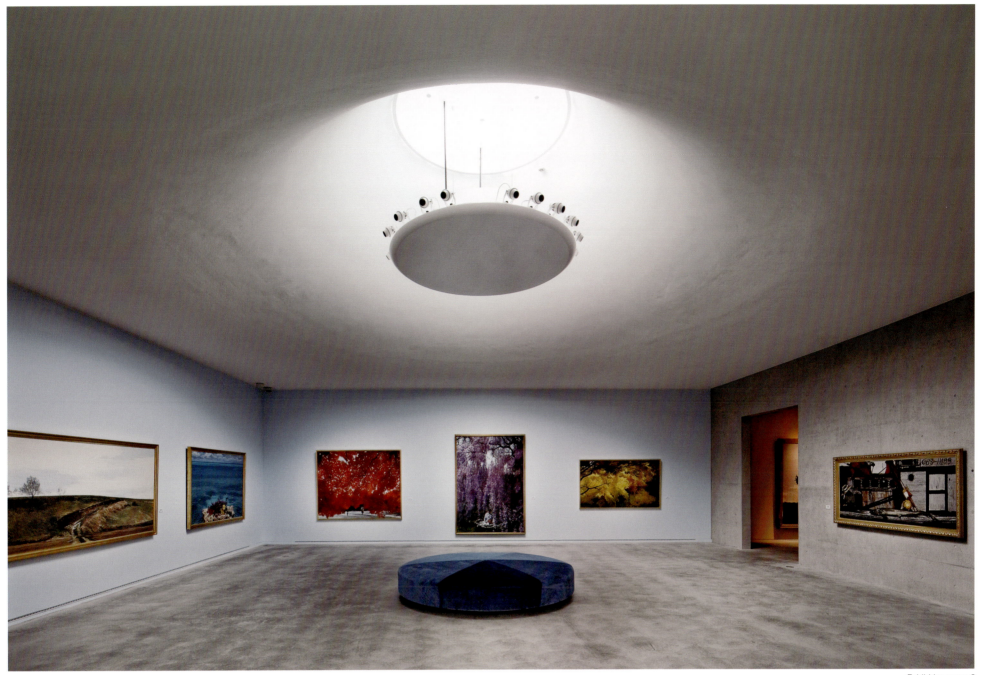
Exhibition room 2

View toward reception counter from entrance

Lounge

Exhibition room 1

1 ENTRANCE
2 EXHIBITION ROOM 1
3 EXHIBITION ROOM 2
4 LOUNGE
5 STORAGE
6 REST ROOM

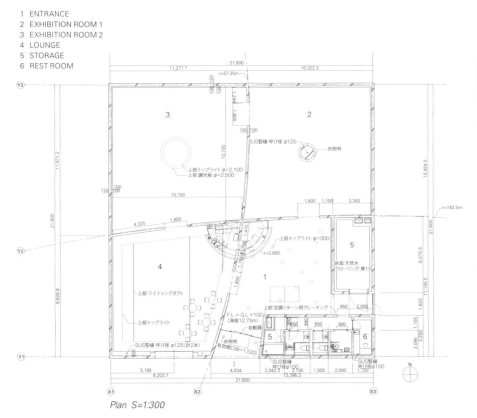

Plan S=1:300

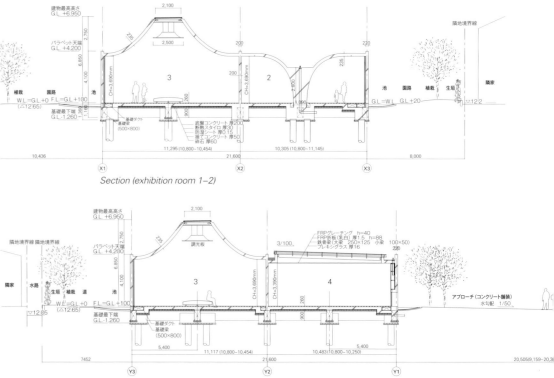

Section (exhibition room 1–2)

Section (exhibition room 2–lounge) S=1:300

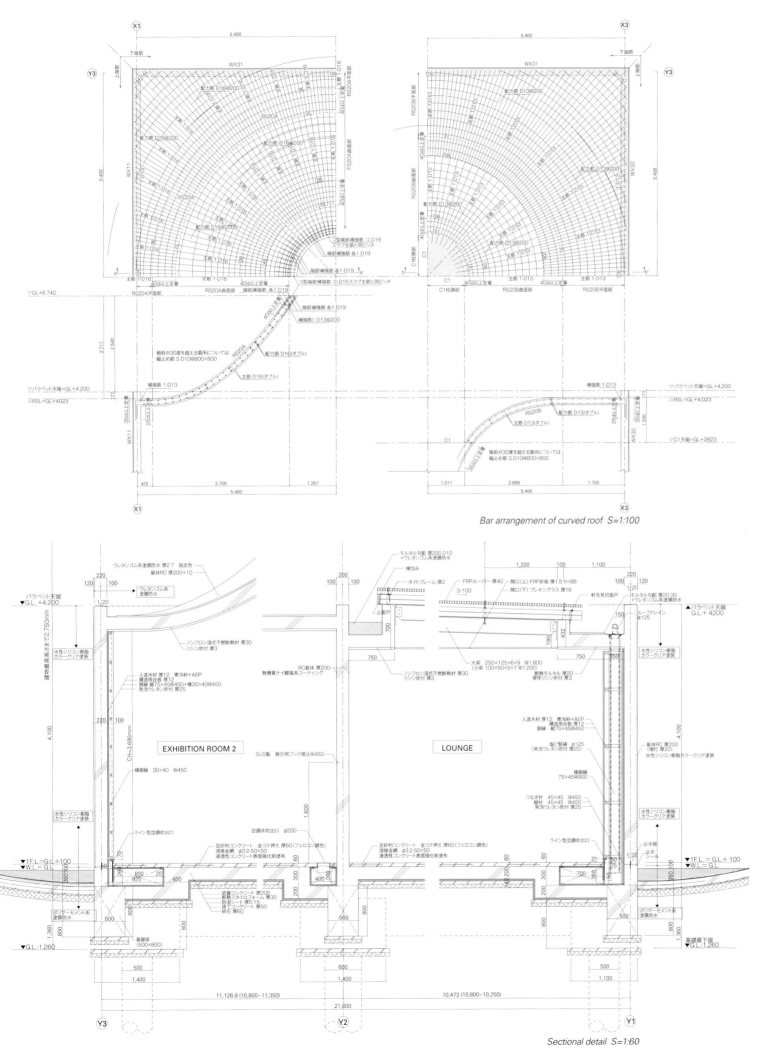

Bar arrangement of curved roof S=1:100

Sectional detail S=1:60

depicted in the artist's works is amplified, especially in the two exhibition spaces where the roofs protrude and sink to create contrasts between light and dark, reflecting the type of artworks on display in the respective spaces.
A collection of simple elements comes together to create the museum, such as the roof that rises towards the sky, another roof that sinks into the ground, curved walls that continue from the approach, wall colors and paintings that surround the internal spaces, and water elements and rich greenery that surround the building. This ensemble has created a museum in which the exterior and interior continue effortlessly, where light, color, and atmosphere of each room evolve through a gentle transition.

ヤオコー川越美術館（三栖右嗣記念館）
小江戸と称される埼玉県川越市は，江戸時代の蔵造りの町並みが今も残され，訪れた人々が町歩きを楽しめるまちである。この川越に本社をおき，埼玉県を中心に展開するスーパーマーケットがクライアントである。創業120周年を記念する文化事業として，永年コレクションしてきた洋画家・故三栖右嗣氏の作品を，近隣の方々に気軽に親しんでもらえるような美術館をつくりたいという思いから，この建築は計画された。
我々は，今回のような特定の個人の作品のみを扱う美術館の展示室は，均質さのみを追求したホワイトキューブではなく，作品の印象や作風の変遷を反映させた展示室の方が適切であると考えた。具象の油絵を多く描いてきた三栖右嗣氏の作品や経歴を読み解いていく中から，「光を媒介にしながら空間の性格が絵と響きあうような関係」をつくり出していくこととした。
20m四方，4mの高さのRC外壁で囲まれた空間が，アプローチの曲線とそのまま連続する緩やかな弧を描く十字のRCの壁で，二つの展示室，エントランス，町の人々が気軽に集えるラウンジの四つの空間に分けられている。各部屋の屋根形状や素材，壁面の色の違いから建物を1周巡ることで，それぞれ特徴的な光の表情の変化が体現される。特に二つの展示室では，凹凸の屋根形状がつくり出す光の明暗や方向性が，展示される絵画と重なりあうことで，三栖作品に表現される生命力の輝きが溢れる空間となっている。
空に向かって上昇する屋根と地中に向かって降りてくる屋根，またアプローチから連続した曲線を持つ湾曲した壁面，室内を囲む壁面の色と絵画，建物の周りを囲む水面と豊かな植栽，ひとつ一つのシンプルな要素が重なり合う。そのことで，外と内が無理なく連続し，各室内の空気，光，色が緩やかに変化しながら展開していく美術館を生み出した。

Tokyo Mather's Clinic
Setagaya, Tokyo, Japan
2009–11

Overall view from southeast

Built within a quiet residential area in Yoga, Tokyo, this is an obstetrics hospital that specializes in painless childbirths and prenatal checkups. The client started the business in Hiroshima, and gained know-hows and experiences of painless birth that prevails in the West, for over 20 years. This building was planned as their branch. By limiting the number of beds to only nine, the hospital is able to pursue their motto to pay fullest attention to each patient, and they requested for a scheme that embodies the same gentleness and careful attention.

To do so, we arranged the waiting hall to be in the center of the building. Surrounding that, there are the counseling rooms, checkup rooms and office, and on its periphery there are corridors that act as a working space for the doctors and staffs. By positioning the waiting hall where expecting mother spend a long time in instead of placing the checkup rooms in the center of the building, we intended to create a space where expecting mothers can feel secured under the warm attention of the doctors and staffs. Moreover, we were able to create a calm and stable environment by incorporating a radiation air-conditioner on the floor that has stable temperature conditions and by setting a toplight leading diffused light through the louvers on the ceiling. By establishing corridors at the periphery of the building, we were able to functionally connect the counseling rooms, checkup rooms and gynecological examination rooms together, and also secure a bright working space that is 24 m-long, facing south.

In contrast with the first floor, rooms on the second floor are arranged surrounding the courtyard—the wards are placed on the south with sunlight, whereas the labor rooms and delivery rooms are placed on the north. Considering the need to transfer mothers to other rooms on stretchers after the painless delivery process, the wards arranged on the same floor, but separated by a courtyard to keep the area quiet. This courtyard allowed us to achieve an open space that is full of light, even within a residential area that emphasizes privacy.

We hope that the light in the hospital wards that are turned on in the evening will illuminate the town, symbolizing the birth of a new life and the happiness of the family.

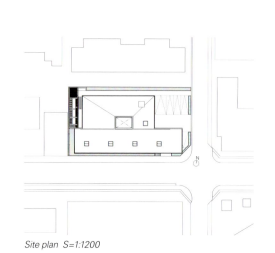

Site plan S=1:1200

East view

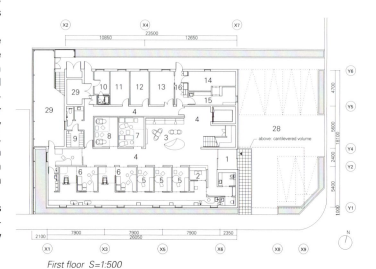

First floor S=1:500

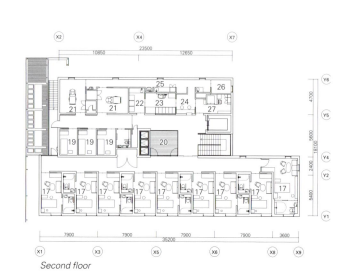

Second floor

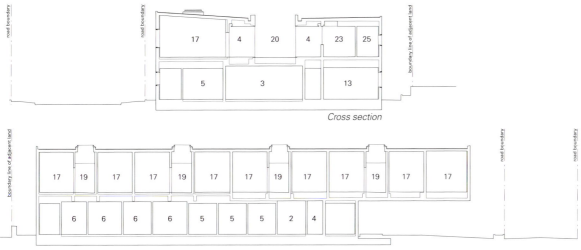
Cross section

Longitudinal section S=1:300

1 WIND BREAKING ROOM
2 INFORMATION
3 WAITING HALL
4 CORRIDOR
5 COUNSELING ROOM
6 OUTPATIENT OBSTETRIC CONSULTATION ROOM
7 ULTRASONIC EXAMINATION ROOM
8 LABORATORY ROOM
9 LOCKER ROOM
10 DUTY DOCTOR'S ROOM
11 DIRECTOR'S ROOM
12 OFFICE MANAGER'S ROOM
13 MULTI-PURPOSE ROOM
14 KITCHEN
15 LAUNDRY
16 STORAGE
17 MATERNITY WARD
18 BATHROOM
19 LABOR ROOM
20 COURTYARD
21 DELIVERY ROOM
22 SUCKLE ROOM
23 NURSERY ROOM
24 NURSES' STATION
25 PREPARATION ROOM
26 RESTING ROOM
27 SERVICE ROOM
28 CAR PARKING
29 MECHANICAL

東京マザーズクリニック

東京用賀の閑静な住宅地に建つ，専門医による胎児診断と無痛分娩を専門とする産婦人科医院の計画である。クライアントは広島で開業されており，20年以上に渡るノウハウとともに，欧米では主流である無痛分娩を専門とする分院として計画された。病室を敢えて9床に絞ることで，目の行き届くきめ細かい専門医療を提供することをモットーとされており，建築計画にもその優しさと気遣いは要求された。

そこで，待合ホールを建物の中心に据え，それを囲むようにカウンセリング室や診察室，事務室を配置し，そして外周に先生やスタッフの作業場となる回廊を設けた。診療行為が行われる部屋ではなく，妊婦さんが長い期間にわたり通う待合ホールを中心にすることで，先生やスタッフに暖かく見守られながらお産ができるという安心を感じられるスペースとした。さらに，床には温度ムラの少ない輻射による冷暖房空調を，天井にはルーバーによって拡散された光を導く天窓を採用することにより，安定した穏やかな環境をつくり出している。また，外周に回廊を設けたことにより，カウンセリング室や診察室，内診室などを機能的に結びつつ，南に面した全長24mの明るく快適な作業スペースを確保している。

1階とは対比的に2階は中庭を囲むように，陽あたりの良い南側に病室を，北側に陣痛室や分娩室を並べている。無痛分娩後のストレッチャーによる移動を考慮し，同じフロアに病室と分娩室を配置しつつ，中庭によって分けることにより，病室エリアの静寂さが保てるように配慮した。この中庭を介して，近隣とのプライバシーが重視される住宅地においても，光に満ち溢れた開放的な場を実現している。

夕暮に病室に点る明かりが，小さないのちの誕生と，家族の幸せを表象するかのように，街を灯すことを願いたい。

Courtyard on second floor

Waiting room

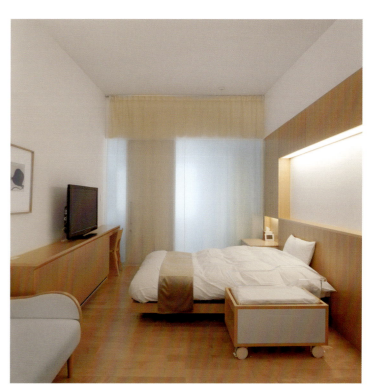
Maternity ward

ITO JUKU Ebisu Studio
Shibuya, Tokyo, Japan
2012–13

This is the main base for Ito Juku, NPO Initiative for Tomorrow's Opportunities in architecture that is in its sixth year of operation.

The studio opened in June, 2013 within a residential area in Ebisu, Tokyo, as a place for architecture education in order to realize Ito's vision "to create a place like a salon where people can discuss about community and architecture", as well as connecting Omishima in Seto Inland Sea where *the Toyo Ito Museum of Architecture (pp.156-161)*, Imabari City stands. With the three year-round workshops (open lectures for members, Architecture School for Children, exclusive course for Ito Juku students) as the key program, the studio is like a house with a large *doma* (earth floor) that can accommodate a range of different activities including various architecture-related events, exhibitions, meetings and workshops.

On top of a salon space where people are able to gather, the studio also practices an environmental approach "to open up to nature while living within the city". The pit between the foundation and the concrete *doma* that extends from the entrance to the back of the studio enables thermal energy to circulate, bringing in warm air in the winter and cool air in the summer. By building two layers of bricks with high heat accumulation capacity for the outer walls that creates an air layer, it creates an airway and functions as an insulator throughout the year by sending warm air that is accumulated near the roof down to the floor. The west-facing entrance is fitted with large wooden lattice sliding doors and glazed doors that help natural ventilation through the high-side windows of the raised roof at the center while keeping a steady indoor air velocity of 3 m/s. A mechanism that allows the building to breathe using nature's power was created by minimizing artificial air-conditioning. For the materials and construction methods, we aimed to create a space where people could feel the warmth of nature, for example by installing a natural slate roofing, plaster walls and a brick fireplace.

Many activities have been carried out day and night at the studio since its completion three years ago. One day, students are here to make a mockup of a wooden hut at the spacious *doma*, on another day, about 20 children make colorful models, or on a weekday night, people come in after work for discussions. Sometimes, there are also students from abroad who come in for classes on to learn about community development. There are also food-related events of small markets that

View from west

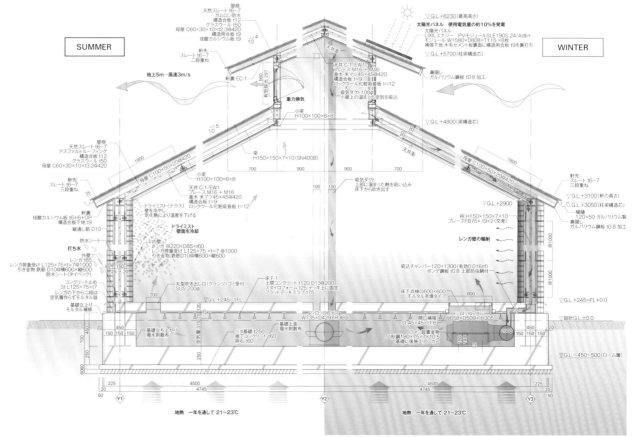

Sectional detail S=1:100

1 APPROACH
2 ENTRANCE
3 TERRACE
4 LECTURE HALL
5 KITCHEN
6 LIBRARY

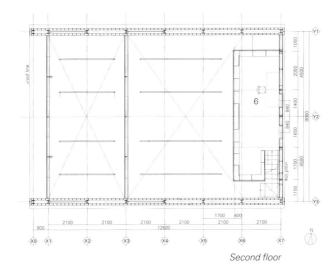

Second floor

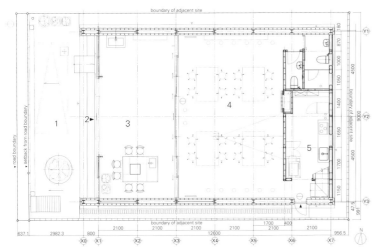

First floor S=1:200

anyone can join, and all of this create a strong community that former students from both the exclusive course and children workshop to gather at different events. Nowadays, regional activation seems to be necessary for us, and the activities at the small studio that started with personal thoughts is becoming an accumulation of enthusiasm and developing into a great swelling which generates community and architecture for the future.

伊東建築塾 恵比寿スタジオ

今年で活動6年目となる、伊東建築塾「NPOこれからの建築を考える」の活動拠点である。

「地域づくりや建築を語り合うサロンのような場所をつくりたい」という、塾長である伊東の思いを携え、瀬戸内海の大三島にある「今治市伊東豊雄建築ミュージアム」（pp.156-161）と結ぶ建築教育の場として、2013年6月に東京都恵比寿の住宅地の一角にオープンした。伊東塾の年間を通した三つの活動〔会員向けの公開講座/子ども建築塾/塾生限定講座〕を軸として、関連するイベントや展覧会、ミーティングや製作活動など多種多様な活動ができるよう、大きな土間をもった家のようなスタジオとした。

人々の集うサロンであると同時に、「都会に居ながら自然に開いた生活」を実践する環境的な試みも行っている。入口から一続きに奥まで続くコンクリート土間と基礎の間につくられたピットでは、地中熱による安定した空気を循環させて、冬は温かく夏は涼風を床下から室内に吹き出している。外壁は蓄熱性能の高い煉瓦を二重に積み壁内に空気層を設けることで、通年の断熱効果と暖房時に天井付近に溜まる温かい空気を床下に送りこむ風道として機能する。西に向いたエントランスは、光や風の調節ができる大きな木製の格子引戸とその奥にガラス戸を嵌め込み、中央の屋根を持ち上げてつくったハイサイドの窓によって、約3m/sの定常風を捉えながら室内の自然換気を促す。人工的な空調を最小限にし、自然の力を借りて建物が深く呼吸する仕組みをつくっている。屋根は天然のスレートを葺き、室内には左官の壁と煉瓦の暖炉も設え、素材や工法についても自然の温かみを感じられる空間を目指した。

完成して3年を迎えるスタジオは、昼夜を問わず常に活動が行なわれている。ある日は広い土間で塾生たちが木の小屋のモックアップに試行錯誤し、別の日は20人程の子供たちがカラフルな模型づくりに奮闘し、平日の夜は仕事後に集まった有志が輪となり熱く議論を交わす。海外の大学生が訪れて、まちづくりの授業を連日行うこともある。誰でも参加できる食のイベントやマルシェも時折開催され、塾生OB・OGや子供塾の卒業生など、様々な立場の人々が集い繋がる場として、層の厚いコミュニティが形成されている。地方創生が叫ばれる今、個々の想いから始まった小さなスタジオの活動は、熱いエネルギーの集積となって、これからの地域づくりや建築を生み出す大きなうねりとなりつつある。

Above: downward view from east; below: lecture hall

"Home for All" Projects in Tohoku
Miyagi, Iwate, Fukushima, Japan
2011–

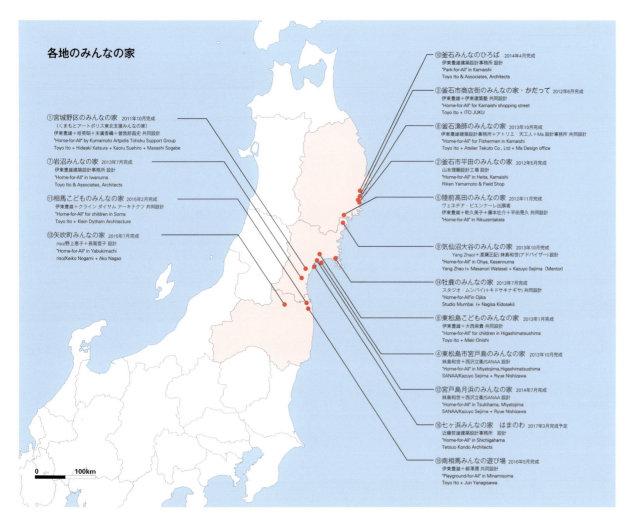

"Home-for-All" by Kumamoto Artpolis Tohoku Support Group
in Miyagino-ku

Home for All is a project initiated by *Kishin no Kai*, a group of 5 architects who stepped up after the Great East Japan Earthquake of March 11, 2011 with a common ambition to search for what we can do. Having witnessed the harsh realities of life in temporary housing, we began to seek a way in which we could help as human beings who wanted to share their grief and heartache, and also as professionals who have found their vocation in architecture. The concept, which embodies our initial aim to create a humble haven where people can gather, warm themselves, eat, drink and talk, is outlined by the following three points:

- The shelter is a place where those who have lost their home can gather and talk, and find peace of mind.
- The shelter is realized by both the people who live there (users) and the people who build it (architect, contractor)
- It is a platform for people to discuss disaster recovery

The first *Home for All* center was completed in October 2011 amongst temporary housing in Sendai, Miyagi, with support from Kumamoto prefecture. From then on, Toyo Ito, Kazuyo Sejima and Riken Yamamoto took initiative in calling out to young architects. By May 2016, 15 *Home for All* centers had been completed in disaster-stricken areas, with one more under way. These are located in temporary housing sites and around devastated shopping arcades or fishing ports, and accommodate diverse functions, such as meeting place for temporary housing residents, restoration of the community, playground for children, and base of operations for NPO organizations who aspire to revive the agricultural and fishing industries.

However, the operation of *Home for All* is now facing a difficult situation with issues such as funding. In order to enhance coordination amongst the *Home for All* centers and to continue supporting them, we founded an NPO named HOME-FOR-ALL together with the architects involved in construction, as well as the local people.

As time passes after the disaster, *Home for All* centers are being given no choice but to be transferred or taken apart due to integration or abolition of temporary housing sites and implementation of new local disaster prevention plans. *Home for All in Rikuzentakata* has already been dismantled, and its components are being stored for reassembly in 2 years' time. *Home for All in Miyagino-ku* is to be reestablished as a local meeting place at the relocation site of residents who leave the temporary housing site.

In this way, *Home for All* reaches beyond its role of supporting the affected areas. It has a potential to become a new model of public facilities, and furthermore, society itself. We consider the significance of *Home for All* hereafter to be as follows:

1. It demonstrates significance as a public facility in its basic form: a place that soothes grief, provides warmhearted communication and strengthens the bond between people. Therefore, it will set an example of how public facilities should be even during times of peace.
2. Users (residents), architects and contractors come together as one for construction, displaying an ideal form of participatory process.

"Home-for-All" for children
in Soma

"Playground-for-All"
in Minamisoma

"Home-for-All"
in Rikuzentakata

3. "The spirit of being considerate and rendering good service to others" allows us to break away from the supremacy of economy, and offers people hope for the future.

In expectation of further development of *Home for All*, we intend to continue our diverse activities and to carry on calling out to people around the world.

東北の「みんなの家」

「みんなの家」は，2011年3月11日の東日本大震災を受けて「自分たちにできることを模索しよう」と集まった，5人の建築家グループ「帰心の会」によって提唱されたプロジェクトである。仮設住宅での厳しい暮らしを目の当たりにした時，悲しみや心の痛みを共有したい一人の生活者として，同時に建築を生業とする者としてできることを考え始まった。当初は家を失った人々が集い，暖をとり，飲み，食べ，語り合えるささやかな憩いの場をつくることを目指し，以下三つをコンセプトとした。

− 家を失った人々が集まって語り合い，心の安らぎを得ることのできる小屋である
− 住む人（利用者）と建てる人（建築家，施工者）が一緒につくる小屋である
− 利用する人々が復興を語り合う拠点である

最初の「みんなの家」は熊本県の協力の下，宮城県仙台市の仮設住宅の中に，2011年10月に完成した。その後，伊東豊雄，妹島和世，山本理顕が中心となって若い世代の建築家たちに呼びかけ，2016年5月までに被災各地に15軒の「みんなの家」が完成し，現在も1軒の計画が進んでいる。それらは仮設住宅地内や被災した商店街，漁港の周辺に建てられ，その主たる用途も仮設住民たちの集まり，コミュニティの回復，子供たちの遊び場，農業や漁業を再興しようとするNPO団体の拠点としてなど，多岐に亘るようになっている。

しかし，「みんなの家」の運営体制は，資金的なことを含め，徐々に厳しい状況になりつつある。そこで，それぞれの「みんなの家」の連携を促し，サポートしていくために，「みんなの家」の建設に携わった建築家，および地元の方々と共に，NPO法人「HOME-FOR-ALL」を立ち上げ活動している。

また，現在，被災からの時間の経過とともに，仮設住宅地の統廃合や地域の防災計画により，「みんなの家」は移転や解体を余儀なくされている。すでに「陸前高田のみんなの家」は解体され，2年後の再築に備えて資材を保管することとなった。また「宮城野区のみんなの家」も仮設住宅を出た方々の新しい移転先の地域の集会所として生まれ変わることになっている。

このように，「みんなの家」は単に被災地支援という役割を超えて，これからの公共施設，さらにはこれからの社会のあり方に言及しうる可能性を秘めている。今後の「みんなの家」が持つ意味を，次のように考える。

①人々の心を癒し，人と人を結ぶヒューマンな場として，原点とも言うべき公共施設の意味を持つ。したがって，それは平時の公共施設のあるべき姿を示している
②利用者（住民），設計者，施工者が一体となって考え，つくることにより，住民参加の理想的姿を示す
③「他者を想い，他者に尽くそうとする精神」によって経済至上主義の社会から抜け出し，人々に未来への希望を育む可能性を持つ

「みんなの家」のさらなる発展のため，私たちは世界の人々に呼びかけ，様々な活動を行っていくことを目指している。

"Home for All" Projects in Kumamoto
Kumamoto, Japan
2016–

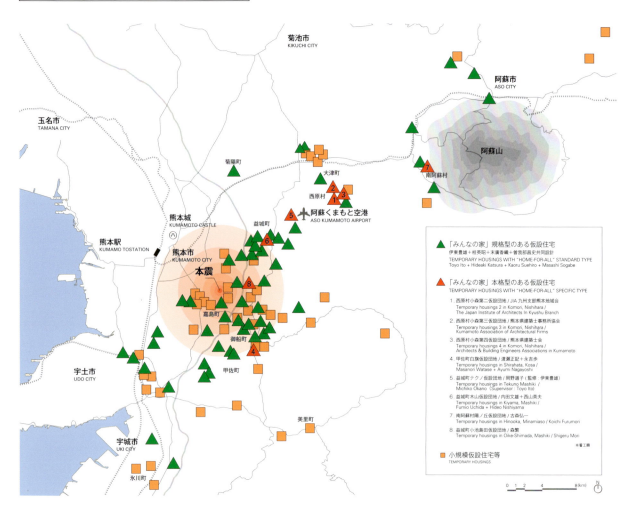

Temporary housing units built of wood

Home for All, implemented in Tohoku after the Great East Japan Earthquake of 2011, is a project which was established from a different standpoint to that of a governmental or prefectural recovery scheme. Construction was funded by supporters of the *Home for All* concept, and through discussion with local residents, the project was carried forward by people in various positions including users, designers and contractors who worked closely together. The first centers to have been built after the earthquake were located in temporary housing sites. In order to provide a warm architecture within a neighborhood of prefabricated box houses without eaves, we initially proposed a simple, wooden shelter with a deep roof overhang and verandah. This proposal of a timber construction posed a question to governmental and prefectural recovery schemes which principally employ standardized prefabricated structures.

It was Kumamoto prefecture that had donated construction materials and funds for the first *Home for All* center in Tohoku, known as *Home for All in Miyaginoku* (*Home for All* by Kumamoto Artpolis Tohoku Support Group). The experience acquired in Tohoku was then put to use in Kumamoto in the recovery scheme after the severe flooding of July 2012, when two *Home for All* centers in Ichinomiyamachi Miyaji district, Aso were completed with the lead of Kumamoto Artpolis.

After the Kumamoto Earthquake of April 2016, the network of the three *Home for All* centers in Tohoku and Aso was enforced to support reconstruction. Thanks to Ikuo Kabashima, the governor of Kumamoto prefecture who has a deep understanding of the *Home for All* project, and to Kumamoto Artpolis's accomplishment over the years in community development, a powerful recovery scheme is under way in Kumamoto. Under this scheme, 15% of the 4,000 temporary housing units will be built of wood, and a wooden *Home for All* center that serves as a meeting place (60 m²) or common room (40 m²) will be constructed for every 50 homes, making a total of more than 80 centers. *Home for All in Kumamoto* was therefore realized as a result of the government and architects working together from an early stage in the scheme.

Home for All in Kumamoto includes "Standardized Home for All" centers which are constructed together with temporary housing sites, and of "Authentic Home for All" centers which are designed through conversation with temporary housing residents and those involved in management.

The 80 *Home for All* centers are currently in the process of design and construction, following the lead of the Kumamoto Artpolis Commissioner (Toyo Ito) and Advisors (Hideaki Katsura, Kaori Suehiro, Masashi Sogabe), as well as young architects working locally and in Tokyo. With students members of KASEI (Kyushu Architecture Students Supporters for Environmental Improvement) starting to use the completed *Home for All* centers as a base of operations to support reconstruction, we have high hopes for further development of the project.

"Standardized Home for All"
(60 m² type)

"Authentic Home for All"
(100 m² type)

Plan and elevation S=1:250

熊本の「みんなの家」

2011年の東日本大震災以来の東北で実践された「みんなの家」は，国や県の行政主導の復興とは異なる立場で，「みんなの家」の趣旨に賛同していただいた寄付者の方々から建設資金を募り，地元の住民と話し合いながら，建築を使う立場，設計する立場，施工する立場の人々が一体となってつくり出されたものであった。大震災後の初期のものは仮設住宅の中に建てられ，庇もないプレファブの箱状の住居が建ち並ぶ仮設住宅の中で，少しでも暖かみのある建築を，簡素ではあっても，深い庇と縁側を備えた木造の小屋を提案したことから始まった。さらに木造の提案は，プレファブを前提としてマニュアル化された国や県の復興プログラムに対して，一石を投じるものであった。

東北の「みんなの家」第1号である「宮城野区のみんなの家」（くまもとアートポリス東北支援「みんなの家」）の建設木材と資金を提供していただいたのが熊本県であり，引き続いて発生した2012年7月の熊本広域大水害の復興計画では，東北支援の経験を活かして，くまもとアートポリス主導のもと，阿蘇市一の宮町宮地地区に2軒の阿蘇「みんなの家」が完成した。

東北と阿蘇で実践された3軒の「みんなの家」が，2016年4月に発生した熊本地震の復興支援のための「みんなの家」として繋がっていくこととなった。「みんなの家」に対する蒲島郁夫熊本県知事の深い理解と，くまもとアートポリスの長年のまちづくりへの取り組みの実績から，約4,000戸の仮設住宅のうち15％を木造住宅とし，仮設住宅内で50戸ごとに，集会所（60m²）や談話室（40m²）として木造の「みんなの家」を80棟以上建てる，積極的な復興計画が熊本県で進行している。実行計画の最初期段階から，行政と建築家が一体となって，熊本に「みんなの家」がつくり出されることとなった。

熊本の「みんなの家」には，仮設団地開設時に建設される「規格型みんなの家」や，仮設団地に住まい始めた住民，運営者と意見交換しながら設計を進める「本格型みんなの家」などがある。

計80棟の「みんなの家」は，くまもとアートポリス・コミッショナー（伊東豊雄）とアドバイザー（桂英昭氏，末廣香織氏，曽我部昌史氏）をはじめ，地元や東京の若手建築家たちの手により，続々と設計，建設が進行中であり，建築が竣工した後も，KASEI（九州建築学生仮設住宅環境改善プロジェクト）の学生たちが，「みんなの家」を拠点に復興支援の活動を開始しており，今後の展開が期待されている。

View toward entrance

Hermés Pavilion
Basel, Switzerland
2011–13

This pavilion is to be used by Hermès at the world's largest luxury watch and jewelry trade show, Baselworld, which is held annually in Basel, Switzerland. As a place to unveil and sell new luxury watches, the structure needed to be cleverly designed so that it can be easily assembled and disassembled, as well as efficiently packed and transported repeatedly over the next 10 years. 22 negotiation rooms, a meeting room, lounge and kitchen are arranged within a 19 m-wide, 34 m-deep, 2-story steel framework.

The pavilion is entirely covered by a latticed facade made of 634 laminated beech timber slats. The facade maintains durability while creating an organic waving elevation by overlaying two layers of curved and straight timber slats in a crisscross pattern. The joints needed to be hardwearing, and were designed so that the pavilion can be assembled quickly and frequently. More than 167 plants are arranged inside the facade to "pop out" between the lattices, creating a calming atmosphere for visitors to the interior fair site. The curtains inside the pavilion are made of plant-dyed fabrics, and the milled aluminum showcase has been carefully hand-polished and finished by craftsmen.

Hermès' appreciation of the elegance of natural materials and commitment to craftsmanship became the main guiding factors in designing this project. Despite having to design for repeated assembling and disassembling, we tried to steer away from the industrial ethos, and aimed to create a home (maison) that embraces the warmth and gentleness of nature.

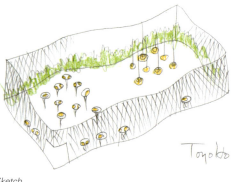

Sketch

エルメス パヴィリオン

毎年，スイス・バーゼルにて開催される世界最大規模の時計と宝飾品の見本市バーゼルワールドにおける，エルメスのパヴィリオンである。このパヴィリオンは，新作時計の発表と商談の場として10年間，毎年再設置できるよう簡便な組立・解体，効率的な梱包・運搬を考慮した設計が求められた。幅19m，奥行34mの鉄骨による2階建てフレーム構造の中には22室の商談室，会議室，ラウンジ，キッチンなどが配されている。

パヴィリオン全周は，634本の木（ブナ集成材）によって格子状に覆ったファサードに囲まれている。直線材と湾曲材で構成された2層のレイヤーを格子状に重ね合わせることで，堅牢性を担保しながら，揺らいでいるような有機的なファサードが形成された。木材の接合部は，短期間に設営できる工法と繰り返し使える強度が必要とされた。ファサード内側に配された167本の植栽は，格子の合間から時折顔を出し，屋内展示場という環境で人々に安らぎを与える。パヴィリオン内部のカーテンには草木染めの布が使われ，アルミ削り出しのショーケースは職人の手により丹念に磨かれ，仕上げられている。

エルメスが大切にする自然素材のもつ優美さへの愛着，手仕事によるこだわりは，プロジェクト全工程におけるデザインの指針となった。繰り返し解体・組立可能という条件下で，工業的イメージに陥ることなく，自然のもつ柔らかさ，暖かさを感じられる家（メゾン）のようなパヴィリオンを目指した。

Exhibition space

1 ATRIUM
2 PRIVATE LOUNGE
3 CONFERENCE ROOM
4 MEETING ROOM
5 STAFF ROOM
6 KITCHEN
7 DIRECTOR'S ROOM

First floor

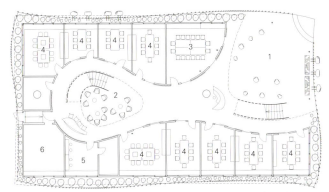

Ground floor S=1:400

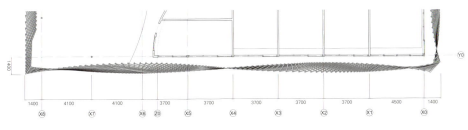

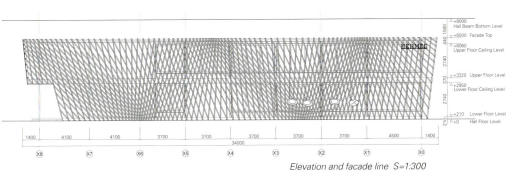

Elevation and facade line S=1:300

Lounge

Facade

PRODUCTS

Modular Bench "Naguisa"
2005

This piece of urban furniture was commissioned by Escofet, Spain's leading precast concrete maker.

This bench was designed to be a stand-out piece while still adapting to its surroundings, whether that be a large plaza or park, or a narrow sidewalk. It can be freely arranged with other 4 m bench pieces to create a large ring and other shapes, depending on the direction of the arcs.

Each piece has seats chiseled out from concrete in gently flowing curves, with the rest of the bench shaped into backrests and armrests.

Modular Bench "Naguisa"

スペインを代表するPCメーカーEscofet社より依頼され，実現したアーバンファニチャーである．

大きな広場や公園にあっても，狭い歩道にあっても，存在感をもち順応するものとして，4m程のピースを並べて配置することで大きなリング状になるようにデザインされた．リングに限らずとも円弧の向きを自由につなげていくことができる．

それぞれのピースは，水の流れのような柔らかい曲線でコンクリートの座面を切り出し，残りの部分は背もたれや肘掛けに適した形状としている．

Architecture for Dogs
2012

This was a project to create *Architecture for Dogs*. Under the direction of designer Kenya Hara, 14 teams of architects and designers came up with DIY designs.

We thought about dogs who were eager to go out for walks with their owners come rain or shine, even after growing frail in their old age. In order to improve these dogs' lives by even a tiny amount, we designed homes in which they could easily go out for walks. We attached tires to a wooden cage which lets through the breeze, laid down a fluffy cushion, and attached a retractable fabric to keep out direct sunlight and rain — thus creating a space much like the shade of a tree.

We lowered the duckboard flooring as close as possible to the ground to make it easy for dogs to climb on and off. The structure can be brought indoors, and can even be used as a bed — a moveable dog home. Dogs will love the gentle swaying of their boat-shaped baskets when going for leisurely walks with their owners.

Architecture for Dogs

「犬のための建築」をつくるプロジェクト．デザイナー原研哉氏ディレクションの元，14組の建築家やデザイナーが，DIY可能なデザインを提案した．

「どんな日でも，たとえ足腰弱い老犬になっても，飼い主と共に散歩へ出かけたい」．そんな犬の負担を少しでも和らいであげられる，散歩するための犬の家を考えた．風通しの良い木製のかごにタイヤを付け，ふかふかのクッションを敷き，日差しと雨を和らげる開閉式の布のシェードを取り付けて，木陰のような場所をつくる．

スノコ状の床はできるだけ低く地面へ近づけ，犬が自ら乗り降りできるようにした．玄関や室内に持ち込んでベッドにもできる，まさに移動する犬の家．船のような形のかごに揺られ，飼い主と一緒に優雅な散歩を楽しみたい．

URUSHI plates in an acrylic case
2016

This is a serving dish and case designed with modern sensibilities towards lacquerware. *The REVALUE NIPPON PROJECT* launched by Hidetoshi Nakata aims to spread awareness of Japanese craftwork and culture, and has set lacquerware as its theme for 2015. For his contribution, Toyo Ito reached out to woodturner Yasuhiro Satake and designer Nao Tamura in order to explore and create new forms of lacquerware.

The three team members came up with numerous ideas and images for everything from the presentation of the lacquer to the shape and finish of the vessel, and carried out several rounds of trial and error. Their finished pieces comprised of three differently sized wooden plates for everyday use, created using Satake's woodturning technique; and a transparent storage case made from 30 mm of acrylic layering.

The vessels were made using horse chestnut and Mongolian oak. The horse chestnut has a graduated two-tone wax color lacquer finish, while the Mongolian oak is finished with both wipe-lacquer and polyurethane. The way in which the delicate lightweight vessel is contained within the transparent acrylic case creates the illusion that it is floating in space.

Yasuhiro Satake passed away in April, 2016. Despite not being in the best of health, Satake poured all of his artisan's spirit into his pieces. We would like to once again offer our heartfelt gratitude for the superb one-of-a-kind pieces he created.

漆の器とアクリルケース

「漆」を，現代の感性でデザインした器とケース．中田英寿氏主催による，日本の工芸・文化を広める活動「REVALUE NIPPON PROJECT」の2015年テーマ「漆」について，伊東豊雄は漆の新しいあり方を模索実現すべく，木地師・佐竹康宏氏とデザイナー・田村奈穂氏に声をかけた．

漆の表現から器の形状・仕上げまで，3人でイメージや案を出し合い試行錯誤を重ねて実現した作品は，佐竹氏のろくろ成形による3種類の大きさの日常使いの木皿と，厚さ30mmのアクリルを積層した透明な収納ケースからなる．

器の材質はトチノキとミズナラ．トチノキはグラデーショナルな2色の蝋色（ろいろ）漆仕上げ，ミズナラは拭き漆とウレタンの2種類の仕上げが施された．繊細で軽やかな器が透明のアクリルケースに収められた様は，まるで宙に浮遊しているかのようである．

2016年4月に佐竹康宏氏が逝去された．体調が万全でない中で，佐竹氏は作品に職人の魂を込められた．唯一無二の素晴らしい作品が生まれたことを，改めて心から感謝申し上げたい．

Modular Bench "Naguisa"

URUSHI plates in an acrylic case

Architecture for Dogs

SET DESIGN

"Le nozze di Figaro" set design

"Le nozze di Figaro" set design
2005

Every year in the summer, the Seiji Ozawa Matsumoto Festival is held in Matsumoto City, Nagano Prefecture. One event taking place during this festival was a performance of the opera "The Marriage of Figaro," staged in *the Matsumoto Performing Arts Center (pp.38-47)* which we designed. We were entrusted the task of designing the stage set by director of the center as well as stage manager Kazuyoshi Kushida.

We made the walkway from twisted Lauan plywood to resemble a Möbius strip, and had it trace an arc connecting the back of the stage to the audience seating. The stage, orchestra pit and audience became drastically closer as a result of this walkway. It also served as a subtle model of our architectural theme, which aims to nullify the connection between inside and outside, surface and interior.

オペラ"フィガロの結婚"舞台デザイン

長野県松本市では、毎年夏に「セイジ・オザワ松本フェスティバル」が行われる。その催しのひとつとして、私たちの設計した「まつもと市民芸術館」(pp.38-47)で、オペラ「フィガロの結婚」が演じられた。演出家であり館長である串田和美氏より、我々に舞台デザインが依頼された。

ラワン合板を曲げてつくられた、メビウスの輪のような一本の道が、弧を描きながら舞台奥と客席を結ぶ。舞台とオーケストラピット、客席との間の距離はこの道により一気に縮められた。それは内と外、表と裏の関係を無化しようとする、私たちの建築のテーマのささやかなモデルともなった。

"La Mode" set design
2016

We constructed the stage for *the National Taichung Theater*'s *(pp.268-277)* opening performance—Tomoko Mukaiyama's *La Mode*. Guided by the keyword of boundaries, we attempted to deconstruct the codes surrounding fashion, which is also compared to religion of the modern world.

The stage set utilized fabric to replicate the three-dimensional curved catenoid structure of *the National Taichung Theater*. The 700 audience members in the auditorium were able to feast their eyes on an expanding and contracting white mesh catenoid floating above the stage, while one pianist, 10 dancers, and 100 audience members mingled together beneath.

La Mode took a slightly unusual approach to well-established themes such as: the stage and audience areas; architecture and clothing; performers and viewers; self and other; body and body; body and place; and place and place. It was a rare and exciting event in which architectural feats and space became one with the performing arts.

"La Mode" 舞台デザイン

「台中国家歌劇院」(pp.268-277)中劇院のこけら落とし公演、向井山朋子「La Mode」のための舞台構成。「境界」というキーワードを手掛かりに、現代の宗教とも言われる「ファッション」を取り巻くコードの脱構築が試みられた。

舞台セットは、「台中国家歌劇院」の3次元曲面構造体「カテノイド」をファブリックで再現。白いメッシュのカテノイドが浮遊・伸縮する舞台上を、1人のピアニストと10人のダンサーと100人の観客が入り乱れ、オーディトリアムの観客700人がそれを目撃した。

舞台領域と観客席、建築と衣装、演者と観客、自己と他者、身体と身体、身体と場所、場所と場所などといった身近なテーマに、普段とは少し違った角度から向かい合った「La Mode」は、建築行為・建築空間と舞台芸術とが一体となった、稀有でエキサイティングな出来事であった。

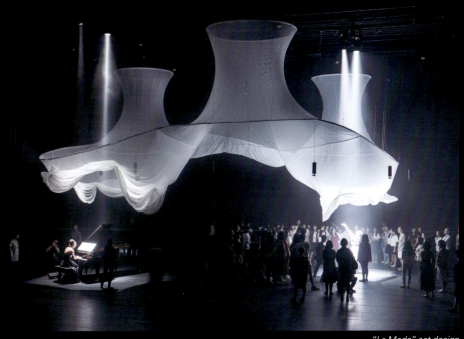

"La Mode" set design
"Commissioned by National Taichung Theater"

Overall view from southeast

New National Stadium Japan, International Design Competition
Shinjuku, Tokyo, Japan
2012

The competition for *the National Stadium* design took place in July, 2012, before Tokyo was selected to host the 2020 Olympic Games. The project was to become the main stadium during the Olympics, as well as a place for hosting a variety of large-scale events such as international soccer matches and music concerts. For this reason, the proposal required sophisticated technical solutions such as systems for growing natural grass and a weatherproof retractable roof. This gigantic facility would encompass approximately 290,000 m² and also include a sports-themed museum, library, and commercial complex. Unlike the recent trend towards suburban stadiums, this one was to be built in the center of Tokyo, with an urban design suitable for the 21st century.

The lush green site, located in the urban Meiji Jingu Gaien, is known among locals as a place of relaxation. We envisaged an open stadium that not only comes to life during events, but expands towards the surrounding Meiji Jingu Gaien like a park. To fulfill this idea, we proposed a semi-outdoors space of water and greenery called the "green loop" that would be open to the public. This large ring of 880 m would connect the Meiji Jingu Gaien and the stadium's main concourse to the surrounding facilities. The loop would also function as a buffer zone to control the flow of visitors entering and exiting the facility. Its double-skin facade would also actively control heat, sound, and airflow in an attempt to reduce the stadium's impact on the environment.

By making the shape of the stadium as simple as possible, and by combining five movable devices (retractable roof system, reflective solar tracker panels, natural grass turf storage device, field floor lifting device, and movable seats), we designed a multi-functional stadium that could be used for various types of events. The solar panels would make maximum use of the 40,000 m² roof and generate 4 MW of natural energy, helping the facility to conserve and supply extra power in times of emergency.

The proposal progressed as we focused on the stadium's impact on the environment, how it would be perceived by pedestrians inside the Meiji Jingu Gaien, and creating a stadium interior that could be changed to meet various needs like a theater. With the "green loop" as the axis, we hoped that the stadium would be continually utilized, not only during events, but also at all other times as a place of relaxation within Meiji Jingu Gaien, a locale that would serve the community as a cafe, restaurant, and park.

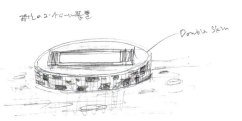

Sketch by Toyo Ito, 12 Aug. 2012

Aerial view from southeast

Arena

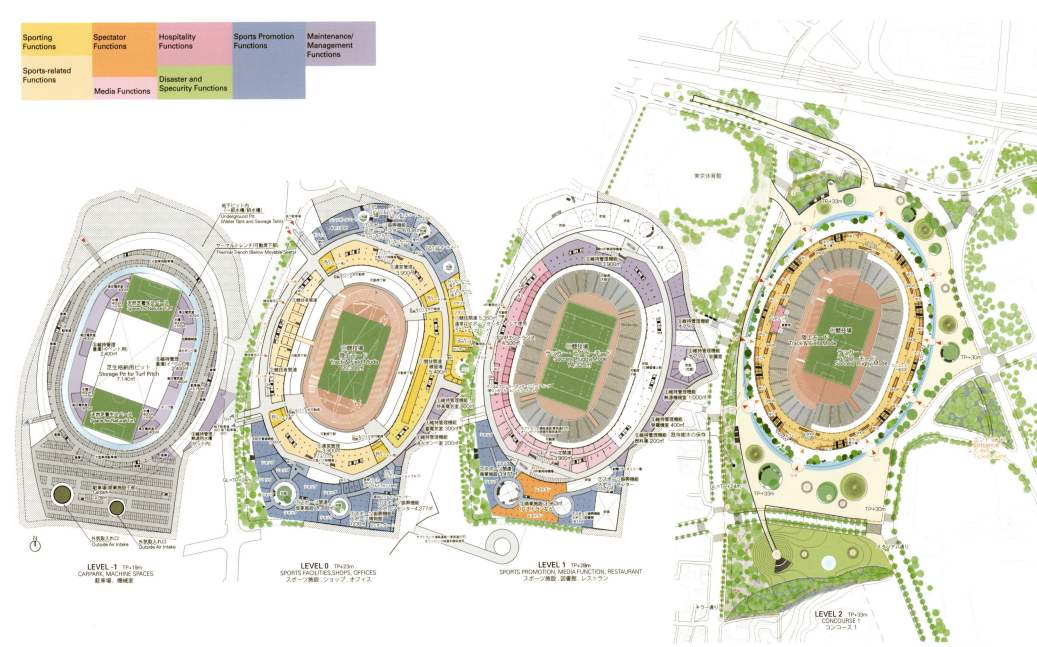
Plans S=1:5000

新国立競技場基本構想国際デザイン競技応募案

東京が2020年オリンピックの開催地に選ばれる前，2012年7月にコンペティションが行なわれた。オリンピックのメインスタジアムとして想定され，さらに大会後もサッカーの国際試合や大規模コンサートなど多種多様なイベントが開催できるように，天然芝育成システムや全天候型屋根開閉装置など，高度な技術的解決策が求められた。スポーツに関連したミュージアム，図書館，商業施設など付属施設を含めると，約29万m²におよぶ巨大な施設であった。近年よく見られる郊外型スタジアムとは異なり，東京の中心にある21世紀に相応しい都心型スタジアムであることが望まれた。

都心にありながら豊かな緑に恵まれた神宮外苑の敷地は，市民の憩いの場である。我々はイベント時だけ活気を帯びるのではなく，神宮外苑に繋がる公園のような開かれたスタジアムをイメージした。これを実現するために，日常的に開放できる「グリーンループ」という水と緑の半屋外の空間を提案した。神宮外苑とスタジアムのメインコンコース，関連施設を結ぶ全周880mの大きなリングである。イベント時の観客の入退場をスムーズに促す緩衝帯であり，さらに熱や音，気流をアクティブにコントロールするダブルスキンとして，環境負荷の低減を図った。

またスタジアムの形状をなるべくシンプルに保ち，五つの可動装置（屋根開閉機構，太陽光追尾反射パネル，天然芝ピッチ格納装置，フィールド床昇降装置，可動式客席）を組み合わせることによって，集客力のある様々なイベントに対応する多機能型スタジアムを目指した。特にスタジアムを覆う4万m²におよぶ屋根を最大限利用した太陽光発電によって，4MWの容量を確保し，自然エネルギーを利用した省エネおよび災害時における電源供給を可能としている。

このように，神宮外苑の歩行者レベルからの視線や環境に配慮した外周部と，劇場のように色々な演出ができる内部に，より焦点をあてながら計画が進められた。イベント時はもちろんのこと，スタジアムが「グリーンループ」を軸として，神宮外苑に開かれたカフェやレストラン，ジョギングやストリートパフォーマンス等の市民の憩いの場として，日常的に利用されることを期待した。

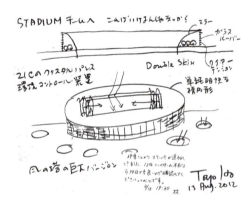

Sketch by Toyo Ito, 13 Aug. 2012

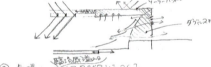

Sketch by Toyo Ito, 20 Aug. 2012

Semi-outdoor space 'Green Loop'

South elevation

West elevation S=1:2000

Downward view of 'Green Loop'

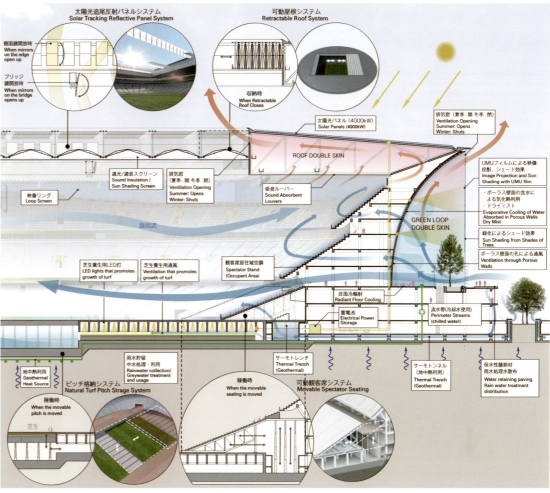
Sectional detail

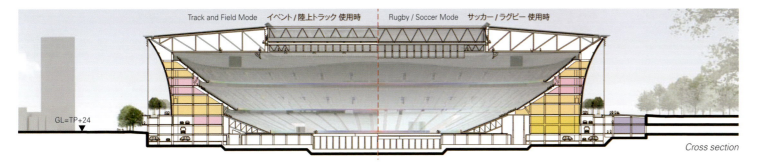
Cross section

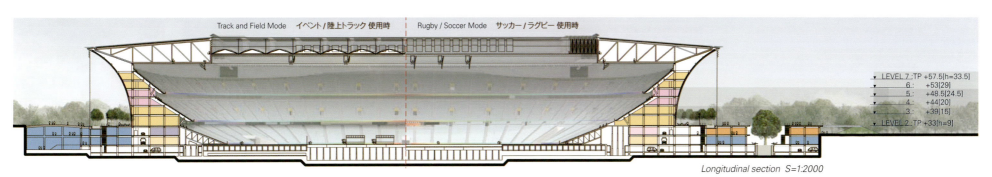
Longitudinal section S=1:2000

Crematorium and Akayama Historic Nature Park in Kawaguchi
Kawaguchi, Saitama, Japan
2011–

This project in Araijuku, Kawaguchi City is an integral scheme that includes a crematorium and an urban park. The site is located on a geographical boundary called "yato", where plateaux and valleys interweave in a complex manner. Despite the area being only a little more than ten minutes away from Tokyo, the views of plant nurseries offer a peaceful scenery. The project is comprised of a central reservoir that is surrounded by three different facilities: urban park, crematorium and a highway oasis.

One of the focal points of the crematorium was making the large facility with its substantial machine room blend into the greenery of the urban park. By positioning the 14 furnaces back to back and gathering all operative functions below ground and in the central core, we allowed the lobby and waiting room to be open to the surrounding park in all directions. The columns which protrude continuously from the freeform roof surface make the building seem as though it is a green hill floating on water. Rain that falls on the roof is guided back to the reservoir through the greenery above the columns and the internal drainpipes. Part of this water is reused for irrigation. The abundant groundwater flowing beneath the site is used as a heat source for the air conditioning system; heat exchange takes place between the groundwater and the heat collection pipes installed in the foundation piles that reach down to 50 m below ground. By integrating the natural flow of the site, we aimed to create a building that becomes part of the cycle of nature. We wish for this space to become a place where those who have lost someone close can surrender themselves to the flow of water, confront nature and grow to accept death as a process of human beings returning to the natural cycle.

Site plan S=1:15000

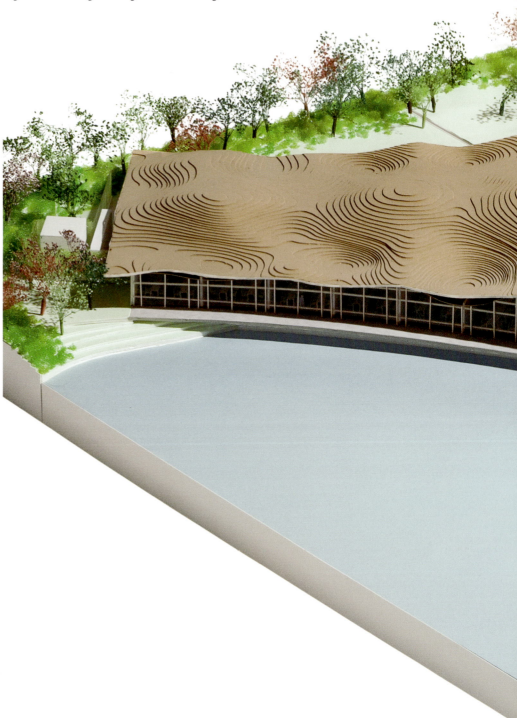

Waiting hall at crematorium

Regarding the planning of the park, workshops involving farmers from local plant nurseries were conducted under the leadership of Mikiko Ishikawa, landscape designer and professor at Chuo University. As a result, the scheme incorporates traditional trees from the Akayama-Angyo area, as well as new varieties that have been cultivated locally, whilst bringing out the best of the existing landscape. Furthermore, gates leading directly to surrounding plant nurseries have been installed in an attempt to create a park that is open to the local public.

(仮称)川口市火葬施設・赤山歴史自然公園

川口市新井宿に整備される，火葬施設と都市公園の一体的な計画である。敷地は谷戸（やと）と呼ばれる台地と谷地が複雑に入れ替わる境界に位置し，東京から十数分にも拘わらず，植木の囲場が広がるのどかな風景が広がっている。中心に調整池を整備し，都市公園・火葬施設・ハイウェイオアシスという三つの異なる施設が取り囲む計画である。

火葬施設においては，大きな機械室をもつ現代の巨大火葬施設をいかに都市公園の緑に溶け込ませるかが，ひとつのテーマとなった。14基の火葬炉を背中合わせに並べ，運営機能を地下と中央コア部分に集約することで，ホール機能と待合機能を公園に対して360°開放した。自由曲面の屋根から連続した柱によって，緑の丘が水上にふわりと浮上しているような建築となっている。屋根上の雨水は柱上の緑から柱内部樋を通って水面に戻され，一部は灌漑設備の水源として再利用される。敷地を流れる豊富な地下水を地下50mまで達する基礎杭内の採熱管によって熱交換することで，空調の熱源として活用した。場所の自然の流れを取り込んで，自然の循環の一部となるような建築をめざした。親しい者を亡くした人たちが，水の流れの上に身を置き風景と対峙することで，人が死を通じて再び自然循環に帰っていくことに向き合うことができる空間になればと考えている。

公園の計画にあたっては，ランドスケープデザインの中央大学・石川幹子氏を中心に，地域の植木農家とワークショップを行い，地形を活かしながら赤山安行の伝統的な植木や地域で開発された新品種を取り入れる計画とした。また，周囲の囲場に直接立ち寄れるゲートを各所に設けて，地域に開かれた公園とする試みを行っている。

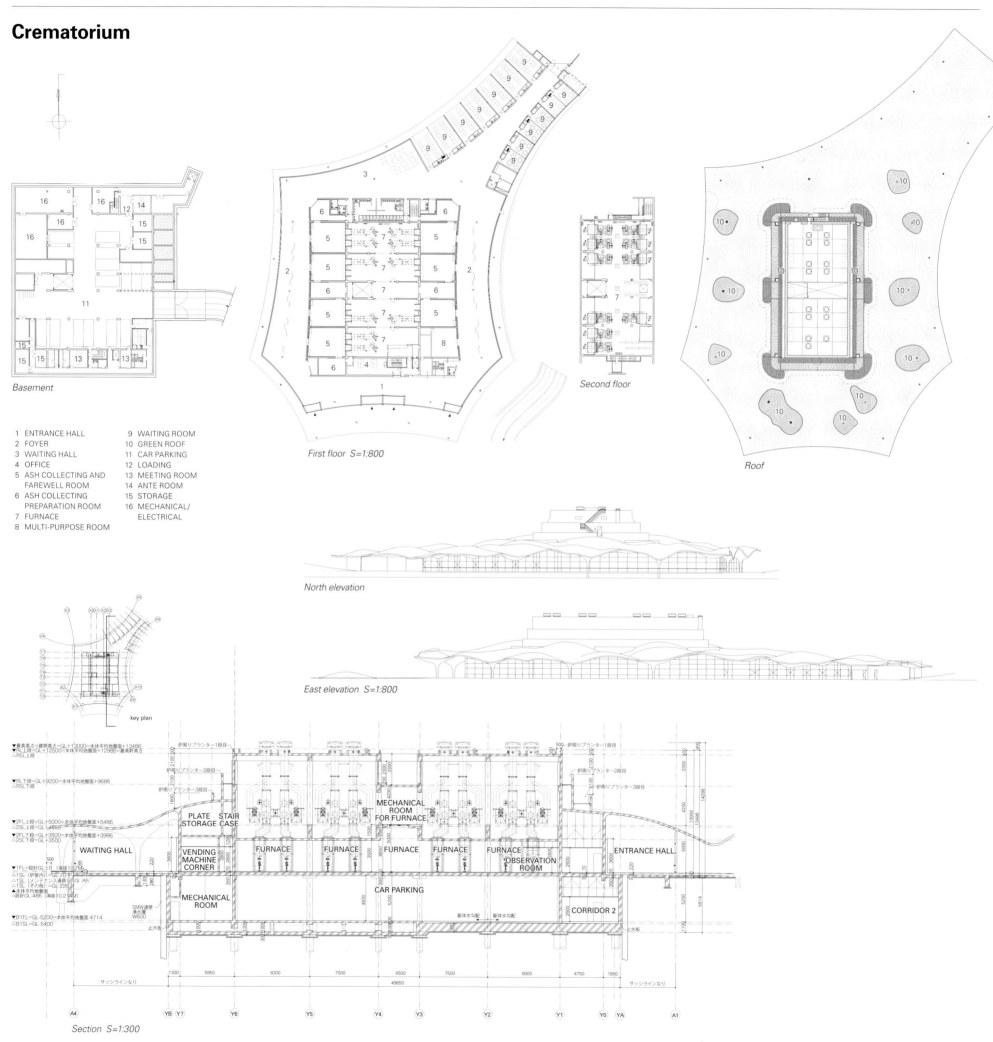

Historical Natural Information Center

Overall view of Historical Natural Information Center

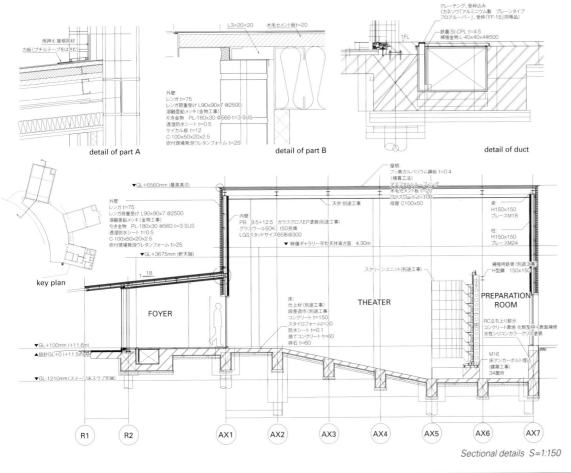

detail of part A
detail of part B
detail of duct

key plan

FOYER
THEATER
PREPARATION ROOM

Sectional details S=1:150

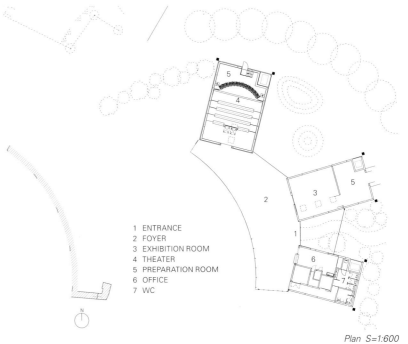

1 ENTRANCE
2 FOYER
3 EXHIBITION ROOM
4 THEATER
5 PREPARATION ROOM
6 OFFICE
7 WC

Plan S=1:600

Regional Products Center

Overall view of Regional Products Center

1 ENTRANCE
2 EXHIBITION AND SALE CORNER
3 EXHIBITION PREPARATION ROOM
4 LIBRARY
5 CAFE / SHOP
6 CONFERENCE SPACE
7 OFFICE
8 KITCHEN
9 STORAGE
10 WC

Plan S=1:600

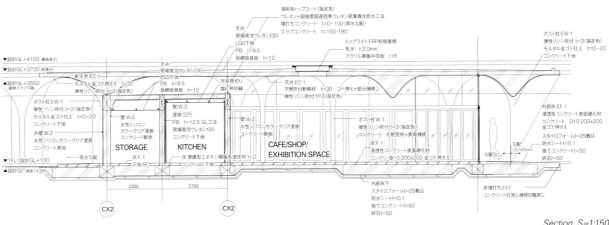

STORAGE KITCHEN CAFE/SHOP/EXHIBITION SPACE

Section S=1:150

National Taiwan University, College of Social Sciences
Taipei, Taiwan, R.O.C.
2006–13

Overall view from southeast

North view of school building

Taiwan University is based on a former Taipei Imperial University, therefore its campus has a symmetrical configuration with a central trajectory also found in a former Imperial University of Japan. Following the building relocation plan of the social study department to the main campus area, which is currently located outside of the main campus, it is requested to give a new design for this wing to be one of the symbols of the university. This new wing program consists of sub departments of the social study department, the department of economics, the department of politics, a research study center, an international convention hall, and a library. The school building is a multi-programed complex, while the building in layered configuration houses smaller units such as classrooms and research laboratories as the building goes up to higher levels.

The first scheme was a symbolic, large one-volume plan; the second scheme was to house each sub department in a tower to be configured in three-tower configuration; the third scheme was to isolate the library to place it as the symbol of the social study department, rather than representing the entire social study department as a symbol. In details, the new wing volume in 168 m long and 31 m high is placed in east-west orientation, while the library wing is projected into the courtyard of the campus block to produce a unity with the existing green area.

The library wing is an one-story building in 6 m high, supported by a tree-like structure system derived from unifying columns and the roof. The library space is related with the naturalistic environment of the courtyard to provide reading spaces under the grove of trees. Those tree-like columns (stems) are distributed based on the autonomous algorithm. It is a double spiral condition often found in plants; those two spirals retain certain distances to each other and form its own growing patterns at multiple points. The intersection of those two spirals becomes the cardinal point, and the space between each cardinal point is further divided in Voronoi pattern to define the forms of each roof slab. The forms of the columns are the repetitive patterns in 3 scales specified by the different spans, in a large, a middle, and a small sizes.

The programed column distribution based on the double-spiral algorithm means to define their coordinates in radial pattern, and the plan in the space is derived from the intersection of three radial coordinates. In other words, the plan has three minor focal points, which are different from the points definable in Euclidean geometry grid. We hope that the library space produced in such operation can provide more natural and peaceful space.

Courtyard on third floor of school building. Roof of library wing on right

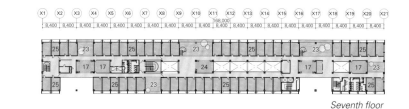

Seventh floor

First floor S=1:1800

Third floor

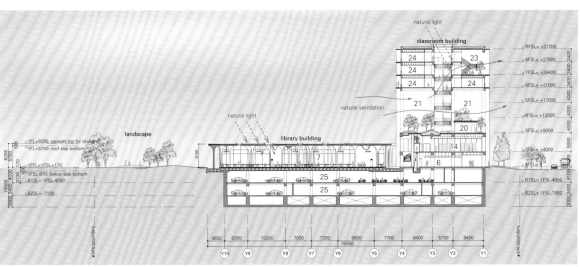

Cross section

Diagram: double spiral

Longitudinal section S=1:1000

1 ENTRANCE OF CLASSROOM BUILDING
2 EXHIBITION SPACE
3 COMMON ROOM
4 ENTRANCE OF LIBRARY BUILDING
5 LIBRARY OFFICE
6 MAGAZINE READING SPACE
7 OPEN STACK READING ROOM (1F)
8 LARGE CLASSROOM (HOLDING 150 PEOPLE)
9 LARGE CLASSROOM (HOLDING 300 PEOPLE)
10 ELECTRIC ROOM
11 TEACHER'S ROOM
12 STUDENT CLUB
13 SERVER ROOM
14 OPEN STACK READING ROOM (2F)
15 COMPUTER ROOM
16 STUDY ROOM
17 MEETING ROOM
18 DEPARTMENT OFFICE
19 INTERNATIONAL CONFERENCE HALL
20 REST ROOM
21 ROOF GARDEN
22 CLASSROOM
23 TERRACE
24 LOUNGE FOR TEACHER
25 LABORATORY

Night view of southeast corner

Stacks are arranged between tree-like columns according to geometry of double spiral

Reading area and open-stacks: 88 tree-like columns and bamboo laminated lumber-made stacks

台湾大学社会科学部棟

台湾大学は戦前の台北帝国大学を前身とし，日本の旧帝大のキャンパスと同様に，中央に軸線を通したシンメトリーの構成をもつ。現在，飛び地にある社会科学部のメインキャンパスへの移転計画に伴い，大学の新しいシンボルとなる校舎棟のデザインが求められた。経済学部，政治学部，研究センター，国際会議室，図書館などが複合された計画である。積層される校舎は，上階へいくほど小単位の教室や研究室となる，複合的なプログラムである。

全体をシンボリックなワン・ヴォリュームとする第1案から，部門ごとに3棟のタワーを構成した第2案を経て到達した第3案は，社会科学部棟すべてをシンボル化するのではなく，図書館を分離して学部全体のシンボルとして位置づけるというものであった。それは，敷地の東西方向に長さ168m，高さ31mのヴォリュームの校舎棟を配置し，キャンパスブロックの中庭側に既存の緑地と一体になるような図書館棟をせり出すという提案である。

図書館棟は高さ6mの平屋であり，柱と屋根が一体となった樹木のような構造体によって構成されている。図書館の空間は，中庭の自然と連続しながら，森の木立の中で本を読むような場として提案された。樹木のような柱(幹)は，自己生成的なアルゴリズムに基づいて配置されている。それは植物に見られるような二重スパイラルであり，二つのスパイラルはある距離を保ちながら複数のポイントで自己生成し，互いのスパイラルの交点が柱の基点になる。さらにその基点間がボロノイ分割されて，個々の屋根スラブの形状が決定されている。柱の形状はスパンによって大中小の3パターンの繰り返しである。

この二重スパイラルを描くアルゴリズムに基づいて柱の位置が決定されることは，放射状座標が設定されることを意味しており，平面は三つの放射座標の交差によって形成される。その結果，ユークリッド幾何学のグリッド上での決定とは異なる三つの小中心を持つ。こうして得られる図書館の空間は，より自然で安らぎを感じる場となることが期待されている。

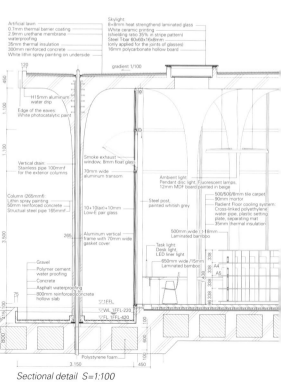

Sectional detail S=1:100

◁ *Reading area and open-stacks*

View from entrance of reading area and open-stacks.
Reception counter, sofa and bench designed by Kazuko Fujie

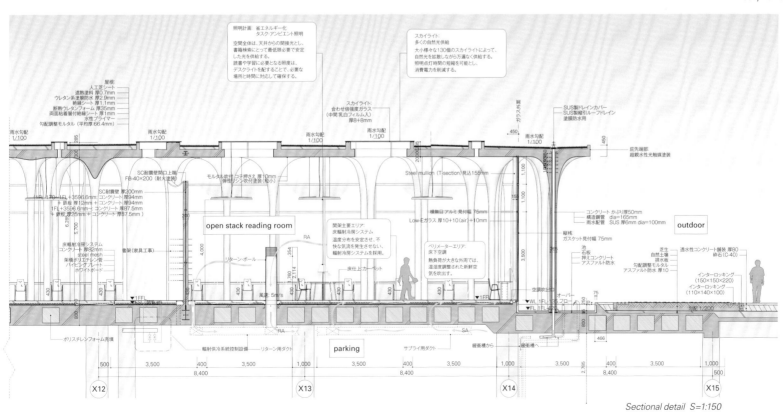

Sectional detail S=1:150

**Songshan Taipei
New Horizon Building**
Taipei, Taiwan, R.O.C.
2008–13

The site of this redevelopment scheme is the historic remains of a former tobacco factory in central Taipei, which was built in the 1930s during the period of Japanese rule. The 100,000 m² complex encompasses office, commercial, hotel and cultural facilities, and aims to conserve and utilize the site, whilst also establishing a platform for cultural activity.

The site embodies not only an urban scale, but also a more human-scale, providing a pleasant overground environment with its low-story factory buildings and rich gardens. In order to accommodate communities of various scale, the 70 m-high and 165 m-long building volume is subdivided by different-sized arcs without undermining its integrity.

On the south side of the building, there is a lively cultural plaza towards the historic site, a tranquil green garden towards the lotus pond, and a sunken garden that leads underground in the center. The arced stepped terraces reduce the sense of oppression imposed by the building, and the green network of the continuous garden leading up to the rooftop of the upper stories integrates the architecture with the landscape. The north facade that faces the elevated road is divided by two large arcs, and is intended to become an expressive landmark with a 6-color scheme corresponding to the facade and roof of the historic remains and the surrounding nature. The northern and southern latticed facades, composed of SRC structures forming a gentle arc, act as brise-soleil to provide sunshade, while ventilating windows in the transom structure allow natural breeze, offering an open and pleasant internal environment.

The underground concert hall and art cinema are an urban oasis of sound and film, serving as a place of relaxation like a cultural salon. The event hall on the uppermost floor is an open space overlooking the city of Taipei, which can be used together with the rooftop garden. The space is covered by a large, gently curving roof that harmonizes with the surrounding mountains, and acts as a new symbol of the cultural facility.

The former tobacco factory was a utopia that pursued ideal working and living environments with welfare facilities, gardens and lotus ponds. Thus, by creating a suitable environment for the functions of the new facility, and by harmonizing with the surrounding environment, we aspire to create a building that becomes a place of everyday recreation for the local people, as well as a place that promotes a new lifestyle.

South elevation divided by three circular arc

Overall view from southeast

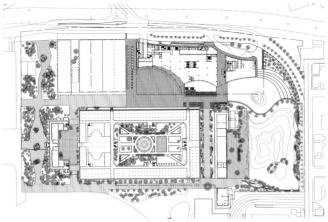
Site plan S=1:5000

1 HOTEL LOBBY
2 RESTAURANT
3 ENTRANCE (14F)
4 PROMENADE
5 SHOP
6 SUNKEN GARDEN
7 OFFICE ENTRANCE
8 MEMBER'S ROOM
9 HOTEL
10 OFFICE
11 TERRACE
12 ELEVATOR HALL
13 HOTEL LOUNGE
14 EVENT HALL
15 ROOF TERRACE
16 MECHANICAL SPACE
17 ART HOUSE
18 CONCERT HALL
19 BICYCLE PARKING
20 PARKING

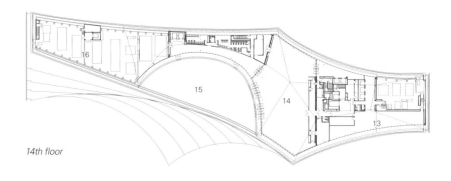
14th floor

South elevation divided by three circular arc

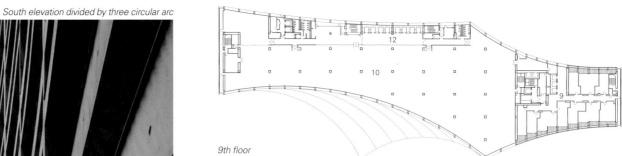
9th floor

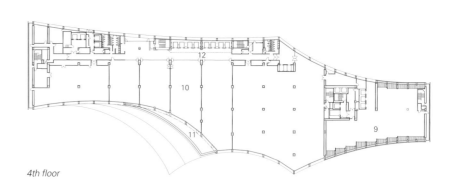
4th floor

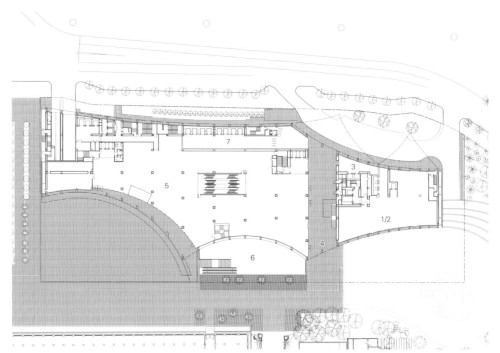
First floor S=1:1500

松山 台北文創ビル

台北市の中心に位置する，1930年代日本統治時代に建設された煙草工場の跡地における再開発計画である。オフィス，商業，ホテル，文化施設からなる約10万m²の複合施設を建設することで，古蹟の保存・活用を行う事業と共に文化的活動の基盤をつくることが求められた。

敷地は都市的なスケールに向き合うだけでなく，低層の煙草工場跡や豊かな緑地などのヒューマンスケールで心地よい空間が地上に広がる。様々なスケールのコミュニティに対応するために，高さ70m，長手方向165mの建物ヴォリュームを，スケールの異なる円弧によって分節しつつ一体的に構成した。

建物南側は，保存される古蹟との間に賑わいある文化広場や荷花池側に静かな緑の庭園，中央には地下へと誘うサンクンガーデンに分節している。また，段々状に円弧をセットバックさせることで建物の圧迫感を和らげつつ，地上の緑を上層部の屋上庭園まで連続させて，建築とランドスケープを緑のネットワークで統合している。一方，高架道路に面する北側ファサードは，大きな二つの円弧で分節し，古蹟の外壁や屋根・周辺の自然と呼応した6色のカラースキームによって，表情豊かなランドマークになることを意図している。そして，緩やかな円弧を描くSRC造による南北の格子状ファサードは，ブリーズソレイユとして日射を遮り，欄間に設けた換気窓からの自然通風により開放的で快適な内部環境をつくっている。

地下に配置されたコンサートホールとアートシネマは，都市の中の音と映像のオアシスとして，文化的サロンのような憩いの場を設けている。最上階のイベントホールは屋上庭園と一体的に利用でき，台北市内を一望できる開放的な空間である。周囲の山々と呼応する緩やかで大きな曲面屋根で覆われ，文化施設としての新しいシンボル性を獲得している。

かつての煙草工場は，福利厚生施設や庭園，荷花池等を併設した居住労働環境の理想を求めたユートピアであった。それゆえ，新しい施設もまたそれぞれの施設に適した環境を整え，周辺環境との調和を図ることで，この地に暮らす人々の日常的な憩いの場になるとともに，新たなライフスタイルを創造し得るものでありたいと考えた。

14th floor
Above: roof terrace
Below: 345 expanded metal floating in event space

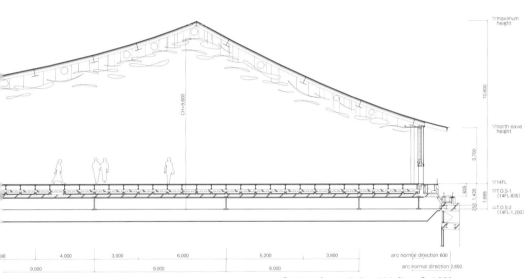

Section of event hall on 14th floor S=1:250

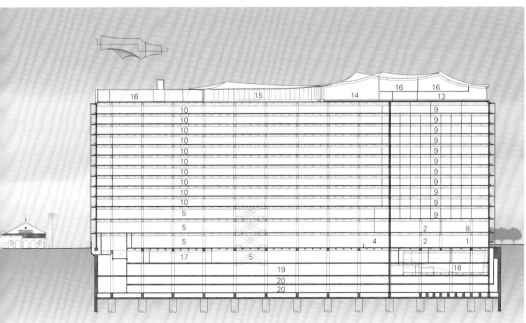

Section S=1:1500

Entrance hall of office area

New Athletic Field and Sports Park in Aomori
Aomori, Japan
2013–

This is a scheme to build an athletics stadium which will serve as a central facility of the Aomori Sports Park located at the foot of the Azumadake hills in the east of Aomori city. The facility will have 1 story below ground and 4 above, with a total floor area of approximately 28,000 m² and a seating capacity of 20,800. It will be certified a Japan Association of Athletics Federations Class 1 facility as well as International Association of Athletics Federations (IAAF) Class 2 for athletics; J3 league for soccer; and Japanese Top League for rugby.

There will be an indoor circuit track with a 540 m lap that incorporates the 100 m running track and dugout, making it possible to practice even during winter snowfall.

The park, surrounded by rich greenery, stretches out over 86 ha, and many visitors come for a walk or to use the neighboring indoor practice center and tennis courts. In order for the stadium to become a familiar presence to these people, the main functions facing the field have been arranged as semi-underground spaces with the construction of an embankment, while the overground volume has been integrated with the landscape to create an open stadium. The main concourse, which can be accessed freely, overlooks Aomori city, and has a friendly atmosphere with louvers made of locally produced pine trees from the prefecture and brick tiles covering parts of the exterior wall.

The main stand and concourse are covered by a large roof with a surface area of 8,700 m² and a cantilever of more than 26 m. The soffit is composed of approximately 4,600 GRC panels, forming a sequence of curved and flat surfaces that extend out from the capital. This becomes a symbol of the facility, displaying strength and dignity that correspond with the trees in the surrounding mountains. The large roof also controls the constant wind blowing into the stadium from the northeast.

The site boasts a rich natural environment, which on the other hand means that the stadium must adapt to harsh winter conditions.

The large roof has a snow drop prevention structure which can hold 350 kg/m², and will collect melted snow and rainwater for reuse. The scheme also makes use of natural energy by employing an underground heat collection system using steel pipe piles, and by reducing load in fresh air intake using heat tubes in the embankment. The project is due for completion in December 2018.

谷戸の優れた自然環境を生かし、
生命の躍動するスタジアムをつくります。

計画地周辺は，里山と低地が相互に貫入し合う谷戸であり，豊かな水資源に恵まれた多様な生物の宝庫です。私たちは，この"大地の力"そのものが生み出すスタジアムを計画します。

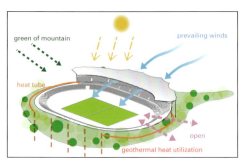

自然エネルギーを利用し，新しい自然を生み出す
オープンスタジアムをつくります。

地中熱や風のコントロールによって，自然エネルギーの徹底した利用を図ります。また，樹木を連想させる屋根によって，周囲の自然と一体化すると同時に，雨や雪，強い日射を防ぎます。

Diagrams

View toward main stand with large roof from east

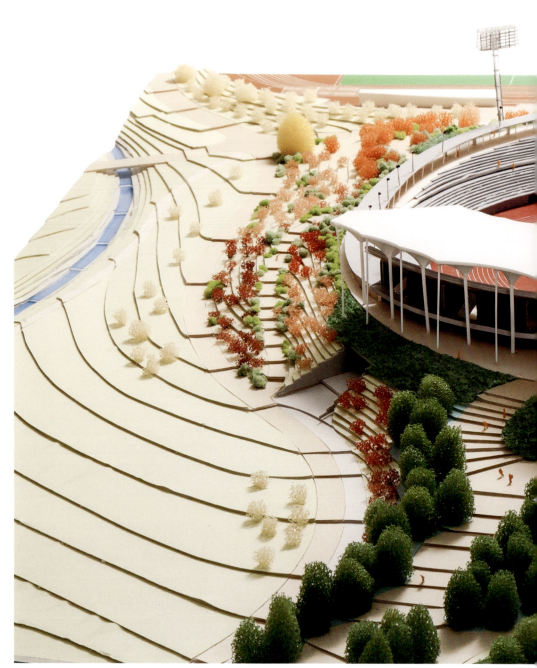

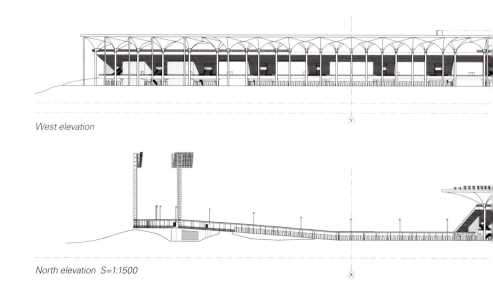

West elevation

North elevation S=1:1500

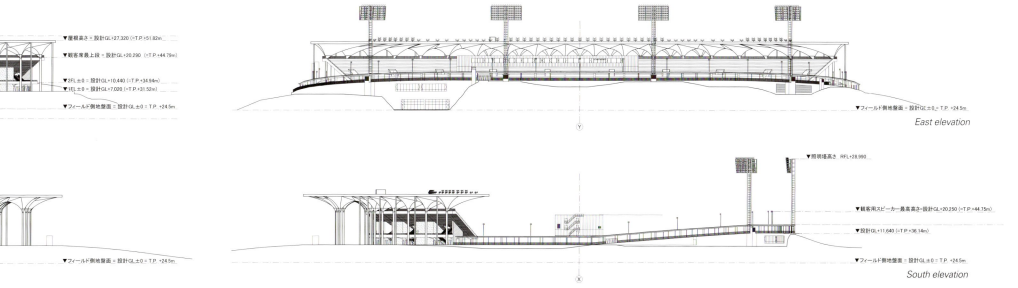

East elevation

South elevation

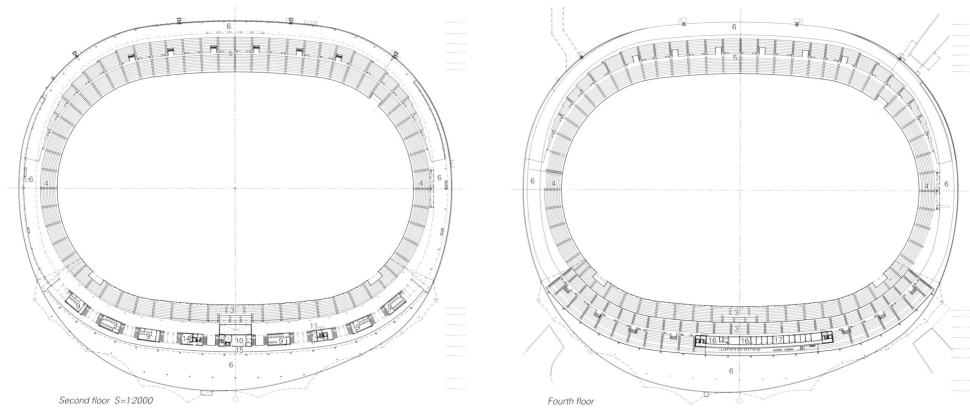

Second floor S=1:2000

Fourth floor

1 GATE
2 TICKET
3 MAIN STANDS
4 SIDE STANDS
5 BACK STANDS
6 CONCOURSE
7 CORRIDOR
8 INFORMATION
9 WC
10 RETAIL
11 FIRST-AID OFFICE
12 NURSING ROOM
13 VIP ROOM
14 NURSERY
15 BRIDGE
16 BROADCASTING ROOM
17 ADMINISTRATION OFFICE
18 MECHANICAL

A MAIN STUDIUM (PLANNING BUILDING)
B SUB STUDIUM (ONGOING)
C MAEDA ARENA
D TEMPORARY ARCHERY HALL (ONGOING)
E GREEN PLAZA (FUTURE BASEBALL GROUND)
F BALL GAME GROUND
G TRAINING FIELD FOR THROWING GAME (ONGOING)
H MULTI-PURPOSE SPORTS PLAZA (ONGOING)
I TENNIS COURT
J ENTRANCE MALL
K 'KOMOREBI' PLAZA
L 'SAKURA' PLAZA
M REGULATING POND
N SCENERY POND
O NORTH GATE

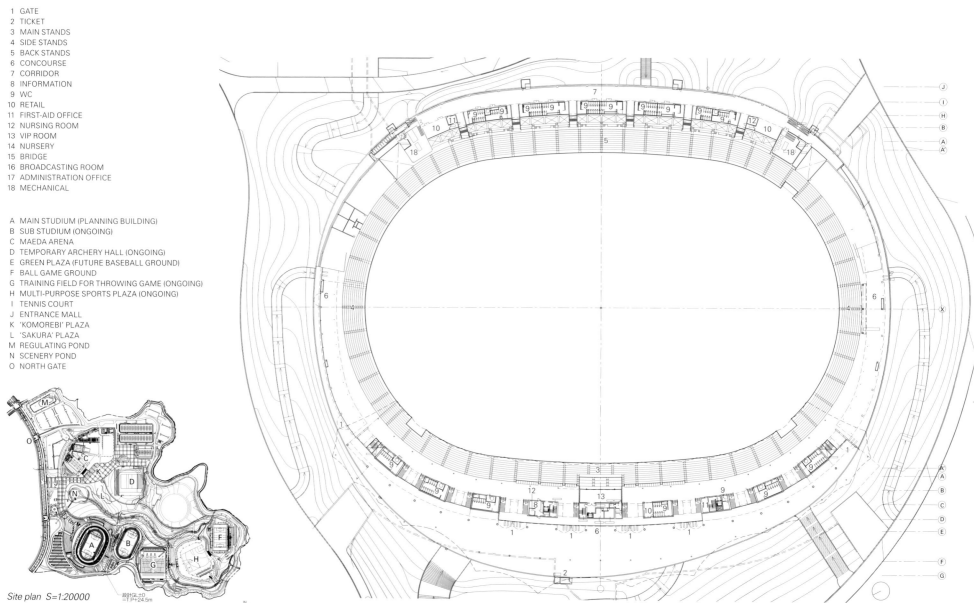

Site plan S=1:20000

First floor S=1:1500

(仮称)新青森県総合運動公園陸上競技場

青森市の東，東岳のふもとの丘陵地にある総合運動公園の中核施設として陸上競技場をつくる計画である。延床面積約28,000m², 地下1階地上4階, 約20,800席の施設で, 陸上は日本陸連第一種公認かつ国際陸連IAAF-class2, サッカーはJ3, ラグビーはトップリーグに対応予定である。

室内には, 100m走路やダッグアウトを利用した1周540mの周回走路があり, 積雪期の練習も可能とした。

緑に囲まれた86haにも及ぶ公園には, 散歩や隣接する室内練習場やテニスコートなどに遊びにくる人々も多い。そんな人々に競技場を身近なものに感じられるように, 盛土によってグラウンドに面する主要機能を半地下空間に収めると共に, 地上部分をランドスケープと一体化させたオープンスタジアムとした。自由にアクセスできるメインコンコースは, 県産材の杉の木ルーバー, 外壁の一部にレンガタイルを用いて親しみやすい空間としており, 青森市内を一望できる場になる。

メインスタンド及びメインコンコースには8,700m²程, 26m以上跳ね出した大屋根がかかる。軒天井は, 約4,600枚のGRCパネルによって柱頭から展開された曲面と平面の組み合わせによって構成され, 周辺の山の樹木と呼応した力強さと凛とした施設のシンボルとなる。大屋根は競技場内への北東からの恒常風のコントロールも行っている。

豊かな自然環境の一方, 冬季の厳しい環境に対応することが求められる。

大屋根は350kg/m²の積雪荷重に耐える無落雪屋根とし, 融雪・雨水は再利用する。また, 鋼管杭を利用した地中熱採取システム, 盛土内に設置したヒートチューブによる外気取り入れ負荷の軽減を行うといった自然エネルギーを利用する計画である。2018年12月竣工予定である。

Main concourse

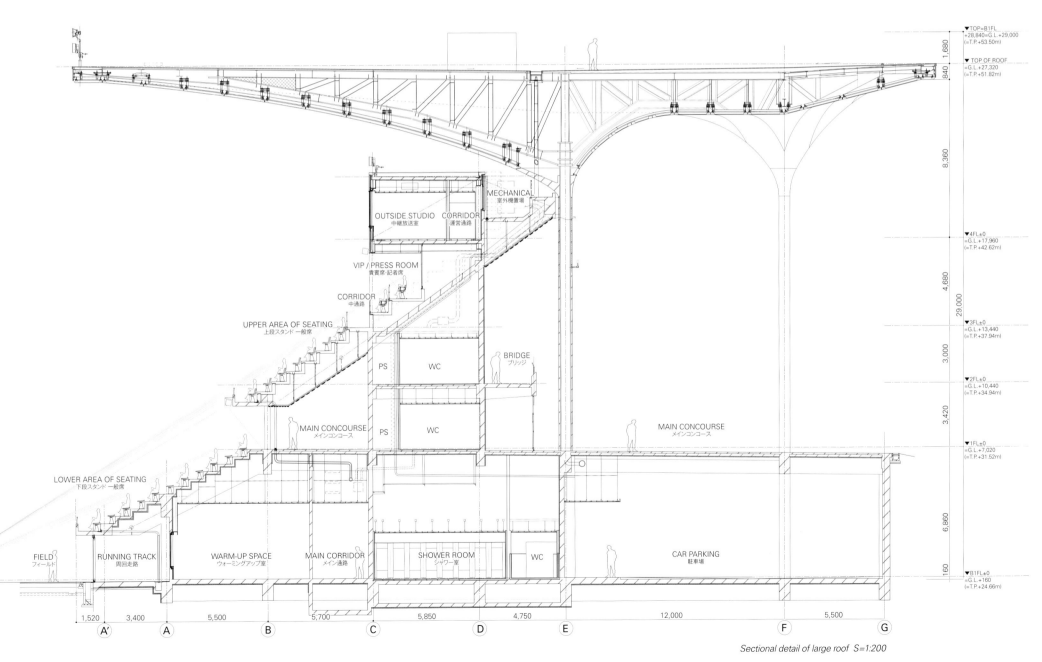

Sectional detail of large roof S=1:200

Museum+ /
West Kowloon
Cultural District,
Competition
Hongkong, China
2013

Aerial view from south

South elevation   *Sketch*

In 2012, the construction of a museum complex (*M+*) was announced by the authority at West Kowloon Cultural District, Hong Kong, following which an open design competition was held. The competition site faces a 23 ha urban park to the west. A concert hall is planned to the east, a 484 m-tall high rise building (*ICC*) stands to the north, and Victoria Harbour borders the south. A station for the bullet train joining Guangzhou and Shenzhen in China has also been planned in the vicinity.

Although *M+* is comprised of diverse and complex programs over a total floor area of 70,000 m², a simple and clear arrangement was required in order to make it easy for all visitors to comprehend. Our proposal divides the complex into three platforms (Art Factory, Art Forest and Art Cloud), each of which has a distinct atmosphere for the visitors to enjoy. The platforms have a simple structural composition; flat slabs held up by the plant-like "Emerging Walls".

Art Factory (1st to 3rd floor) is a combination of programs such as the entrance hall, exhibition hall, industrial spaces and educational facilities. Various activities including exhibition, production, research and workshops take place in the various spaces, and the platform becomes a lively art factory that is connected to the city.

Art Forest (4th floor) is a semi-outdoor space at 32 m above ground. An artificial forest of artwork and a natural forest coexist, creating a surreal and enchanting atmosphere. Visitors can wander around the experimental art space or take a rest in the restaurant and cafe, whilst enjoying the ocean view and the natural breeze.

Art Cloud (5th to 7th floor) is the topmost platform, which is divided into the permanent exhibition and storage floors. The permanent exhibition space, which has a double-height ceiling, is a sequence of abstract white cubes of various scales and proportions. The act of discovering the unknown in this exhibition space is almost like trying to find one's way through white clouds. The storage floor is bordered by office spaces and conservation spaces, at the center of which the collection storage, also a white cube, is placed.

M+ is open to all; it is a museum that provides diverse spaces to be enjoyed by everyone. New possibilities of art are opened up by the integration of various spatial qualities with both generality and technicality. The Emerging Walls that support the platforms symbolize growth towards the future, like sprouting plants. Unfortunately, we were not able to win the competition.

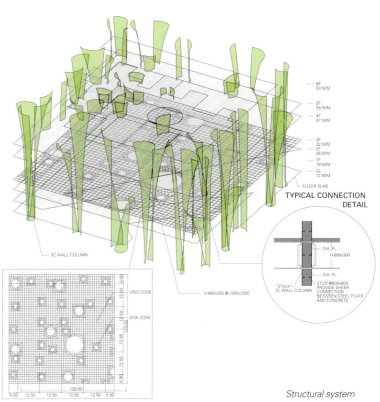

Typical floor slab beam layout   *Structural system*

1 ENTRANCE HALL	GALLERY 1800	20 OFFICE
2 INDUSTRIAL SPACE	10 LEARNING CENTRE	21 IT SUPPORT
3 MUSEUM SHOP	11 TERRACE	22 COLLECTION STORAGE
4 CAFE/BAR	12 SHOP	23 COLLECTION SCREEN 378
5 MULTI PURPOSE HALL	13 RESOURCE CENTRE	24 CONSERVATION
6 TEMPORARY EXHIBITION GALLERY 1200	14 CURATOR OFFICE	25 COLLECTION GALLERY
7 DESIGN GALLERY (RDE TENANT)	15 STAFF CAFETERIA	26 OPEN AIR GALLERY
	16 SCULPTURE GARDEN	27 ROOF TOP GREEN SPACE
8 DESIGN SHOP (RDE TENANT)	17 ART FOREST	28 SOLAR PANELS
9 TEMPORARY EXHIBITION	18 ARTISTS IN RESIDENCE	29 TOP LIGHT
	19 RESTAURANT	

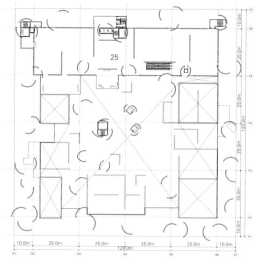

Sixth floor

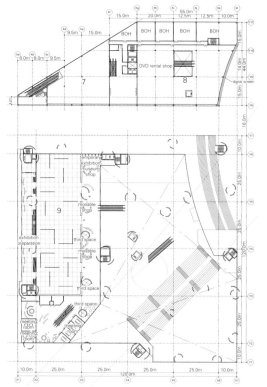

First floor

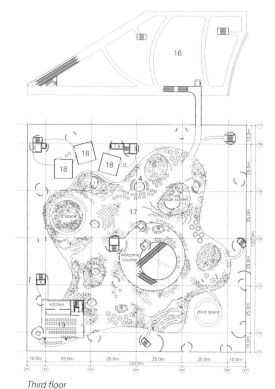

Third floor

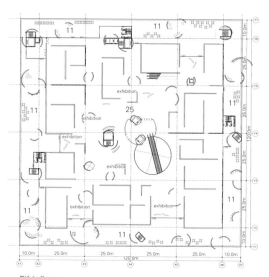

Fifth floor

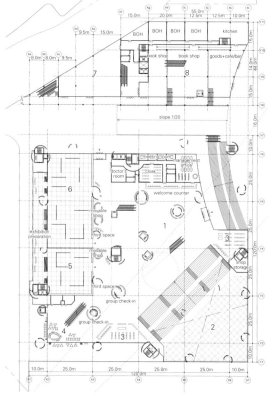

Ground floor S=1:2000

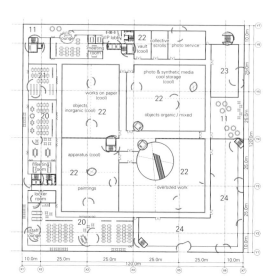

Second floor

Fourth floor

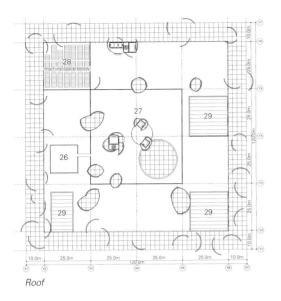

Roof

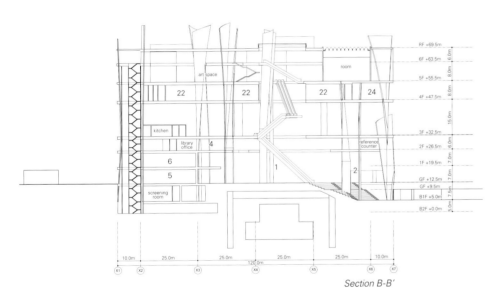

Section B-B'

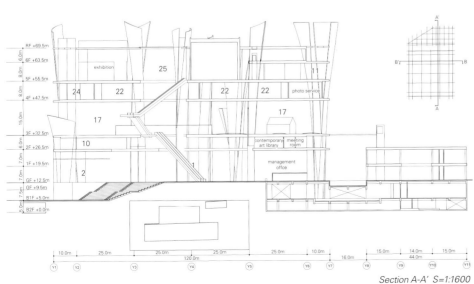

Section A-A' S=1:1600

Art cloud

Entrance hall

Museum＋ /
West Kowloon Cultural District Competition

2012年，香港西九龍文化区の管理局がミュージアム複合施設(M+)を建設することになり，オープンコンペティションが開催された。敷地の西側には23haの広大な都市公園が隣接し，東側にリリックホールが計画されている。北側には高さ484mの高層ビル(ICC)が建っており，南側はヴィクトリアハーバーに面している。近隣には，中国の広州と深圳を繋ぐ新幹線の駅も計画されていた。

「M＋」自体は延床面積70,000m²の複雑で多様なプログラムを持つが，すべての人に分かりやすく単純明快な構成が求められた。我々の提案では施設全体を三つのプラットフォーム(Art Factory, Art Forest, Art Cloud)に分け，そこに全く異なる場が展開し，ビジターはそれぞれの世界を満喫できるようにした。各プラットフォームを構成するフラットな床と，それらを支持する植物のような曲面壁(Emerging Wall)によって，単純明快な構造体となっている。

Art Factory (1階〜3階)は，エントランスホール，企画展示場，インダストリアルスペース，教育施設等が組み合わされた空間。様々な場所で展示，製作，リサーチ，ワークショップ等の活動が常に展開され，街と繋がっている賑やかなアートの工場である。

Art Forest (4階)は，地上32mに設けられた半屋外の空間。アートによる人工の森と自然の緑が混在する，シュールで魅惑的な世界を実現する。海を見下ろし，風を感じながら，実験的なアートスペースを探訪し，レストランやカフェで休憩できるアートの森である。

Art Cloud (5階〜7階)は最上部に置かれ，常設展示階と収蔵庫階に分かれる。常設展示エリアは2層分の天井高を有し，様々なスケールとプロポーションのホワイトキューブが連続する抽象度の高い空間で，純白の雲の中を掻き分けて歩くような，未知の世界を探る行為である。一方，ストレージフロアは，周辺部をオフィスやコンサベーションスペースが囲み，中央部にホワイトキューブのコレクションストレージが設けられる。

「M＋」はすべての人に開かれ，すべての人が楽しめる多様な場を備えたミュージアムである。このような一般性，専門性の双方に開かれた多様な場を統合することによってこそ，アートの新しい可能性は拡張される。また，プラットフォームを支える Emerging Wall は植物の芽のように，「未来に向かって開く成長のシンボル」である。残念ながら我々は，このコンペティションに勝つことができなかった。

Interior Design for the Reconstruction Project of Jikido in Yakushiji Temple
Nara, Japan
2013–

Interiors: view toward "Amida Jodo Henso-zu", describes transformation of Pure Land, with different lighting

This is a restoration scheme of the *Jiki-do* (dining hall) at *Yakushi-ji Temple* in Nara.

Yakushi-ji is an established temple constructed during the Hakuho era at the wish of Emperor Tenmu. Since then, its buildings have been burnt down or damaged by many fires, earthquakes and wars. Aside from the *To-to* (east pagoda) which still stands in its original state, the temple buildings have been undergoing restoration since the late 1960s. As of now, the *Kon-do* (main hall), *Sai-to* (west pagoda), *Kairo* (cloister) and *Daikodo* (lecture hall) have already been reconstructed. The reconstruction of the Jiki-do will complete the restoration of the main buildings at *Yakushi-ji*.

Although the external appearance of the *Jiki-do* will be restored to its original state from the Hakuho era, the internal space has been permitted to host unconventional functions such as various events and exhibits. For this reason, we received a commission for the design of the reconstruction.

The main structure of the building is a steel structure measuring approximately 20 m x 7.3 m, with wood covering the outer side of the columns. Rather than reproducing the four lines of columns along the longitudinal direction, the same span is supported by just a pair of columns placed at either end, opening up a large central space where people can gather. "Amida Jodo Henso-zu" (Mandala of the Pure Land of Amida), a 6 m x 6 m illustration by the great artist Toshio Tabuchi, will be displayed in the center, along with "Yakushi-ji Engi Daihekiga" (Great Mural of the Legends of Yakushi-ji) which will be presented on 14 panels each placed between the columns in the side walls.

The design of the ceiling resembles clouds; it represents the halo of the Amida figure spreading in concentric rings.

The ceiling panels are made of aluminum plates that were laser-cut and treated with alumite dye. The image conforms to the aesthetic concept described in "In Praise of Shadows": floating in dimness and faintly illuminated by pale light.

A traditional roof-laying ceremony has been conducted in July 2016, and completion of the building is scheduled for May 2017.

薬師寺食堂復興計画(内部)

奈良・薬師寺食堂の復興計画である。

薬師寺は天武天皇の発願により白鳳時代に創建された寺院であるが，幾多の火災や震災・兵火等により建物が損壊，焼失した。伽藍の中で建立当初の姿を残すのは東塔のみであったが，昭和40年代より復興が進められ，これまでに金堂，西塔，回廊，大講堂等が再建されてきた。今回の食堂が再建されると，ひとまず薬師寺の主な伽藍はすべて完成することになる。

食堂は，外部は白鳳時代の外観を復元させることになるが，内部は様々なイベントを行ったり，ギャラリー空間として使用できる空間にすることが認められるということで，我々に設計を依頼された。

間口11間，奥行4間の建物の主体構造は，鉄骨造として柱の周囲は木でカバーされる。元々長手方向に4列の柱で支えられていたスパンを外側の2本で支え，中央部分は人々が集まることの可能な大空間とした。中央には田渕俊夫画伯によって6m×6mの「阿弥陀浄土変相図」が，両サイド壁面の柱間14面には「仏法伝来の道と薬師寺」と題する大壁画が奉られる予定である。

我々は阿弥陀像の光背が同心円状に広がる，雲のような天井板をデザインした。

この天井板はアルミ板をレーザーカットでくり抜き，金色のアルマイト染色で仕上げられる。そして「陰影礼賛」の世界のように，うす闇の中で淡い光に照らされて浮かぶイメージを描いている。

この建物は2016年7月に古式豊かな上棟式が行われ，2017年5月に竣工予定である。

View from southeast

1 RECEPTION
2 REFECTORY
3 STORAGE

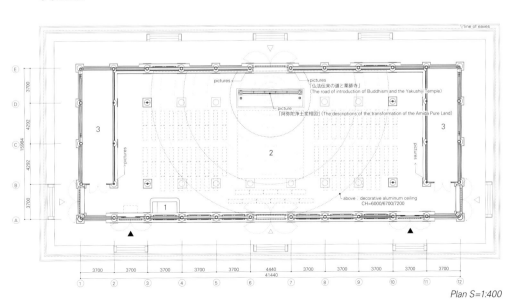

Plan S=1:400

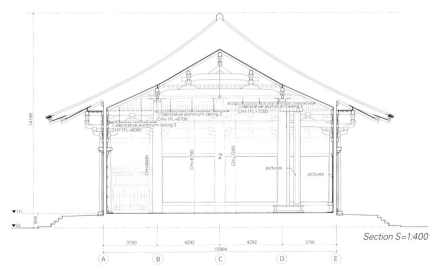

Section S=1:400

The Shinano Mainichi Shimbun Matsumoto Head Office
Matsumoto, Nagano, Japan
2014–

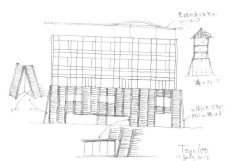

Sketch by Toyo Ito, 17 Jul. 2015

When starting the project for *the New Head Office of Shinano Mainichi Shimbun*, we considered not only office functions but also programs that are open to local citizens. This is a unique project that takes advantage of the company's role as a private newspaper publisher that serves public functions.

The scheme began through hearings with citizens, tourists and the company's employees, followed by public workshops. The recurrent discussion on "what activities should take place here" has been reflected in the architecture.

The 5-story building has a total floor area of 8,000 m². Its programs include "Machinaka Branch Office" for exchange of information between journalists and citizens, "Machinaka Gallery" for cultural or art exhibitions and children's indoor play area, studio space for civic activities, as well as cafes and commercial facilities for enrichment of tourism and everyday life. Our aim is to encourage interaction between individual activities, and to create a place from which new activities emerge.

In the lower stories, GRC and glass louvres provide shade from intense sunlight, and at the same time create an open facade to the public. The third floor has a large terrace facing the plaza adjacent to the city's main street. Here, visitors can watch over ongoing events whilst enjoying a meal or conversation. In the upper stories, natural wind passes through the verandah space behind wooden louvers, providing a pleasant office environment. Furthermore, energy efficiency is enhanced by utilizing water from a nearby river in the floor radiation units for cooling and heating.

We wish for the activities here to be accumulated as a history of Matsumoto, a cultural city, and for them to be passed on to the next generation, in order to develop a pioneer model of local newspapers in collaboration with local citizens.

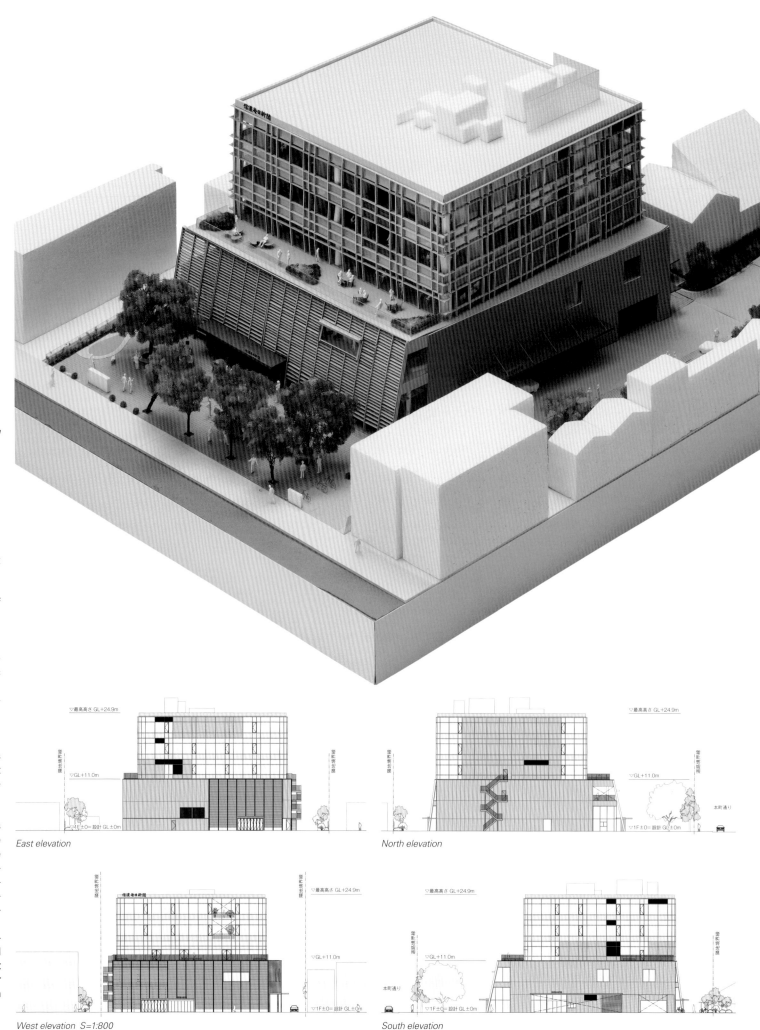

East elevation

North elevation

West elevation S=1:800

South elevation

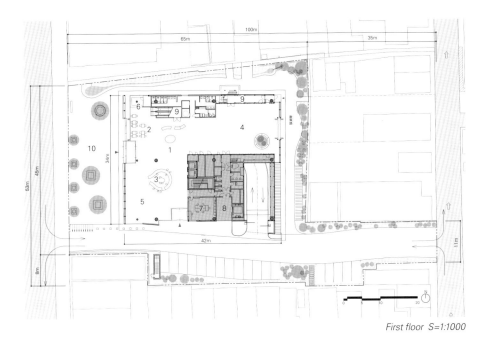
First floor S=1:1000

Fifth floor

Fourth floor

Sketch by Toyo Ito, 8 may 2015

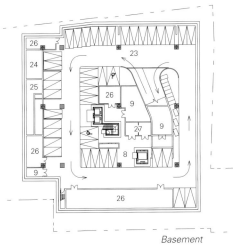
Basement

Second floor

Third floor

'Machinaka Branch Office' and cafe

1	ENTRANCE HALL
2	INFORMATION / NEWSPAPER CAFE
3	'MACHINAKA' OPEN BRANCH
4	'MACHINAKA' OPEN GALLERY
5	RETAIL
6	KIOSK
7	ADMINISTRATION OFFICE
8	LOADING
9	STORAGE
10	PLAZA
11	TERRACE
12	RESTING ROOM
13	RESTAURANT
14	STUDIO
15	KITCHEN
16	SHARE OFFICE
17	ANTE ROOM
18	OFFICE
19	MEETING ROOM
20	LOBBY
21	'ENGAWA' SPACE
22	TATAMI ROOM
23	CAR PARKING
24	STAND PIPE
25	THERMAL STORAGE TANK
26	MECHANICAL
27	GARBAGE AREA

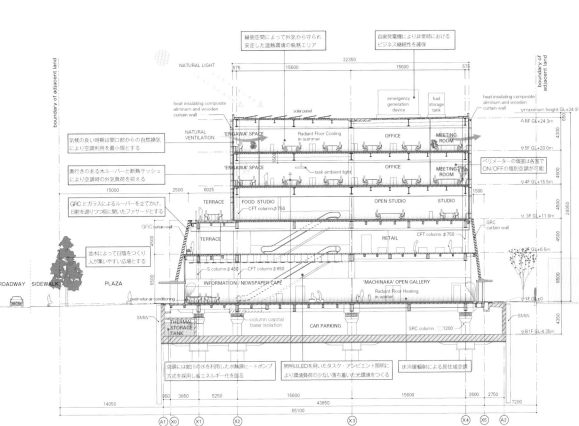
Environmental diagram S=1:1000

信濃毎日新聞社松本本社

「信濃毎日新聞社松本本社」を街の中心部へ建て替えるにあたり，オフィス機能のみならず，市民に開かれたプログラムの検討からスタートした．民間企業でありながら公共的な役割も持つ新聞社という特性を活かした，稀有なプロジェクトである．

計画は，市民や観光客，新聞社社員へのヒアリングに始まり，多様な市民とのワークショップを重ねる中で，「ここでどのような活動がしたいか」ということを繰り返し議論し，建築に落とし込んでいった．

地上5階，延床面積約8,000m²の中には，記者と市民の情報交換の場である「まちなか支局」，文化芸術のイベントスペースやこどもが遊べる屋内広場となる「まちなかギャラリー」，市民活動を支援するスタジオ，観光や日常生活を豊かにするカフェやリテイルを設け，個別の活動が交流し合い，新しい活動が生まれる場となることを意図した．

低層部では，GRCとガラスによるルーバーを立てかけ，強い日射を遮りつつも，街に開かれたファサードをつくり出している．3階では，街の目抜き通りに面した広場側を大きなテラスとし，食事や会話を楽しみながら街のイベントを眺めることができる場を設けている．高層部では，木製ルーバーの縁側スペースを通して，自然風の吹き抜ける快適なオフィス環境が形成されている．さらに，近くを流れる川の水を床輻射冷暖房として活用し，省エネルギー化を図っている．

ここでの活動が，文化都市松本の歴史として蓄積され，次代に発信，継承されていくことで，地方紙の先駆的モデルが市民と共につくられていくことを期待している．

CapitaGreen
Singapore
2007–14

Overall view from north

Even amongst Singapore that has rapidly developed as a central financial city internationally, this project is located on a corner in downtown where modern high-rise buildings are concentrated, and it is a high-rise office building that is 245 m high with a total floor area of approximately 82,000 m^2.

The elevation of the building consists of two elements—an "urban facade" that has a panoramic view with solar shading effects by using double glazed walls, and a "green facade" that acts like tree shades in which people can visually find a peace of mind. The "green facade" looks like as if the lush green that covers the lands of Singapore is rising in a spiral shape, covering around 55% of the whole facade, and while capsuling the "Sky Terrance", it continues to the "Sky Forest" on the top floor that stands at 200 m above ground level.

The fresh air at the "Sky Forest" where approximately 40 different kinds of plants and trees grow to a 15 m level, is around 2 degrees cooler than the air on ground level—it is induced by steady wind power generated from a 45 m tall window catcher that symbolizes the architecture as if it is a breathing body. Through the "cool void" that is installed throughout the whole building, fresh air could be supplied to each office floor and a comfortable and energy efficient workspace could thus be created.

In an increasing homogenized urban environment where priorities are made based on economic theories, we wanted to create a new symbol for the 21st century by restoring our connection to nature and by searching for a way to practice architecture ecologically in this tropical climate.

CapitaGreen

世界的な金融ビジネスの中心都市へと発展を遂げたシンガポールの中でも，とりわけ近代的な高層建築が集中する都心の一角に位置する．高さ245m，延床約82,000m^{2}の高層オフィスビルの計画である．

建物の立面は，ガラスのダブルスキンによる日射遮蔽効果と眺望を併せ持つ「アーバンファサード」，植栽による緑陰効果と視覚的な安らぎが得られる「グリーンファサード」の2種類により構成されている．「グリーンファサード」は，かつてシンガポールの大地を覆っていた豊かな緑がスパイラル状に上昇していくかのように，ファサード全体の約55%を占め，中間階では空中庭園である「スカイテラス」を内包しながら，最上階で「スカイフォレスト」と呼ばれる地上200mの森にまで至る．

15m級にまで成長する樹木をはじめとした約40種類もの植物が生い茂る「スカイフォレスト」では，呼吸する生命体のような建築を象徴する高さ45mのウインドキャッチャーにより，地上よりも2℃程低い清涼で新鮮な空気を定常風の動力を利用して取り込み，建物全体を貫く「クールヴォイド」を介して各階のオフィスフロアへと供給することで，省エネルギーで快適なワークスペースを生み出している．

経済原理が優先され均質化していく都市環境において，熱帯気候独自のエコロジカルな建築のあり方を模索し，自然とのつながりを再生することで，21世紀の新しいシンボルを生み出したいと考えた．

1 COVERED PLAZA
2 INFORMATION
3 LIFT LOBBY
4 CROWN SHUTTLE LIFT LOBBY
5 PARKING LIFT LOBBY
6 OFFICE
7 COOL VOID
8 SKY TERRACE
9 SKY FOREST
10 RESTAURANT
11 RESTAURANT BAR
12 KITCHEN
13 VOID
  (ABOVE SWIMMING POOL)
14 GYM
15 SWIMMING POOL
16 COOLING TOWER
17 FOOD & BEVERAGE
18 PARKING
19 M&E
20 SKY GARDEN

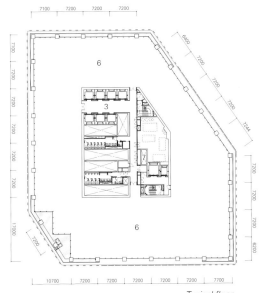
Typical floor

'Sky Terrace' on middle floor

40th floor

14th floor

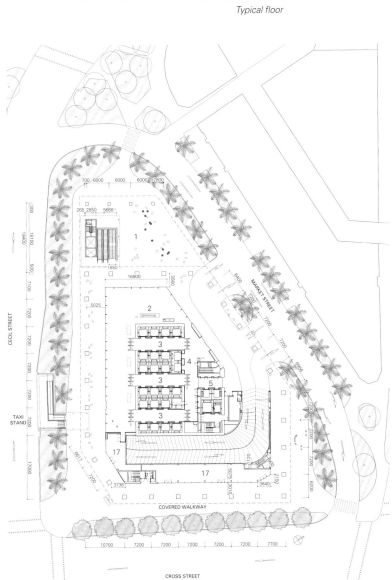
First floor S=1:1000

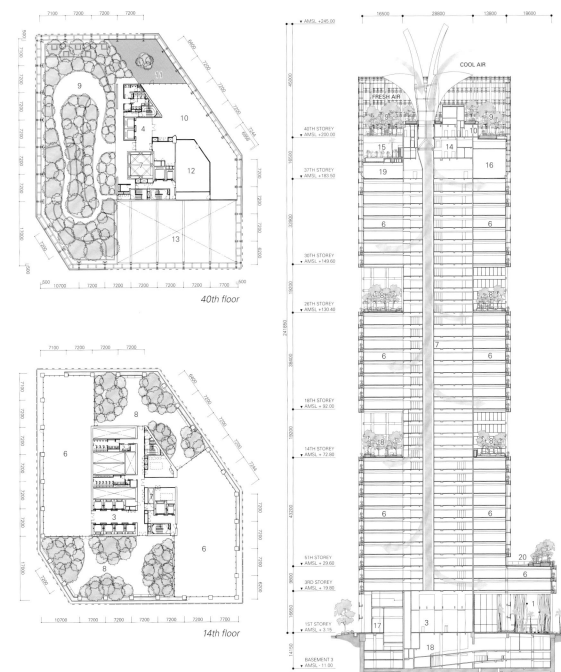
Section S=1:1500

217

South elevation

West elevation S=1:2000

'Sky Forest' on 40th floor

View toward covered plaza from west

Night view toward covered plaza

'Sky Terrace'

Swimming pool

219

Residential Hall at Nanyang Drive, Nanyang Technological University
Singapore
2011–14

Overall view from north

Site plan S=1:2500

The project is for the residential halls inside a rich green campus, located in the suburbs approximately thirty minutes from center Singapore. The residential halls will provide housing for about 1,400 students, faculty and staff members. The halls consist of eight three-way buildings with planar shapes similar to branches spreading out from a tree. Ample water, wind and greenery will run between these buildings to create an "artificial forest" environment.

Building shape and plot planning were determined through repeated environment simulations. The prevailing wind flows smoothly to the south and north between the buildings. The wind is also taken into the hallway, with windows placed on the hallway-side walls to encourage natural ventilation. Aluminum lattice louvers and windows comprise a double-skin facade, with windows that act as "wind catchers" to capture the wind on the building surface. The result is a kind of breathing facade that allows light and wind to flow through, while also shielding from sunlight.

The top floor is for the faculty apartments, middle floors above the second floor are for the students, and the first and basement floors are used as common areas. The building directions are adjusted to face away from each other in a high-density environment. On the

Three-way buildings on landscapes of water and green

Southeast view toward multi-purpose hall and canteen between eight three-way buildings

top floors, TV-lounge and other common spaces are placed in the center intersection to initiate small communities, and half-outdoors terrace called "Sky Terrace" are built in double height to bridge between two floors. In the first and basement floors, larger communities are initiated through the common space built like an organic, networking roots of a tree.

Our hope is that, from the unity of these tree-like buildings and networked common areas, and the landscapes of water and green that utilize the existing geographical features, a living and breathing, ecosystem-like community will emerge.

'Sky Terrace'

Canteen

Apartment: single room

南洋理工大学学生寮

シンガポールの中心部から約30分程の郊外にある緑豊かなキャンパスの中に,約1,400人の学生,教師,職員が暮らす寮の計画である。幹から枝が伸びるような三叉の平面形状を持った建物を8棟配置し,その間にたくさんの緑や水,風が入り込んでくる"人工の森"のような環境をつくる。

環境シミュレーションを繰り返し,建物の配置と形状を計画した。建物の間に南北の卓越風をスムーズに流しながら,積極的に中廊下に風を取り込み,廊下側の壁

Concept

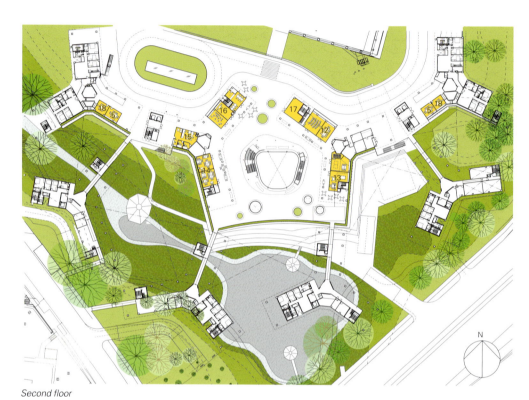
Second floor

1 MULTI-PURPOSE HALL
2 CANTEEN
3 READING ROOM
4 GYM
5 MEETING ROOM
6 JCRC ROOM
7 SEMINAR ROOM
8 COMPUTER ROOM
9 MUSIC ROOM
10 DANCE ROOM
11 GAZEBO
12 MUTI-FUNCTION ROOM
13 RECREATION ROOM
14 TUTRIAL ROOM
15 OFFICE
16 CAFE
17 SHOP
18 SCRC ROOM
19 APARTMENT
20 CORRIDOR
21 BUS STOP

First floor   S=1500

に換気窓を設けることで自然換気を促している。ファサードは，アルミの格子ルーバーと開き窓のダブルスキンになっており，開き窓が建物の表面を流れる風を捕まえる"ウィンド・キャッチャー"の役割を担うことで，光と風を取り入れながら日射を遮蔽する呼吸するファサードを構成している。

最上階が教師用アパート，2階から上の中層階が学生部屋，1階と地階が共用部となっており，各棟の向きを調整することにより，高密度でありながら互いの視線が向き合わない配置としている。上層階では小さな単位のコミュニティが形成されるよう，各階の三叉の中心にTVラウンジなどの共用スペースが配置され，また"スカイ・テラス"と呼ばれる半屋外のテラスが2層吹抜けで階を跨ぐように設けられている。1階，地階には有機的にネットワーク化された樹木の根のように共用スペースが設けられ，より大きなコミュニティが形成される。

樹木のような建物とネットワーク化された共用部，既存の地形を利用してつくられる水と緑のランドスケープとが一体となり，絶えず代謝し呼吸をする生態系のような，新たなコミュニティが創出されることを期待している。

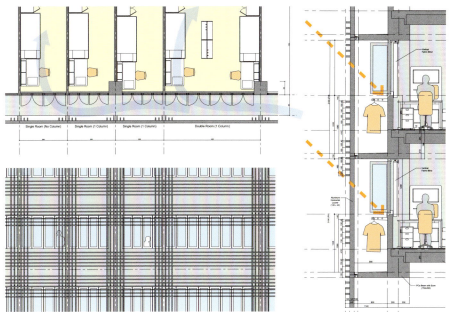

Facade: plan and elevation S=1:200, section S=1:100

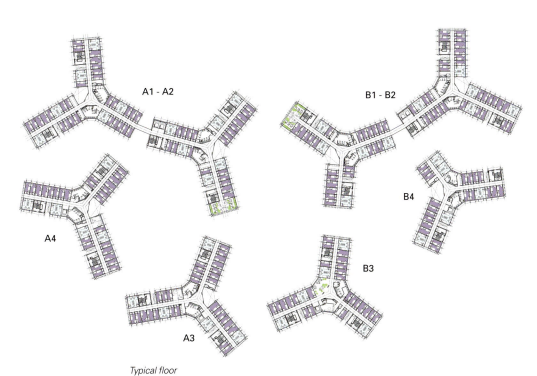

Typical floor

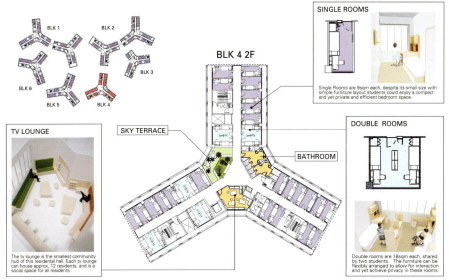

Typical floor layout

Section S=1:500

Overall view from north

K-port / Isoda Suisan Minatomachi 1chome Branch
Kesen'numa, Miyagi, Japan
2013–14

K-port is a cafe and event space built in Kesen'numa, Miyagi. It was planned by the actor Ken Watanabe to support restoration of the city. Although different in both scale and program to the preceding Home for All project, we consider this project as a further development, as it pursues a common purpose: to create a place for interaction of people within the city.

Next to K-port is Isoya Suisan Minatomachi 1-Chome Branch. This is a new store constructed after the disaster by Isoya Suisan Corporation, a seafood wholesaler that has been established in Kesennuma for generations. Naiwan District, the location of the site, is a calm bay about 10 km inland from the sea, where many fishing boats come and go. It is a beautiful place that has been loved by the local people as the "face" of Kesen'numa.

Contributors to the project include Ryuji Ando, president of Isoya Suisan; Akihiko Sugawara, president of a long-established brewery company, who is much engaged in the restoration of his hometown; and Yasutada Onodera, manager of a coffee shop. These local figures were full of life even after the disaster, and it was the interaction between them and Ken Watanabe that led to the idea to create a 'port' that becomes the guiding light of restoration and provides comfort to the heart and soul of the people. Thus, the project was initiated.

By placing K-port and Isoya Suisan side by side within the same site, we aimed to trigger the restoration of the seaside streetscape.

K-port has a curved roof like a circus tent, and wide windows facing the sea. The facade has a serene impression; walls are cladded with burnt pine, and the roof is laid with slate. In contrast, the interior walls are painted red and natural light pours in from the triangular skylight, making the space feel warm and uplifting.

Isoya Suisan has a wide opening towards the sea, and its shopfront is lined with fresh fish. Eaves which are necessary for the unloading of fish extend to K-port, and together the two buildings welcome guests as one.

Whether it be high school students dropping in at the cafe after school, local citizens coming for a play or concert, tourists, or a local sushi chef looking for fresh fish, the project has been embraced in Kesen'numa as a place for interaction of people.

Site plan S=1:5000

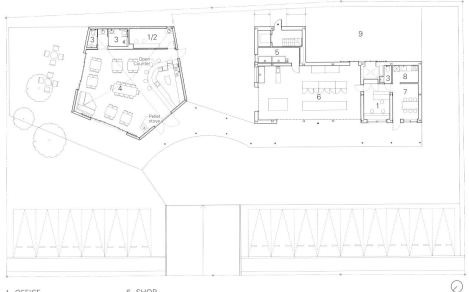

1 OFFICE
2 STORAGE
3 WC
4 CAFE/EVENT SPACE
5 PROCESSING CHAMBER
6 SHOP
7 RESTING ROOM
8 OFFICE KITCHENETTE
9 OUTDOOR WORKING SPACE

Plan S=1:400

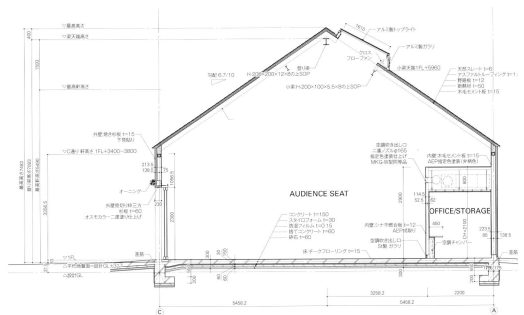

Sectional detail S=1:120

View toward eaves connecting between K-port and Isoya Suisan from west

Cafe/event space

K-port/磯屋水産港町一丁目店

「K-port」は，宮城県気仙沼に建てられた，カフェ兼イベントスペースである．俳優・渡辺謙氏により，街の復興支援のために計画された．それまでに実現した「みんなの家」と比較すると規模も用途も異なるが，「街の中に人と人の交流の場をつくる」という意味で，「みんなの家」の発展形として捉えている．

「K-port」の隣に構える「磯屋水産一丁目店」は，気仙沼で代々魚の卸売業を営んでいた磯屋水産が，被災後に再建した新店舗である．敷地のある内湾地区は，外洋から10km程陸に入った穏やかな湾でたくさんの漁船が出入りし，気仙沼の「顔」として人々に愛されてきた美しい場所である．

その磯屋水産社長安藤竜司氏と，故郷の復興に奔走する老舗酒造会社の社長菅原昭彦氏，コーヒーショップ経営者小野寺靖忠氏など，震災後も力強く生きる地元の人々と渡辺謙氏とが交流を深める中で，「復興の灯火となり，人々のこころの拠り所となる港(=port)をつくろう」という思いが芽生え，このプロジェクトが始まった．

同じ敷地内に「K-port」と「磯屋水産」の二つを並べて配置することで，海沿いに復興する街並みのきっかけとしたいと考えた．

「K-port」は，サーカステントのような曲面屋根を持ち，海に向かって大きく窓をとる構成となっている．外壁は焼杉板貼り，屋根は天然スレート葺きの落ち着いた外観とは対照的に，内部の壁は赤く塗装され三角形のトップライトから自然光が降り注ぐ，暖かくも気分の高揚する空間として計画した．

「磯屋水産」は，海に向かって大きな開口部を持ち，店先には新鮮な魚がずらりと並ぶ．魚の荷下ろしに必要な庇を「K-port」まで連続させることで，二つの建物が一体となって来訪者を迎える構成とした．

カフェを訪れる学校帰りの高校生，芝居やコンサートを聴きに来た地元のおじさんおばさん，観光客，魚を買いに来た地元のお寿司屋さん，といろいろな人々に親しまれ，人と人との交流の場として気仙沼に根付いている．

New National Stadium Japan Proposal

Shinjuku, Tokyo, Japan

2015

In July, 2015, the original plan for *the New National Stadium* designed by Zaha Hadid was cancelled and a new competition was held for selecting a new team to be responsible for both design and construction of the main Olympic stadium. By curious coincidence, we were given the opportunity to participate. The process that led to the cancellation of the original plan aroused much heated debate among the general public in Japan, as well as among architects and historians. While the discussion centered around construction scale and budget, we focused our attention on the history behind Meiji Jingu Gaien (the park on the outer precinct of *Meiji Jingu Shrine*), and tried to envision the ideal stadium appropriate for this context.

Approximately 100 years ago, *the Meiji Jingu Shrine* attempted to create a new holy ground based on traditional philosophy by combining *the Naien* (inner garden) enveloped by a forest, and *the Gaien* (outer garden) that includes a series of sports facilities centered around *Meiji Memorial Picture Gallery*. *Meiji Jingu Shrine*'s dualism fostered a *Naien* that conceals the shrine within a deep forest, and a bright, open Gaien forest that manifests the energetic force of sports and athletics. Our proposal aimed to create a new national stadium to celebrate the rise of new tradition for the coming century, while being respectful of the original philosophy established by *the Meiji Jingu Shrine*.

For the competition entry, our stadium's stands were surrounded by a colonnade of 72 wooden columns made using the most advanced fireproof technology. With this colonnade, we attempted to create a celebratory stage infused with the kind of primeval power of the *Jomon* period found in old Japanese ruins and shrines. These columns were to be gigantic in size, each measuring 1.5 m wide and

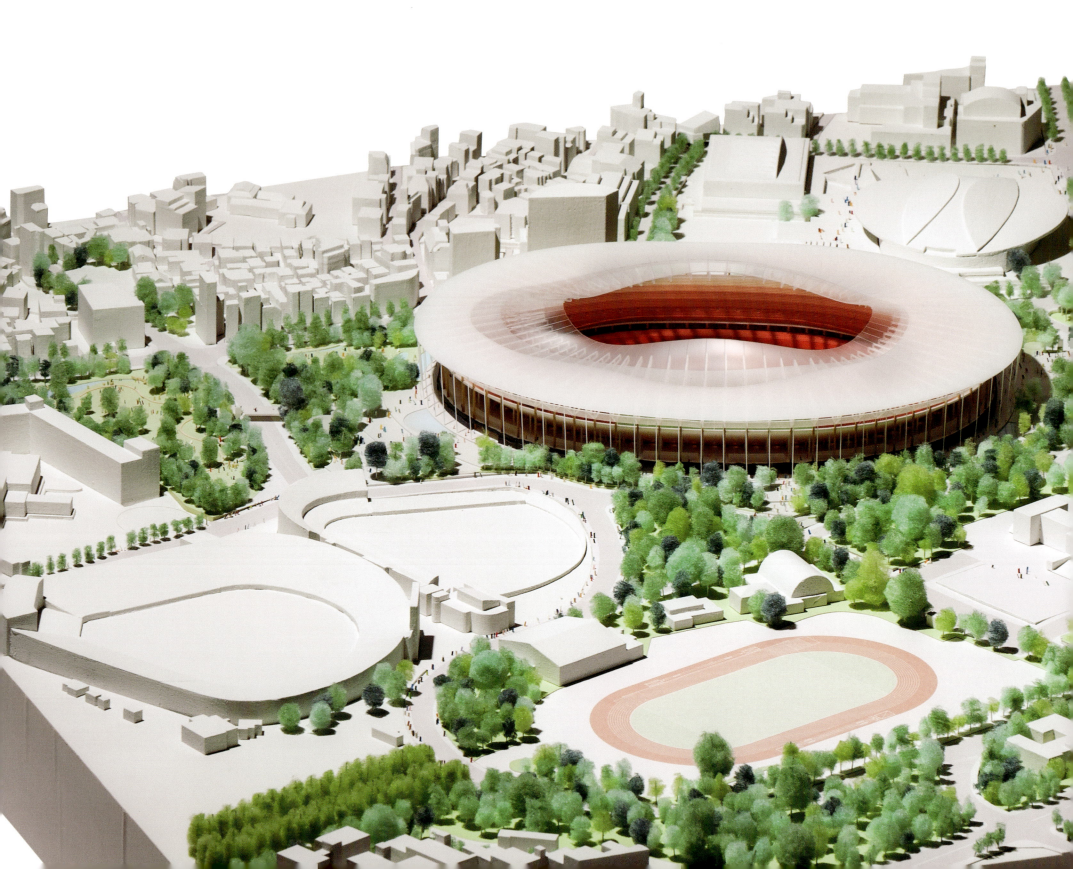

19 m high. The idea was to elicit a kind of symbolism, not only through the columns themselves, but the field and the stands that are surrounded by these columns. Furthermore, we wanted to create a roof with a kind of lightness that would vanish into the sky and not obstruct the surrounding environment. To achieve this, we employed a cantilevered and balanced truss that efficiently supports and maintains the balance of the roof, which runs up to 65 m in length. We attempted to create an architecture that embraces the dual qualities of the powerful columns and the elegant roof.

We also intentionally divided the stands into

Overall view from southeast

Aerialview from east

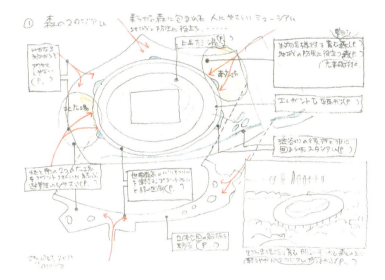

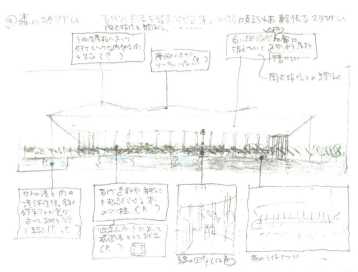

Sketches by Toyo Ito, 25 Oct. 2015

Night view of stadium

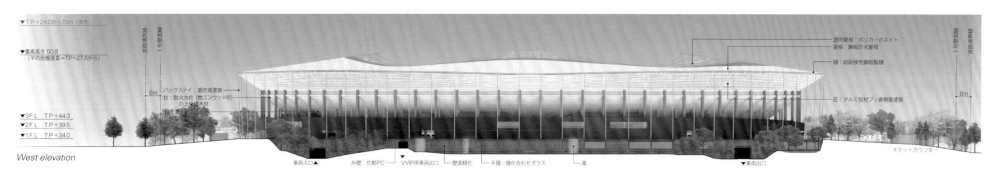
West elevation

South elevation S=1:2000

Seating floor at holding World Cup (about 80,000 seats)

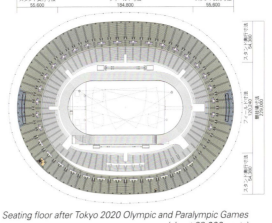
Seating floor after Tokyo 2020 Olympic and Paralympic Games (about 68,000 seats)

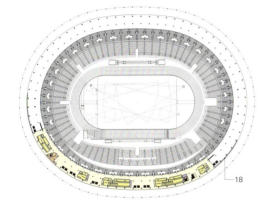
Third floor

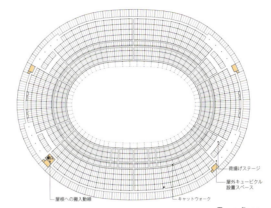
Truss floor

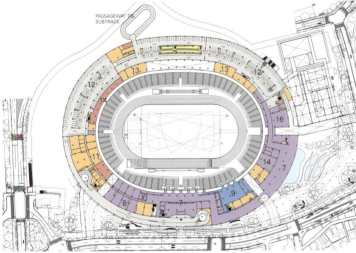
First basement

Second floor

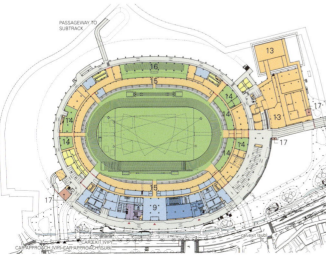
Second basement

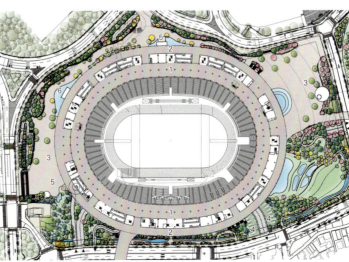
First floor (without deck) S=1:5000

two levels in order to minimize the large walls, a feature commonly seen in large-scale stadium designs. The majority of the lower stands are embedded into the ground, so that only the upper level appears above ground. To ensure safety, we employed a hybrid mid-story seismic isolation system that uses a vibration control device for the lower stands, and a seismic isolation layer between the upper and lower stands. This reduces the volume of the bowl-shaped upper stands, creating a deep and open space between the two levels. There, we designed a Four Seasons' Corridor that opens to the forest, a hallway that connects the Meiji Jingu Gaien's greenery with the main concourse like an *engawa*, or Japanese-style loggia. We designed a vibrant forest that dynamically changes with the seasons along this Four Seasons' Corridor, including northern and southern plazas, water and waterfalls, maple valleys, forests and rice paddies. The idea was to create a place where the local residents could gather for walking, running, and relaxing, so the facility would be utilized not only during sporting events but on a daily basis.

By following the Four Seasons' Corridor, visitors would easily be able to find the nearest stadium entrance, and the simplicity of the double-tiered stands would generate an easy-to-use circulation leading them to their designated seats. The world-leading design proposed not only reducing physical barriers, but also providing peace of mind through safe and clear directions.

Despite our leadership in facility design, which would become crucial after the completion of the stadium, we lagged behind the winning proposal in the areas of construction cost and schedule, and lost the competition by a narrow margin. Had our proposal been accepted, however, we strongly believe that it would have become a "stadium of the forest" that would have withstood the test of time and been much-loved and admired by future generations.

1 CONCOURSE
2 FOUR SEASONS' CORRIDOR
3 PLAZA
4 CAR PARKING FOR MEDIA
5 TICKET
6 SHOP
7 VIP LOUNGE
8 VIP ANTE ROOM
9 PRESS AREA
10 KITCHEN
11 ADMINISTRATION OFFICE
12 CAR PARKING
13 MEP
14 STORAGE
15 UTILITY SPACE
16 TRAINING RUNWAY
17 SECURITY OFFICE
18 SLOPE
19 VEHICLE PATH

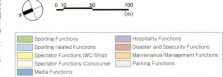

Sectional model

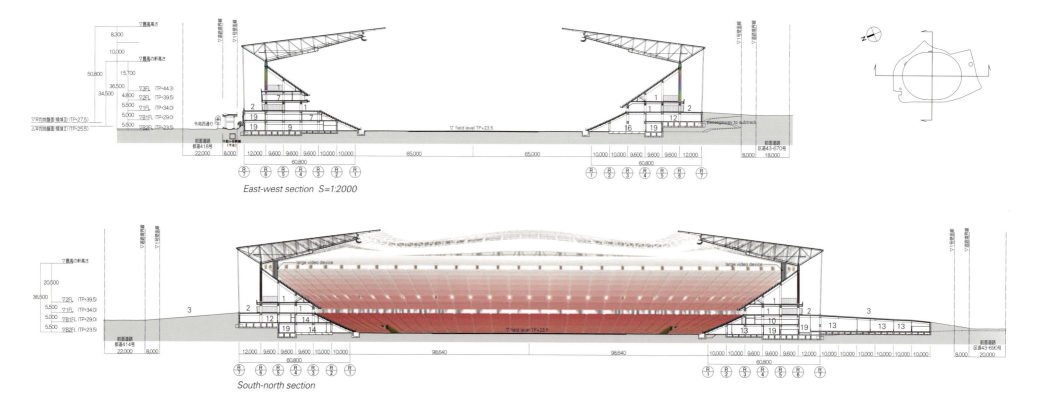

East-west section S=1:2000

South-north section

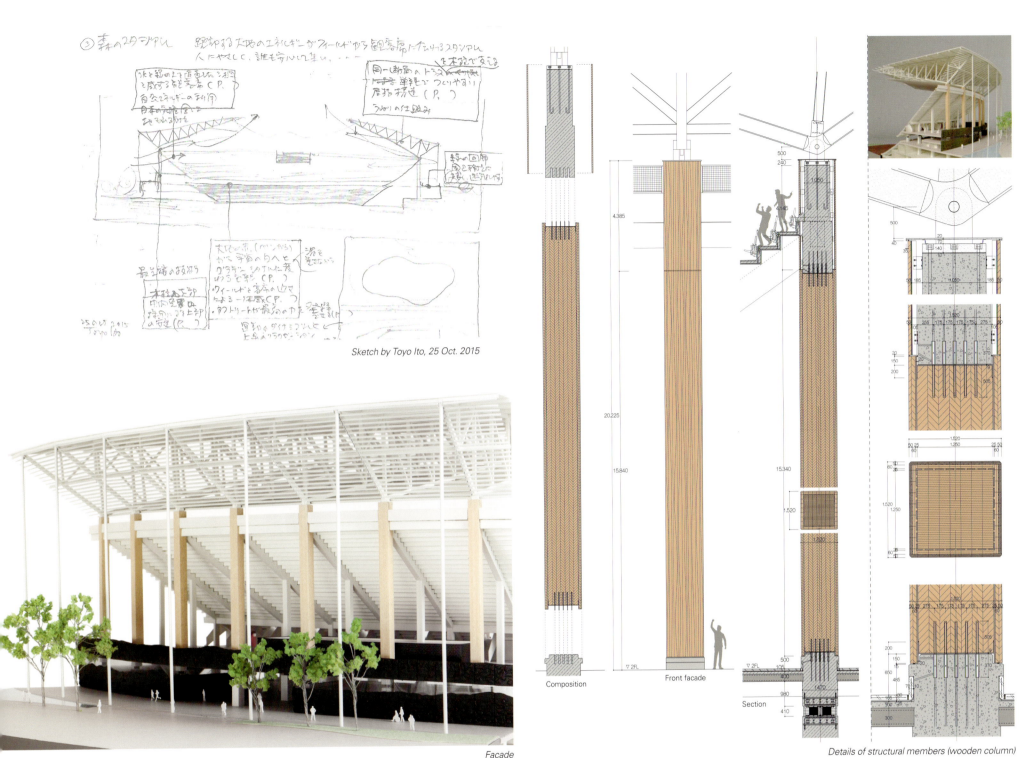

Sketch by Toyo Ito, 25 Oct. 2015

Composition　Front facade　Section

Facade

Details of structural members (wooden column)

新国立競技場整備事業公募型プロポーザル応募案

ザハ・ハディドの基本構想をもとに進められていた新国立競技場の計画が，2015年7月に白紙撤回された。それに伴いオリンピックのメイン会場として，設計と施工が一体となった事業者を選定するコンペティションが開催された。我々は奇しくも参加する機会に恵まれた。白紙撤回に至るまで，市民をはじめ建築関係者や歴史学者なども参加し，盛んに議論が行なわれた。規模や予算の問題が大きく取り沙汰されている中，我々は神宮外苑の創出の歴史に注目し，あるべき神宮外苑のスタジアム像を模索していた。

およそ100年前に明治神宮は，近代都市をめざす東京に，森に包まれた内苑と絵画館を中心にスポーツ関連施設が立ち並ぶ外苑を組み合わせることによって，伝統思想に基づく新しい聖地を創ろうとした。この明治神宮の二元性によって，内苑は社を隠蔽する深い森によって閉じられ，外苑はスポーツなどの躍動する力の顕現する明るい森として開かれている。我々はこのような明治神宮の思想を重んじながら，これからの100年に向けて「新しい伝統」を創出する祝祭の場としての新国立競技場を目指した。

最先端の技術を結集した耐火性能を有する，72本の純木製の列柱によってスタンドを囲み，日本古来の遺跡や神社に見られるような，縄文的な力強い祝祭の場となるように試みた。1辺約1.5m，高さ約19mに及ぶ巨大な角柱であり，柱はもちろんのこと，それによって囲われたフィールドとスタンドが象徴的な存在となることを期待した。また，周辺環境への圧迫感を極力抑えた，空に消えていくような軽快な屋根を実現すべく，天秤のようにバランスを保ちながら，効率的に最大65mの屋根を支える片持ち式天秤トラスを採用した。このように，柱の力強さと屋根の優雅さとを併せ持つ建築を表現しようと試みた。

また，大規模スタジアムによく見られる，スタンドによる大きな壁を極力軽減するために，敢えて2層式スタンドを採用した。下段スタンドの過半を大地に埋め込み，上段スタンドのみが地上に表れる構成とした。安全なスタンドとするために，下段スタンドに制振装置を，上下段スタンドの中間に免震層を設けたハイブリッド中間層免震を採用した。この中間層免震によって器状の上段スタンドはスリム化され，開放的な深い懐スペースを設けることができた。我々は，そこに神宮外苑の杜とメインコンコースをフラットに結ぶ，縁側のような杜に開かれた「四季の回廊」を計画した。この「四季の回廊」に沿って南北の広場，水や滝，もみじ谷や大地の森，さらに田んぼなど，四季に合わせて明るく変化に富んだ杜を配置し，散策やジョギングなど，イベント時以外でも市民の憩いの場として日常的に利用されることを期待した。

この「四季の回廊」によって最寄の入退場ゲートを迷うことなく見つけることができ，シンプルな構成である2層式スタンドによって，観客席への単純明快でわかりやすい動線を実現している。身体的なバリアを減らすだけではなく，安全で迷いにくいという精神的な安らぎを得られる，世界最高レベルのユニバーサルデザインを生み出している。

審査結果は，完成後に重要となる施設計画は優位に立ちながらも，工期とコストにおいて差が開いてしまい，善戦むなしく惜敗してしまった。もし実現していたら，時代を超えて愛される，風化することのない「杜のスタジアム」となっていたであろうと強く信じている。

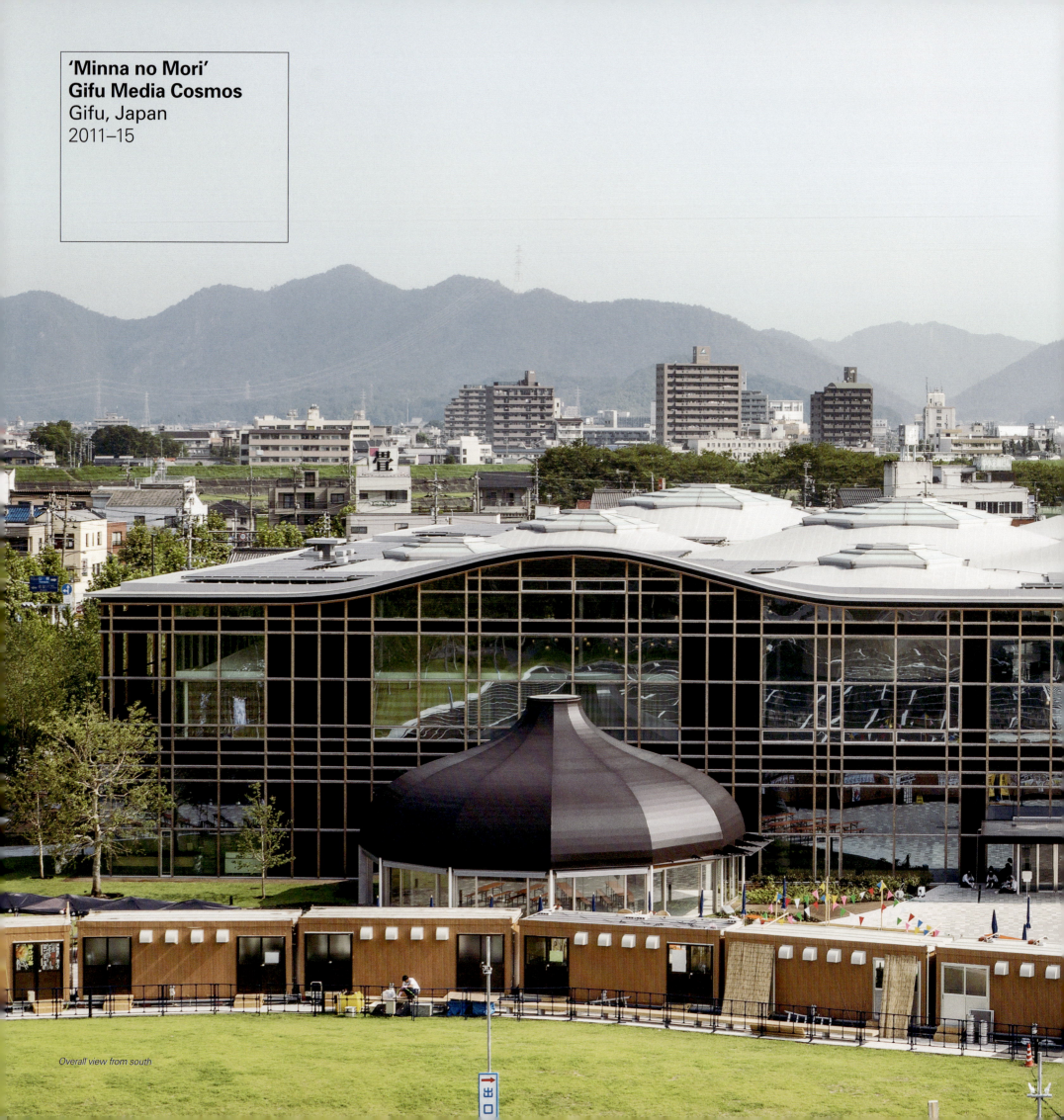

'Minna no Mori'
Gifu Media Cosmos
Gifu, Japan
2011–15

Overall view from south

Night view of north elevation: illuminated 'Globes' on second floor appear

Staircase to second floor: 'Hon no Kura (closed stacks)' on right

Northeast view on children's book area: 'Children Globe' on right

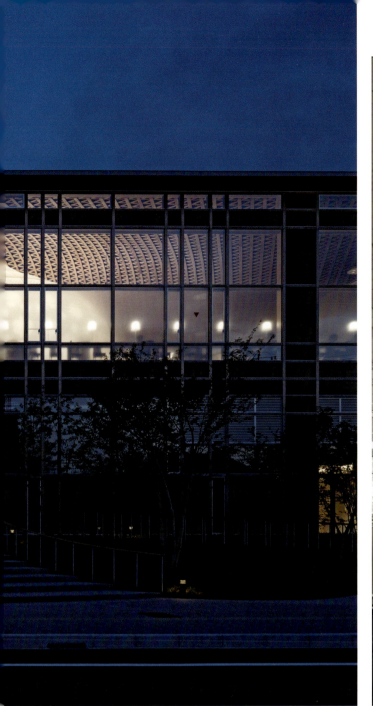

'Entrance Globe' above elevator

'Paperback Globe' on left and 'Literature Globe' on right

'Watching and Listening' seats designed by Kazuko Fujie

'Literature Globe'

'Minna no Mori' Gifu Media Cosmos, which opened its doors on July, 2015, is a cultural complex that mainly includes a public library. The site is located about 2 km north of the Gifu Station, and has a view of the town's symbolic Mount Kinka. The land receives ample underflow from the nearby Nagara River.

The building is composed of two planes in a 2-level structure, with each plane measuring 80 m by 90 m. The first floor includes the closed stacks section, housing 600,000 books, that is surrounded by glazd wall in a temperature-controlled environment. The stacks section is also connected to and encircled by the exhibition gallery, multi-purpose hall, and community center. The second floor is a large open-stacks section with 300,000 books and a total of 910 reading seats designed in various styles.

Hanging above the circular reading areas and the help desk are large "globes," which are semi-transparent shades made mainly of polyester fabric. A total of 11 globes, each measuring around 8 to 14 m in diameter, improve the interior environment by creating airflow and filtering light down into the spaces below.

The curved roof canopy is made of wooden material; the cross sections of these strips of thin wood measure only 120 mm by 20 mm, and they were bent and layered in three directions into a lattice. The roof arches at the top of the globes to amplify the effects of the light and wind. This also expands the span of the entire structure so that the exterior of the building is in response to the surrounding mountain ranges. Trees were planted throughout the project site. There is a tree-lined road on the western side that stretches to a length of 240 m, and an open space on the southern side that is 45 m wide.

The project uses natural elements as part of its design: the globes make use of natural energy; the radiant floor heating/cooling system takes advantage of the heat from the underflow water; and solar energy. By balancing these elements, the project is expected to cut the building's primary energy use by 50% or more (in comparison to a building of similar scale built in 1990). To limit the building's energy consumption, the project deviates from an excessively subdivided, covered space design. Rather, it achieves a comfortable and energy-efficient environment by seeking to connect with nature as the public building of tomorrow.

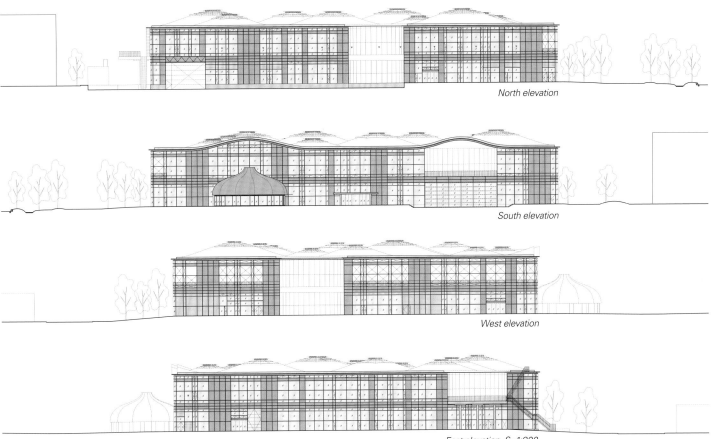

North elevation

South elevation

West elevation

East elevation S=1:800

1	ENTRANCE	23	MORI NO TERRACE
2	ENTRANCE HALL	24	WAI WAI TERRACE
3	RESTAURANT	25	KIDS TERRACE
4	SHOP	26	MINNA NO NIWA (GARDEN)
5	KANGAERU (THINKING) STUDIO	27	ENTRANCE GLOBE
6	ODORU (DANCING) STUDIO	28	INFORMATION COUNTER
7	TSUKURU (CREATING) STUDIO	29	PARENT & CHILD GLOBE
8	WAI WAI TATAMI AREA	30	CHILDREN GLOBE
9	WAI WAI CIRCLE	31	YOUNG ADULT GLOBE
10	KIDS ROOM	32	PAPERBACKS GLOBE
11	COOPERATIVE PROJECTS ROOM	33	LITERATURE GLOBE
12	TSUNAGARU (BOUNDING) STUDIO	34	REFERENCE GLOBE
13	ATSUMARU (GATHERING) STUDIO	35	HISTORY & GEOGRAPHY GLOBE
14	SCHOOL COOPERATION OFFICE	36	DISPLAY GLOBE
15	LIBRARY OFFICE	37	RELAXING GLOBE
16	MINNA NO HALL	38	WATCHING AND LISTENING SEATS
17	KOMICHI GALLERY	39	READING CAFE
18	MINNA NO GALLERY	40	CHILDREN BOOK'S STACKS
19	GALLERY FOYER	41	STORY ROOM
20	HON NO KURA (CLOSED STACKS)	42	OPEN STACKS READING AREA
21	DOKI DOKI TERRACE	43	NAMIKI TERRACE
22	OUTDOOR GALLERY	44	KINKAZAN TERRACE
		45	HIDAMARI TERRACE

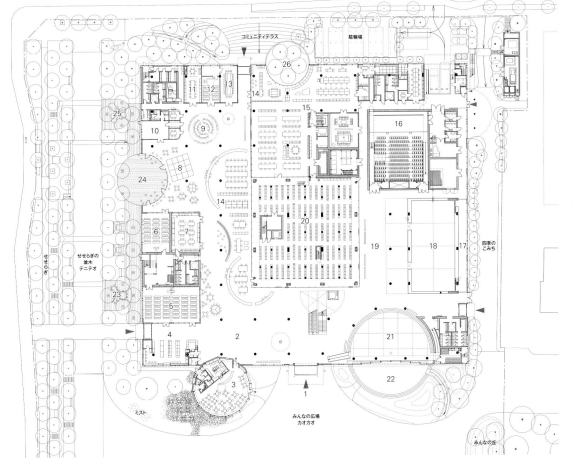

First floor S=1:1000

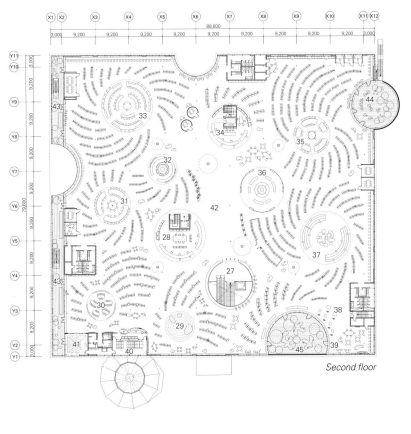

Second floor

237

Reading room on second floor: undulating ceiling and various size of 'Globes' are hanging from there

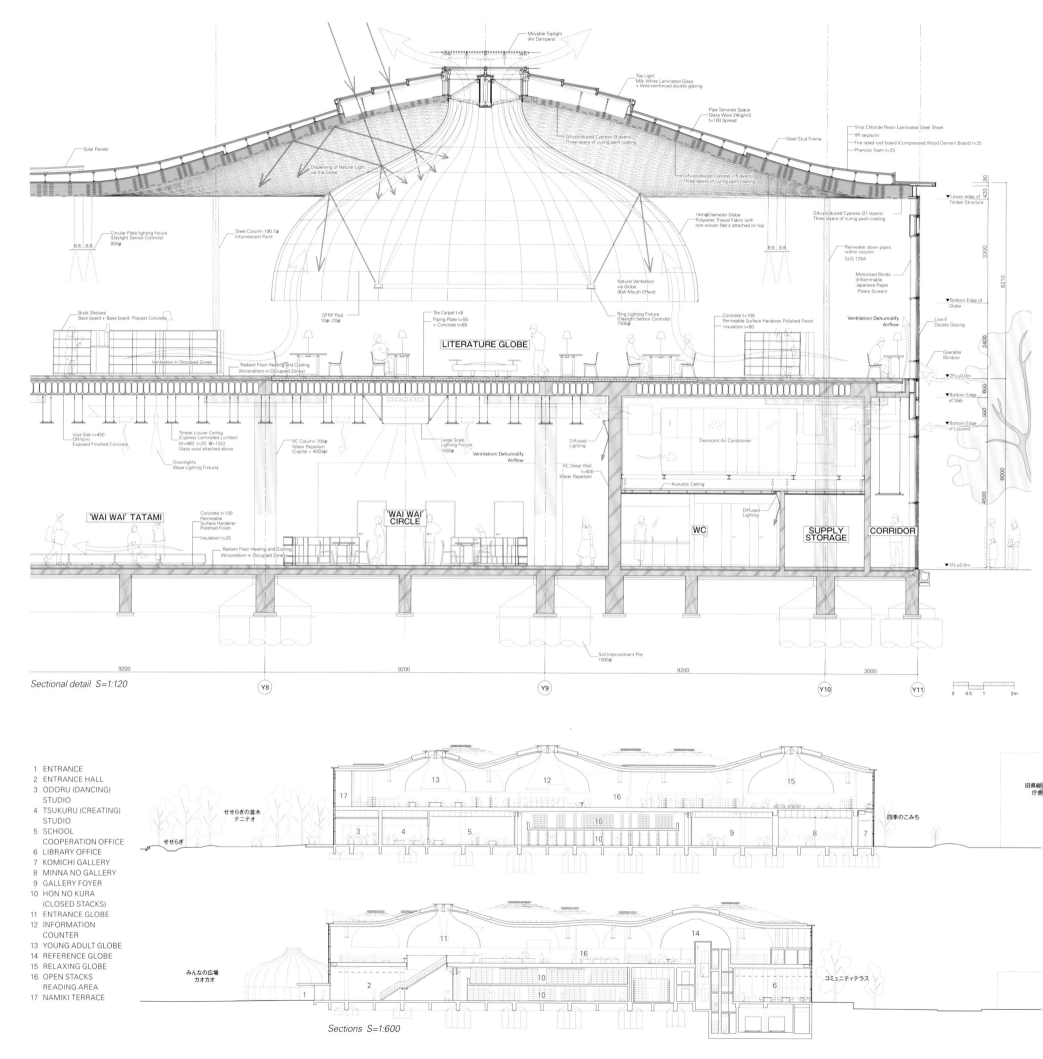

'Watching and Listening' seats designed by Kazuko Fujie

'Parent & Child Globe'

みんなの森 ぎふメディアコスモス

2015年7月に開館した，図書館を中心とする文化複合施設である。敷地は，街のシンボルである金華山を望むJR岐阜駅から約2km北上したところに位置し，近傍の長良川からの豊富な伏流水が地中に流れている。

建物は約80m×90mという大きな平面形が2層積み重なる構成である。1階は温熱環境の安定した中央部にガラスで囲まれた閉架書庫(60万冊収容)を据え，その周囲を展示ギャラリー，多目的ホール，市民活動交流センターなどがつながりを持って取り囲む。2階は壁の無いワンルームの開架閲覧エリアであり，30万冊分の書架や，合計910席の多様なスタイルの閲覧席が設けられている。

サークル状の閲覧エリアや受付カウンターの上部には「グローブ」が吊られている。グローブはポリエステル製のファブリックを主材とした半透明の大きなカサである。直径8m～14m，合計11個のグローブが，その形状によって風の流れを生み出し，上部からの光を柔らかく拡散するなど，室内環境を向上させる役割を担う。

ゆるやかな起伏を持つ木造の屋根は，120mm×20mmという小さな断面サイズの木材をしならせながら，3方向に積み重ねることでできている。グローブ上部でむくり上がることで，風や光の効果を高めると同時に構造スパンを広げ，周囲の山並みと呼応した外観をつくり出している。敷地全体には樹木を豊富に植える計画とし，建物西側は全長240mに渡る並木道，南側は幅45mの広場とした。

グローブが導く自然エネルギーの活用や，伏流水の温度を利用した床輻射冷暖房，太陽光利用などをバランスよく組み合わせることで，建物が消費する一次エネルギーを50%以上削減できる見通しとなった(1990年の同規模建物との比較)。消費エネルギーを減らすことを目的として室内を過度に仕切り・覆うのではなく，自然とのつながりを求める中で快適で省エネルギーな環境をつくることに取り組んだ，これからの時代の公共建築である。

Yamanashi Gakuin University International College of Liberal Arts
Kofu, Yamanashi, Japan
2013–15

Overall view from south

In order to commemorate the 70th anniversary of the founding of Yamanashi Gakuin University, a new school wing and student dormitory were constructed for the Faculty of International Liberal Arts. There had been great demand for a facility which would act as a "global house" welcoming students and teachers from all over the world, and where Liberal Arts teaching would cultivate all-round talented individuals who are active on the global stage.

Students are able to spend all 24 hours of their day inside this combined school wing and dormitory, from waking up in the morning to lessons, mealtimes, club activities, studying, and finally relaxing in the evenings. With this in mind, we have filled the building with various habitats and expanses, and devised it so that the space can be utilized in diverse ways.

In the 52-m-diameter circular school wing, we designed hexagonal classrooms which can be arranged in different ways to accommodate discussion-style lessons in small groups, while a glass-walled laboratory encircles the northern side. This space allows for open areas of varying sizes thanks to its multidirectional axis, and also creates pockets of passageway-type areas.

The dormitory which houses our multinational students contains 3 sets of 8-student units (a total of 24 students) per floor, and the 3-spoked arrangement of the rooms allows light and fresh air to enter the building from every direction. Depending on their needs, students can choose to pass time in their own private rooms, the living area, or the common room—areas which are situated within easy reach of each other.

Due to a height restriction brought about by the high-tension wires crossing the air above the building premises, we decided on a structure with a plain flat slab, and were thus able to create an expansive space with a large interior volume. The earth-colored facade complements the surrounding mountains and forests, while establishing itself as a distinguishing characteristic of the new faculty.

We believe that our creation of gathering spaces and graduated habitats via the use of a building structure which incorporates a centripetal circular school wing and multidirectional axis is truly fitting for a "global house" which sees diverse interactions taking place within its walls.

山梨学院大学 国際リベラルアーツ学部棟

山梨学院大学創立70周年記念事業として、「国際リベラルアーツ学部」の校舎・学生寮の新設である。国際的に活躍する総合的な人才を育てる「リベラルアーツ」の学び舎として、世界中の学生・教師が共に集う、「グ

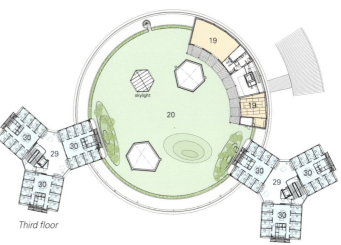

1　ENTRANCE LOBBY
2　LECTURE ROOM
3　ART COURTYARD
4　BAMBOO COURTYARD
5　CAFETERIA
6　COOKING STUDIO
7　KITCHEN
8　STAFF OFFICE
9　ADMINISTRATIVE OFFICE
10　CAREER DESIGN / STUDY ABROAD OFFICE
11　CONFERENCE ROOM
12　DEAN'S OFFICE
13　MUSIC STUDIO
14　STUDY LOUNGE
15　ART STUDIO
16　LECTURE THEATER
17　SCIENCE LAB
18　SCIENCE RESEARCH LAB
19　JAPAN STUDIES
20　ROOF GARDEN
21　POLOTI
22　LOBBY OF DORMITORY
23　YOUTH LEARNING CENTER
24　LAC-LANGUAGE EXCHANGE LOUNGE
25　LAC-LANGUAGE MEDIA CENTER
26　LAC-READING CENTER
27　QUIET SPACE
28　SELF-STUDY ROOM
29　LOBBY
30　DORMITORY
31　LAUNDRY
32　MECHANICAL

Third floor

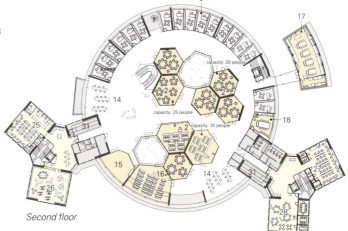

Second floor

First floor S=1:1000

ローバルな家」のような施設が求められた。
　学生は朝起きてから授業，食事，クラブ活動，自習，夜の憩いまで，校舎と学生寮を一体としたこの建物の中で24時間を過ごすことができる。そのため，環境や広がりの異なる空間を散りばめ，様々な過ごし方ができるよう考えた。
　直径52mの円形校舎には，少人数対話形式の授業に合わせて様々にレイアウトが可能な六角形の教室を配置し，ガラス張りの研究室が北側エリアを放射状に取り囲む。多方向の軸を持った空間が大小様々なオープンスペースを生み，路地のようなポケット状の空間をつくり出している。
　多国籍な学生が共同生活を行う学生寮は8人ユニット×3戸＝24人で1フロアを共有し，3戸が三ツ矢状に向かい合うことで各方面からの光や風を受け入れる。個室・リビング，共用ロビーが緩やかに繋がる空間を，学生たちは状況に応じて選択しながら日々を過ごす。
　敷地上空を高圧線が縦断することによる高さ制限があるため，フラットスラブによる躯体を仕上げとして，大きな気積をもつ開放的な空間を実現した。アースカラーのファサードは周辺の山々やキャンパスの樹木と呼応しつつ，新学部のシンボル性を獲得している。
　ここでは，多様な交流を包含する場所を求心的な円形校舎と多方向の軸による構成によって，集い方と環境のグラデーションを創ることが「グローバルな家」として相応しいと考えている。

Entrance lobby

Bamboo courtyard

1 ENTRANCE LOBBY
2 LECTURE ROOM
3 BAMBOO COURTYARD
4 KITCHEN
5 STUDY LOUNGE
6 ROOF GARDEN
7 LOBBY OF DORMITORY
8 LAC-LANGUAGE
  EXCHANGE LOUNGE
9 LOBBY
10 DORMITORY

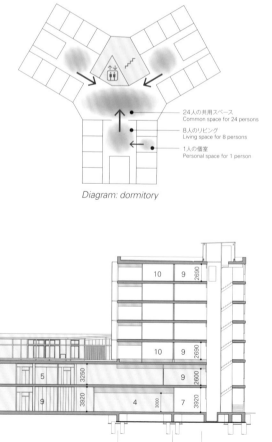

Diagram: dormitory

longitudinal section S=1:600

Corridor on second floor

Cafeteria: bamboo courtyard on left

Plan of dormitory S=1:250

Sectional detail S=1:200

Fubon Sky Tree
Taichung, Taiwan, R.O.C.
2010–16

This is a 155 m tall, 39-floor condominium in Taipei City, Taiwan. There are two units on each floor, and the top two floors are used as a shared space for a lounge and swimming pool.

At the time when we received this offer, it was very popular to build luxurious condominiums called *háo zhái* that are aimed towards the high-end market in Taiwan. However, these apartments were traded for financial purposes and not used for living, and the view of these buildings lining up along the streets was almost deserted. Our aim was to take a step away from economical reasoning, and to practically realize a condominium that would accommodate the active lives of the residents.

As a first step, we tried to minimize the construction area as much as possible within this rich greenery site that is rare within the busy city center, in order to realize a condominium that has a private forest with a big pond.

On each floor, the condominiums have an overhanging balcony and a deep terrace, and the canopy effect helps to block out strong direct sunlight. On top of that, the balconies are covered with a louvered glass screen which helps to prevent strong winds—a characteristic of high-rise buildings—from pressure equalizing from winds around the building. Therefore the balconies can be used as an outdoor living space that continues from the inside. From the mid- to the high-level floors, we planned eight floors with green terraces that three-dimensionally connect to the greenery just under our eyes. We were able to provide a space that is closely connected to the natural environment outside despite the fact that it is a high-rise condominium.

The curvature of the whole volume represents rising waves rhythmically, and the lively motion gets stronger towards the top. This symbolizes strong vitality, like a big tree growing towards the sky.

The houses will be handed over to its owners very soon, and we heard that most of the owners are planning to move in to live there. Within the rapid urban development and capitalism in Taiwan, we are expecting this new residence to become a symbol where people and nature can closely intervene with each other.

Overall view from east ▷

View over Ecological Pond from east

Pavilion floating on Ecological Pond

North elevation　　　*East elevation S=1:1500*

247

Entrance hall

Elevator hall (above); view toward elevator hall from parking (below)

35th floor

38th floor

39th floor

1 SOUTH GATE
2 NORTH GATE
3 GUARD HOUSE
4 CAR PORCH
5 ENTRANCE HALL
6 ELEVATOR LOBBY
7 MEETING ROOM
8 OFFICE / EMERGENCY CENTER
9 WATER FOUNTAIN
10 GARDEN TERRACE
11 CULTURAL PLAZA
12 ECOLOGICAL POND
13 PAVILION
14 SPRING
15 FOREST PROMENADE
16 MAINTENANCE GATE
17 OBSERVATORY LOUNGE
18 SWIMMING POOL

Typical floor (forth floor)

27th floor

First floor S=1:1000

Sky Garden

Balcony: covered with glass louvers

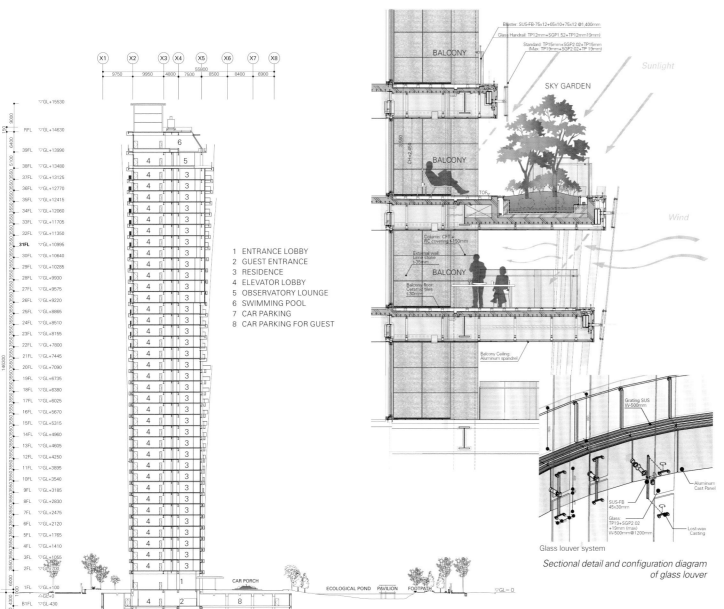

1 ENTRANCE LOBBY
2 GUEST ENTRANCE
3 RESIDENCE
4 ELEVATOR LOBBY
5 OBSERVATORY LOUNGE
6 SWIMMING POOL
7 CAR PARKING
8 CAR PARKING FOR GUEST

Section S=1:1200

Sectional detail and configuration diagram of glass louver

Glass louver system

富邦天空樹

台湾台中市に建つ，高さ155m，地上39層の高層集合住宅の計画である。住戸は各層に2戸，最上階2層はラウンジやプールの共用スペースとして利用される。

　設計のオファーを受けた時，台湾では「豪宅」と呼ばれる高級志向で華美な高層住宅の建設が盛んに行われていた。しかし実際は，投資目的で売買されるばかりで住まわれることがなく，これらが建ち並ぶ街の様相は非常な寂しさを呈していた。その中で我々が課した命題は，経済思考と切り離され，実際に人々が生き活きと暮らす高層住宅の実現であった。

　まず我々は，都心では稀な緑豊かな敷地の中，建築面積を可能な限り抑えて，大きな池をも取り込んだプライベートな森を携える高層住宅をつくり出した。

　各層の住宅は，外周に張り出したバルコニーと奥行のあるテラスを持ち，その庇効果によって強い直射光から守られる。さらに，バルコニーはルーバー状のガラススクリーンで覆われ，建物外周との「風の等圧化」によって高層建築特有の強風の侵入が和らげられ，内部と連続して利用できる安定した屋外空間となっている。中層から高層には，眼下にひろがる緑が立体的に繋がるような緑化テラスを持つ8層分の住戸も計画した。高層住宅でありながらも，外部の自然環境と密接な住空間を提供している。

　建物全体のヴォリュームは，曲面がリズミカルに波立ち，上方に行くほど躍動感を増して広がっていく。それは空に向かって成長する1本の大木のようであり，力強い生命力をシンボライズしている。

　現在，計画は引渡しを目前に控え，多くの人々がここで暮らすために入居する予定だと聞いている。今後も都市化と資本経済が進展していく台湾の街中で，この高層住宅が，人と自然が生命力を持って親密に関わることができる新しい住まいの象徴となることを期待している。

Overall view from southeast forest

Miyagi Gakuen Preschool "Mori no Kodomo-en"
Sendai, Miyagi, Japan
2014–16

This is a relocation and construction plan to add a new nursery to the existing affiliate kindergarten of *Miyagi Gakuin Women's University*, as a project to celebrate the school's 130th anniversary. Located within the site of *Miyagi Gakuin*, "Mori-no-kodomoen" is surrounded by a forest from every direction. We were asked to design a nursery that allows us to feel close to nature.

This is a single story wooden building that uses a conventional post and beam structural system of 1,000 m², and playgrounds with different characteristics are placed in the south and north of the building.

The nursery rooms for children aged 3-5 line up surrounding the playground in the south. We are aiming to achieve a place that accommodates the activities of the children according to their development with an irregular layout of the nursery room, the play corner and toilet. On the other hand, the nursery rooms for children aged 0-2 line up facing the quiet fields on the northern side. Problems like the noises that are caused by different age groups and things like infections were also taken into consideration.

The respective nursery rooms are arranged continuously by incorporating an engawa and a deep eave, so that the activities of the children can easily extend into the playground and forest.

At the center of the building, there is a room that serves as a lunch hall and playroom, and by connecting it to the kitchen and the playground with the farming fields on the north, not only can we expect a place that encourage food education, but it also becomes the main space for activities such as prayer services and other events for the children.

The building is covered by a large undulated roof. The large and small convex curve of the roof wraps the place created for the children like a dome, and connects the building to create a sense of unity.

We will achieve a light structure by bending 20 × 90 mm residential-scale timber and by stacking them in 8 to 12 layers. By setting them in 900 mm pitches in grid form with braces at 45 degrees, it adds rigidity to the roof. The weaved timber of the ceiling and roof gives us comfort like as if we were inside a cradle.

Through conversation with the teachers from different specialties of *Miyagi Gakuin Women's University*, and also teachers from the existing kindergarten, this is a plan that fully utilizes the environment of *Miyagi Gakuin*.

Model

Engawa (veranda) along south court

Club room

宮城学院女子大学付属認定こども園「森のこども園」

宮城学院の創立130周年記念事業として，従来の附属幼稚園に保育園の機能を追加し，認定こども園として移転新築する計画である。

宮城学院敷地内の四方を森に囲まれた場所に，自然にふれ合い，自然を感じることができる「森のこども園」をつくることが求められた。

今回の計画は，約1,000m^{2}の在来軸組工法で計画された木造平屋の建物であり，南側と北側に性質の異なる園庭を配置している。

南側の園庭を囲む様に，3〜5歳児の保育室が並んでいる。保育室のヴォリューム，遊びのコーナーやトイレの配置などに変化をもたせ，こどもの発達に応じた活動ができる場を実現している。また，畑が並ぶ静かな北側の園庭に面し，0〜2歳児の保育室が並んでいる。保育室間の距離をとることで，年齢別の活動音や感染症などの問題にも配慮した。

それぞれの保育室は，縁側と深い軒により内外が一体的に連続し，こどもが園庭や森へと活動を広げやすくなっている。

園舎の中心には，ランチルーム兼遊戯室を配置し，調理室や，畑のある北の園庭と繋げることで，こどもたちの食育の場として期待すると共に，礼拝や，こども園のイベントなどの活動の中心となる。

園舎は1枚の起伏のある大きな屋根で覆われている。大小のむくりは，ドームのようにこどもの居場所を包み込みながら，建物全体を繋ぎ，こども園の一体感を生んでいる。

屋根は，20×90mmの住宅スケールの木材をしならせながら8〜12層積層することで，軽やかな構造を実現している。平面割りに合わせて900mmピッチで格子状に積層し，45度にふられた斜材が筋交いとなり，屋根の剛性を高めている。木材が編み込まれた様子は，揺りかごの中にいるような安心感を与える。

宮城学院女子大学の様々な専門分野の先生，既存の幼稚園の先生との話し合いを重ねることで，宮城学院の環境を最大限に生かした計画となった。

1	APPROACH	10	ENGAWA (VERANDAH)
2	MAIN ENTRANCE	11	LUNCH ROOM + PLAYROOM
3	CHILDREN'S ROOM (0 YEARS OLD)	12	KITCHEN
4	CHILDREN'S ROOM (1 YEARS OLD)	13	OFFICE
5	CHILDREN'S ROOM (2 YEARS OLD)	14	CLUB ROOM
6	CHILDREN'S ROOM (3 YEARS OLD)	15	CHIIDCARE SUPPORT
7	CHILDREN'S ROOM (4 YEARS OLD)	16	PARKING
8	CHILDREN'S ROOM (5 YEARS OLD)	17	SUB ENTRANCE
9	PLAYING CORNER		

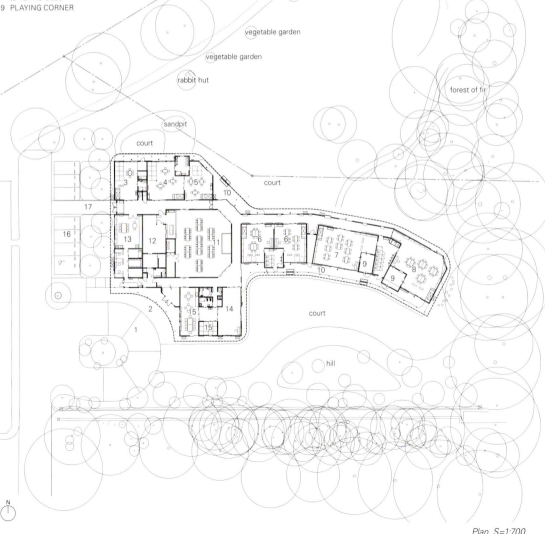

Plan S=1:700

Children's room (5 years old)

Corridor across north court

West elevation

East elevation

North elevation

South elevation S=1:400

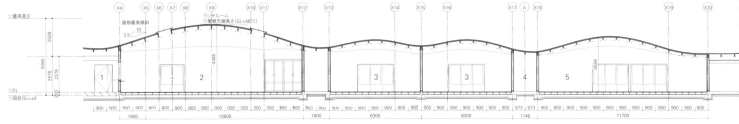
Section S=1:250

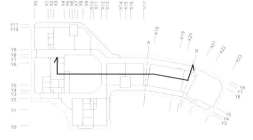

1 KITCHEN
2 LUNCH ROOM + PLAYROOM
3 CHILDREN'S ROOM (3 YEARS OLD)
4 STORAGE
5 CHILDREN'S ROOM (5 YEARS OLD)

Lunch room/playroom

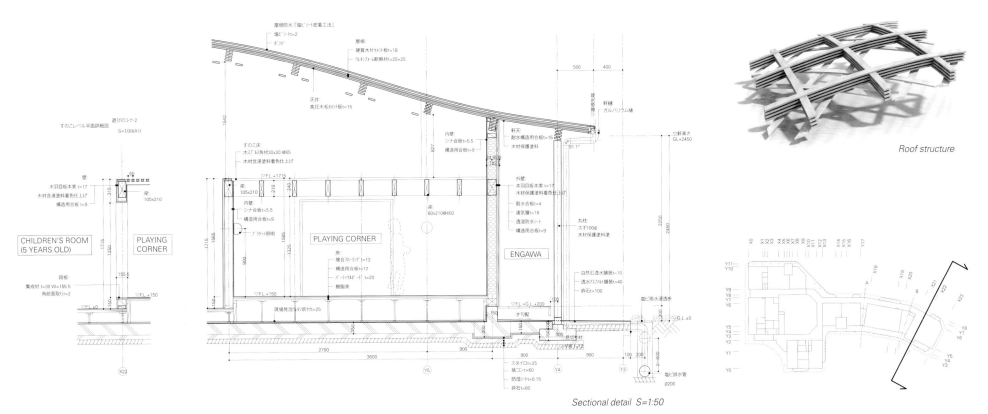

Sectional detail S=1:50

Roof structure

Museo Internacional del Barroco
Puebla, México
2012–16

Overall view from west

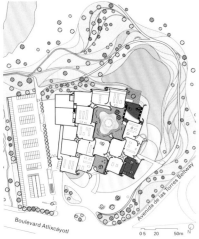
Site plan S=1:5000

The expansion of the European trade route over the Atlantic and the Pacific ocean was driven by the discovery of the new continent. Due to this movement, Baroque came to be known as the world's first artistic style. The city of Puebla, Mexico, which became a UNESCO World Heritage Site in 1987, was at the center of this expansive trade network. *Museo Internacional del Barroco* (*MIB*) is a museum that has been planned inside this historic city. The museum features Baroque art and Baroque-inspired objects and ideas in the current world.

Our work is to express through architecture the Baroque way of thinking that continue to exist in the world today. We planned the project around three goals. First, a space where order begins to unravel and flow, and a space that is fluid and free-flowing; second, beautiful lighting; and third, consideration for the environment and its ecological systems. Baroque itself is a form of response to the static and intelligent Renaissance movement. For this reason, the Baroque theme revolves around constant motion and change, with water as its primary symbol. Those who are led by the light (God); an emotionally moving drama; and experiences that are understood through the senses, rather than through logic.... Our aim is to create a space that stimulates movement and change, and to unravel the system that is ruled under the modern architectural grid. Once each grid is given a particular functionality, they are untied from each other. Light and scenery begin to flow in through the open seams, allowing people to rediscover their connection to the outer world and drift through the spaces.

If Baroque is a kind of order that had evolved from the human-centric, Renaissance system to a kind of order that identifies with God, then a similar shift is occurring in today's society as well. The restoration of nature-to-human conversation is the most important theme of our century, and *MIB* is an expression of such a shift in formality. Rather than being bound to the cold and rigid grid system, the spaces are held together by an order that is just about to be released, exuding a sense of fluidity as a whole. We shall begin to comprehend the essence of Baroque when we experience the space in such a state.

Second floor S=1:1500

First floor S=1:1500

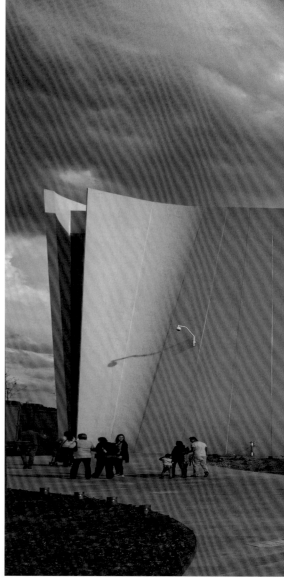

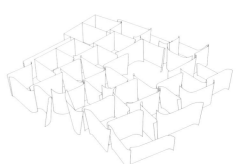
Conceptual axonometric

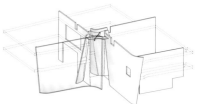
Axonometric: open (p.261, right)

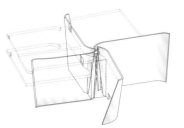
Axonometric: close (p.261, left)

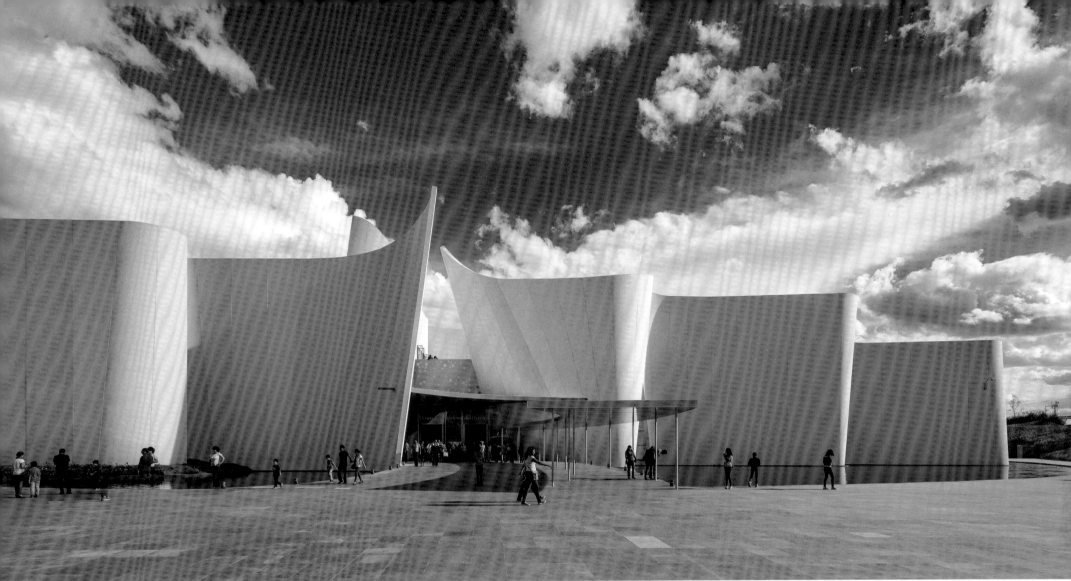

Overall view from north

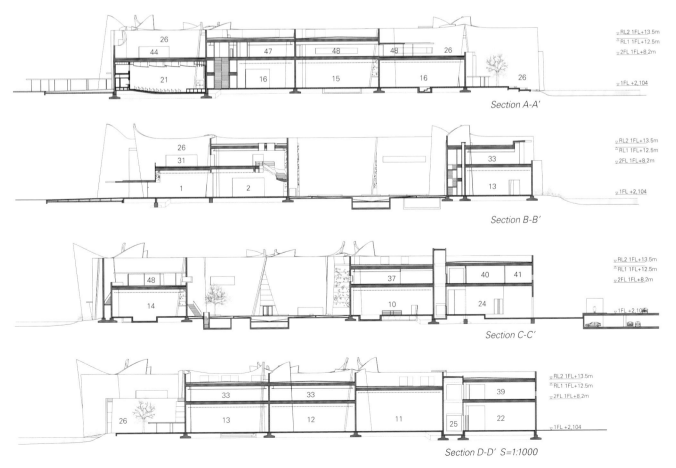

Section A-A'

Section B-B'

Section C-C'

Section D-D' S=1:1000

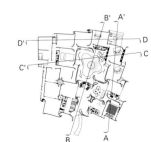

1 ENTRANCE HALL	11 ROOM 3: BAROQUE FEELING	23 QUARANTINE ROOM
2 LOBBY / STAIRS	12 ROOM 4: NEW ORDER OF TIMES	24 LOADING BAY
3 ELEVATORS	13 ROOM 5: ALLEGORIES OF KNOWLEDGE	25 SERVICE LIFT
4 CLOAKROOM		26 TERRACE
5 INFIRMARY		27 FILM OF WATER
6 EXHIBITION LOBBY	14 ROOM 6: TO ENTERTAIN AND IMPRESS	28 KIOSK
7 TEMPORARY EXHIBITION HALL		29 POND
		30 RESTORATION WORKSHOP
8 SPECIAL COLLECTIONS HALL	15 ROOM 7: ARTIFICES OF EAR	31 EDUCATIONAL AREA
9 ROOM 1: THEATRUM MUNDI	16 ROOM 8: BAROQUE TODAY	32 EDUCATIONAL SERVICE OFFICE
10 ROOM 2: PUEBLA DE LOS ANGELES	17 MUSIC BOX	33 OFFICE
	18 SHOP	34 LOCKERS
	19 PATIO	35 SERVER ROOM
	20 AUDITORIUM LOBBY	36 LIBRARY ACCESS
	21 AUDITORIUM	37 LIBRARY
	22 TRANSIT STORAGE	38 LIBRARY FILE
		39 MUSEOGRAPHY WORKSHOP
		40 MUSEOGRAPHY MATERIAL STORAGE
		41 PAINT AND VARNISH AREA
		42 COLLECTION STORAGE
		43 CULTURAL PROMOTION
		44 INTERNATIONAL CONFERENCE ON BAROQUE
		45 MEETING ROOM
		46 COFFEE SHOP
		47 KITCHEN
		48 RESTAURANT

View from southwest

Entrance ▷

Staircase at lobby

Entrance hall

Lobby on upper level: restaurant on left

Above: upward view of toplight with four walls converging closely
Below: view from exhibition lobby toward full-height void between four walls converging closely

Above: upward view of toplight between shop and auditorium
Below: between shop and auditorium: natural light falls from toplight

Terrace on north

View from room 2 to room 4

Patio

バロック・インターナショナルミュージアム・プエブラ

バロックが人類初の世界様式となったのは，新大陸発見により大西洋と太平洋が結びつき，交易ルートが拡大したことによる。その交易ネットワークの中心に位置していたのが，ユネスコの人類世界遺産に1987年に登録されたメキシコのプエブラだ。「バロック・インターナショナルミュージアム・プエブラ(MIB)」は，この歴史的な街プエブラに計画され，バロック芸術や現代にも生きるバロック的なものを世界の人々に紹介するミュージアムである。

私たちの取り組みは，現代にも生きるバロック的な思考を，建築を通し表現することである。そこで「秩序が解け始め，流出する空間。空間全体が流動的な印象をもつ空間」「美しい光」「エコロジーの機構，環境に対する配慮」という三つの目標を立てた。そもそもバロックは，スタティックで知的なルネサンス的なるものへの反動であり，そのテーマは常に動きや変化，水はそのシンボルである。光(神)に導かれ改心する人々。心を揺さぶるドラマ。理論的に理解されるのではなく，感性を通して体験されるもの。私たちは現代建築特有の機能的なグリッドに支配された秩序を解き放ち，空間が動きや変化を触発させるものになることを狙った。グリッドの一駒一駒にそれぞれの機能を与えた上で，グリッドの結び目をほどき，その綻びから光や景色が流入することで，人々は外界との繋がりを再発見しつつ，各部屋を流れゆくように移動する。

バロックがルネサンス的な人間中心の秩序から神を踏まえた秩序への変化だとすれば，これと同じような変化が私たちの暮らす現代にも生じている。自然と人間との対話の回復は，今世紀最大のテーマであり，この「MIB」はそうした秩序の変化を表現している。固く冷たいグリッドに支配されるのではなく，今にも溶け出そうとする秩序をもって，空間全体が流動的な印象をつくり出す時，それを体験することがバロック的な空間エッセンスを体感することに繋がるであろう。

This is a scheme for a new civic hall centered around a grand theater that seats 2,000 people. Following the presentation of proposals in March 2016, our practice was selected as the winner.

The site is located in the city center, approximately 1.5 km northwest of Mito Station. It is between two distinct buildings: *Art Tower Mito* designed by Arata Isozaki to the north, and a very popular 7-story commercial complex to the south.

The building measures 110 m x 70 m in plan. The theater, which faces and aligns with the plaza of *Art Tower Mito*, is positioned in the center. Other programs are wrapped around the theater: a large-volume indoor plaza (Yagura Plaza) to the north, and 4 stories of shops, exhibition studio, conference room and multifunction hall to the south.

Boasting sites such as *Kodo-kan* and *Kairaku-en*, Mito is a beautiful city full of history. In order to revive and inherit the memories of the Mito Domain castle town, our proposal encompasses the building with a stout timber framework. As for the indoor plaza, a double-grid scaffold-like structure surrounds the space to support the long span. Joints are simple butt joints without any carving, and all timber material used in the project has been tested for fire resistance.

As an overall scheme, materials have been selected according to their suitability and practicality; the walls of the grand theater which requires acoustic insulation is concrete, whilst steel is used overhead and in the floor structure.

By showing a presence rooted in the historical culture of Mito City, and even overcoming the notion of time, the project aims to restore interactions and the bond between people, and to create a building that citizens feel close to and are proud of. The project has been initiated, and is due to open in 2021.

Mito Civic Hall
Mito, Ibaraki, Japan
2016–

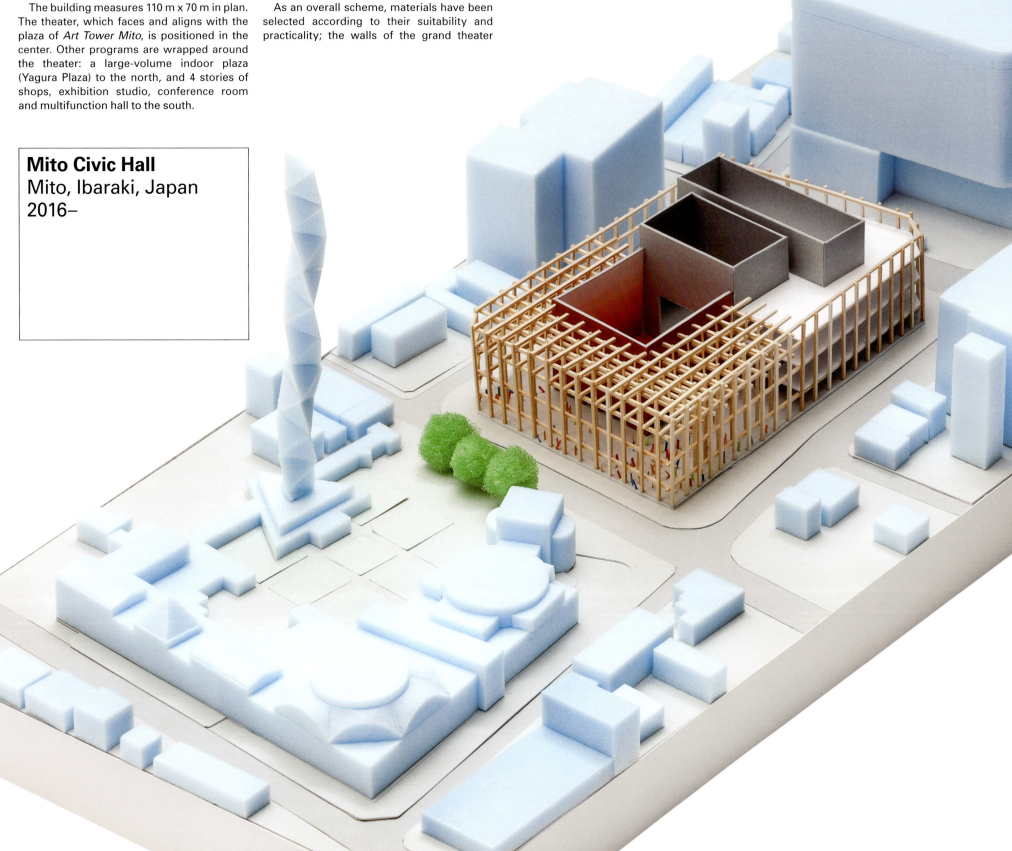

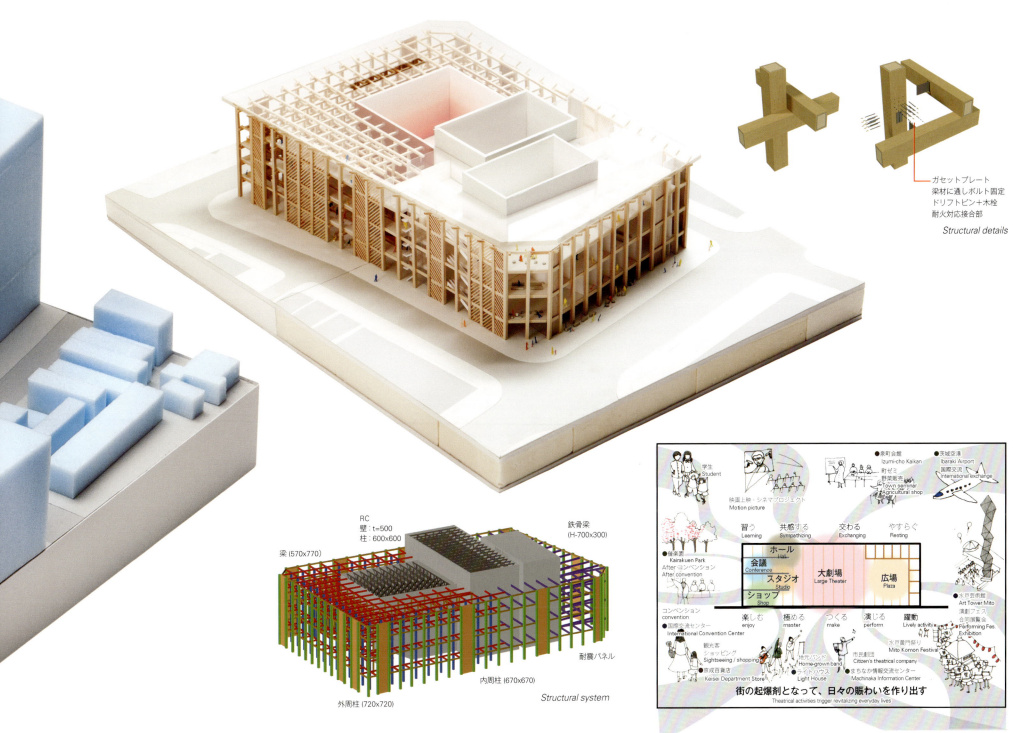

Structural details

Structural system

Concept diagram

North elevation

West elevation

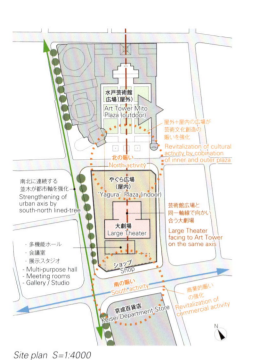

Site plan S=1:4000

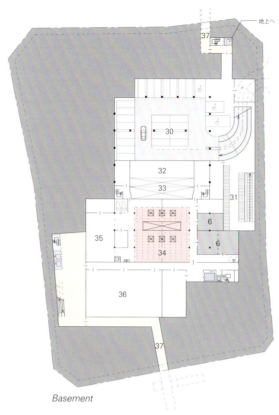

Basement

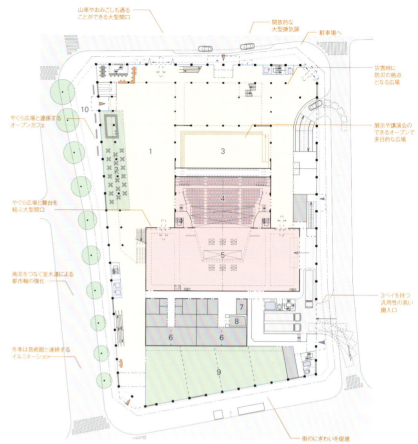

First floor S=1:1200

(仮称)水戸市民会館

2,000人を収容できる大劇場を中心とした，新たな市民会館である。2016年3月にプロポーザルが行われ，我々が設計者として選定された。

敷地は，JR水戸駅から約1.5km北西に進んだ街の中心に位置し，北側に磯崎新氏設計による「水戸芸術館」(1990年)，南側は街で一番の集客力がある7階建ての商業施設，この二つに挟まれた場所にある。

建物は約110m×70mという大きな平面形状とし，その中央に「水戸芸術館」の広場と軸をそろえて向かい合うように大劇場を配置した。この周囲に，北側には気積の大きな屋内の広場(やぐら広場)を，南側にはショップ，展示スタジオ，会議室，多機能ホールを4層に重ねて配している。

水戸は弘道館や偕楽園など，歴史を強く感じさせる美しい街である。このような水戸藩城下町の記憶を蘇らせ，継承すべく，純木製の骨太な柱・梁によって建物全体を取り囲むこととした。また，屋内広場の大スパンになる部分は，2重のグリッドとなるやぐら状の架構で包み込む計画とした。木材同士の仕口は，欠損のない接するだけのものとしている。また，これらの木材はすべて耐火の認定を取得したものを用いる計画である。

建物全体としては，遮音性の求められる大劇場の壁をコンクリートとし，その上部やその他の床組みに鉄骨を用いるなど，適材適所の構造計画としている。

水戸という街の歴史文化に根差し，時の経過を超えるような存在感を持つことで，人と人との関係や絆を取り戻し，市民の人々に親しみ，愛され，誇りを持ってもらえるような建物となるよう，2021年の開館を目指して設計が始まったところである。

1 'YAGURA' (FRAME TOWER) PLAZA
2 CAFE
3 EXHIBITION PLAZA
4 SEATING OF LARGE THEATER (FIRST FLOOR)
5 STAGE OF LARGE THEATER
6 DRESSING ROOM
7 STAFF ROOM
8 VOCAL ROOM
9 SHOP
10 TREE-LINED PLAZA
11 FOYER / GALLERY
12 BUFFET SPACE
13 LOUNGE / GALLERY
14 ADMINISTRATION OFFICE
15 GALLERY / STUDIO
16 STUDIO / FOYER
17 ARCHIVE / LIBRARY
18 STUDIO
19 SEATING OF LARGE THEATER (SECOND FLOOR)
20 STUDIO / GALLERY
21 PRACTICE ROOM
22 TATAMI ROOM
23 MEETING ROOM
24 MINI-THEATER
25 MEETING / FOYER
26 SEATING OF LARGE THEATER (THIRD FLOOR)
27 MULTI-PURPOSE HALL
28 LOUNGE / FOYER
29 CAFE BAR
30 CAR PARKING
31 BICYCLE PARKING
32 STORAGE FOR SEATING
33 ORCHESTRA PIT
34 TRAP CELLAR
35 STAGE SETTING ROOM
36 MECHANICAL
37 PASSAGE WAY
38 MUNICIPAL PARKING LOT

Yagura Plaza

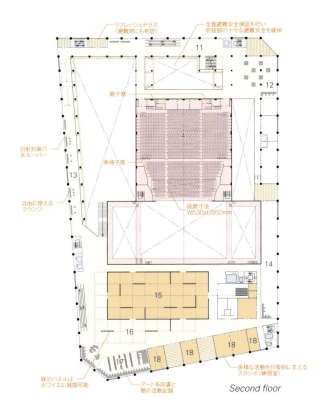
Second floor

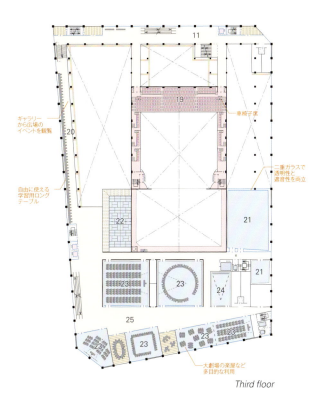
Third floor

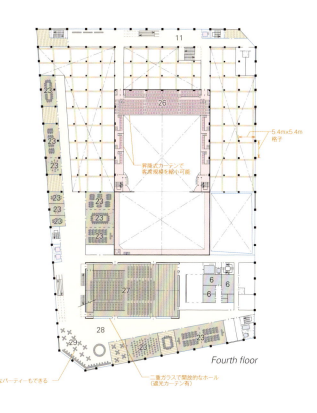
Fourth floor

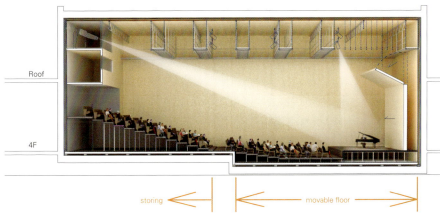
Sectional detail of multipurpose hall

Exhibition plaza

Section S=1:800

National Taichung Theater
Taichung, Taiwan, R.O.C.
2005–16

Overall view from south

This is a theater complex planned in Taichung City, a major city in the central area of Taiwan. The requirement includes; series of theater spaces with the seating capacity of 2014, 800, and 200; enough practice rooms and back spaces; a restaurant and commercial facilities, and a public park space around the building for the daily bustle of activities.

This project has the most complex configuration in its structure system after our *Sendai Mediatheque* project. In detail, there is a huge cave-like space produced by three-dimensional curve surfaced reinforced concrete shells, whose curved surfaces were derived from the grid that repeats itself in a simple regularity. The cave space is transformed in complex manner by housing three theatrical spaces inside of the cave space, and it develops two pairs of tubal space in either vertical or horizontal orientations. We named this structural system as Catenoid. Two layers of Catenoid forms a single pair, while those layers repeatedly open or close in reversal manner. This pair is then repeatedly stacked in vertical orientation to form the whole unit.

This is based on the spatial concept of the unrealized *Forum for Music, Dance and Visual Culture in Ghent (pp.52-57)*, but there are some different points; because of the close relationship of the building programs to the surrounding urban environment in *Ghent* case, we suggested a space based on the concept of a three-dimensional networking of city streets to bring in the urban context into the interior space. In addition, its external form is derived from the surfaces, adapting to the site boundary by getting a polygonal section-cut—therefore the notion of the continuity from the inside space of the building and the outside space is strong; in Taichung case, the surrounding condition is the proposed park space with a little existing context, therefore the sectional detail of those four facade surfaces have more sense of abstraction and independence of themselves from the surrounding, which is similar to the case of *Sendai*. Still, the grid of the interior space spills out to the exterior space to establish networked garden spaces along with the roof garden, thus the sense of continuity between the interior space and the exterior space is maintained.

The theaters were required to introduce a system, which divides the space considering the centripetal, complete quality of the theatrical space. We named this system as a "Plug", a two-dimensional surface fitting onto the three-dimensional Catenoid either in horizontal or vertical orientation. Horizontal Plug functions mostly as a floor slab, but it also represents a condition as a water surface poured onto the Catenoid space. The Horizontal Plug can become either a continuously allocated element or an independently distributed element, depending on their water surface level and the relative relationship of a Plug with other Plug. The Vertical Plug can also considered as a section-cut surface of a cube filled with water, which repeatedly appears on the facades or the section surface.

We considered this cave-like primitive space that sympathizes with nature can be created by the organic spatial network, and such space will be a suitable for a theater play—an original form of human expression.

Night view of entrance

Southeast elevation

Basic geometric generative system. Simple rules leading to a spatially highly complex structure. A regular grid with alternating A and B zones is pulled apart to open up interstices separated by the surface.

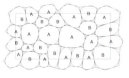

A transformation into a "Flexible Grid" allows for a strategic redistribution according to programmatic needs of area/volume and local adjacencies.

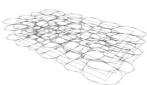

Structural concept

The flexible grid system is applied on a per level basis responding to specific needs in local programmatic changes. Eventually, structural links evolve between the flexible grids.

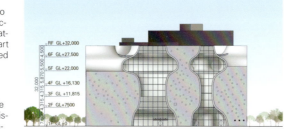

Southwest elevation

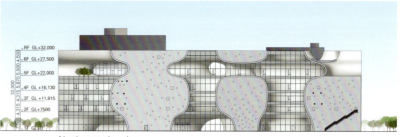

Northwest elevation

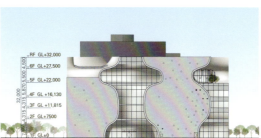

Northeast elevation S=1:1500

Southeast elevation

First floor S=1:2000

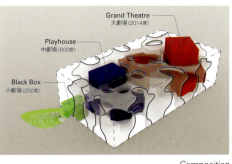

Composition

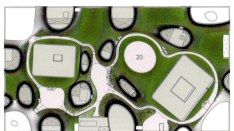

Sixth floor

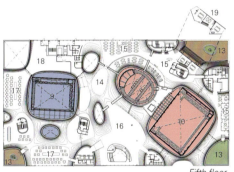

Fifth floor

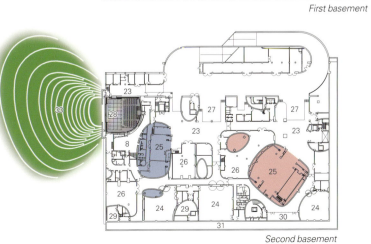

First basement

Fourth floor

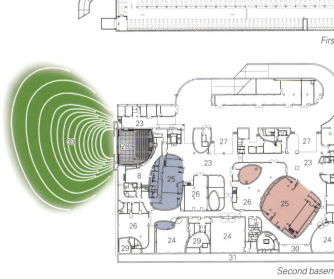

Second basement

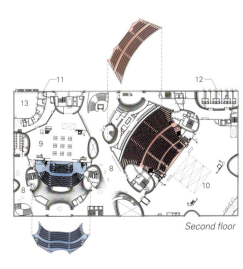

Second floor

1 INFORMATION COUNTER
2 TICKET COUNTER
3 GALLERY (TENANT)
4 FLOWER SHOP (TENANT)
5 SHOP (TENANT)
6 CAFE (TENANT)
7 EVENT SPACE
8 FOYER
9 PLAYHOUSE
10 GRAND THEATER
11 DRESSING ROOM
   (PLAYHOUSE)
12 DRESSING ROOM
   (GRAND THEATER)
13 TERRACE
14 GALLERY
15 OFFICE
16 BOOK STORE (TENANT)
17 RESTAURANT (TENANT)
18 KITCHEN (TENANT)
19 MEETING ROOM
20 SKY GARDEN
21 PARKING (STAFF)
22 PARKING (GUEST)
23 ASSEMBLY WORKSHOP
24 REHEARSAL ROOM
25 MACHINERY PIT
26 MACHINE ROOM
27 LOADING
28 BLACK BOX
29 STUDIO
30 SUNKEN GARDEN
31 COOL PIT
32 STORAGE
33 OUTDOOR THEATER

271

First floor. View toward main entrance

Grand Theater

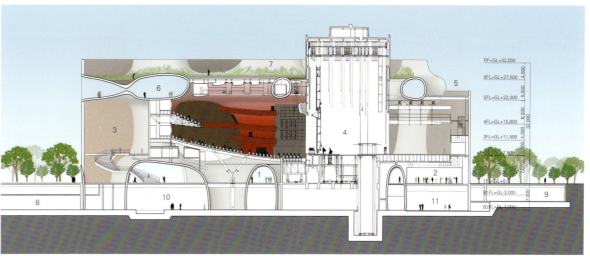

1 SHOP (TENANT)
2 EVENT SPACE
3 FOYER
4 GRAND THEATER
5 TERRACE
6 OFFICE
7 SKY GARDEN
8 PARKING (STAFF)
9 PARKING (GUEST)
10 ASSEMBLY WORKSHOP
11 REHEARSAL ROOM

Section: Grand Theater S=1:1000

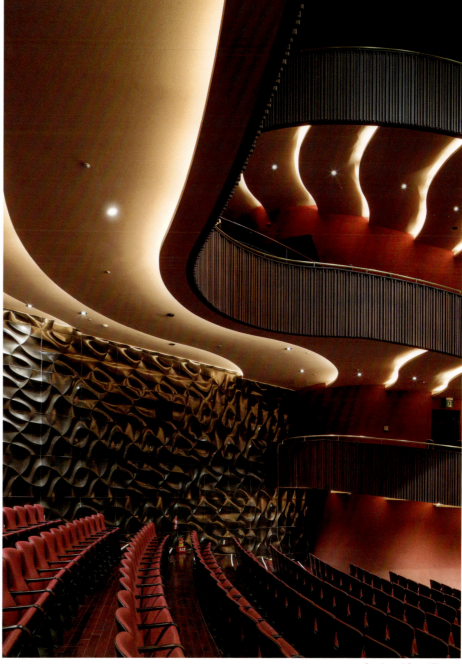

Seating of Grand Theater

Foyer on second floor. Playhouse on left

From Simple Grid to Finished Surface

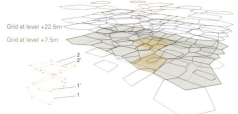

Control Grid
The catenoids are defined by a simple polygonal grid, superimposed over 5 levels. At each level, the grid slightly adjusts to accommodate local variation. Based on this simple control grid, the final complex geometry is thus controlled by a mere 74 polygonal curves or 423 control points.

Crude Mesh
Each of the 58 catenoids is defined by four polygons: a set of corresponding polygons of adjacent levels (bottom [1] and top [2]) and their offsets ([1'] and [2']). The Crude Mesh is the translation of this control grid into the aggregate of all catenoids in their initial state (i.e. as derived from the four polygonal lines). This simple mesh provides the basis for the final geometry.

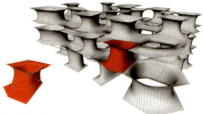

Smoothed Surface
The final geometry is the result of several iterations of a smoothing algorithm. In each iteration, every facet of the crude mesh is divided in half relative to all its adjacent facets.

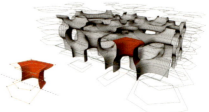

Finished Surfaces
To obtain the final surfaces with the correct thickness, the smoothed surface is offset in the necessary distance, e.g. 115 mm on either side for the truss walls or 200 mm on either side for the structural thickness. These resultant surfaces are then trimmed at façade, roof and basement boundaries.

Foyer in front of Grand Theater on second floor: elevaor on southeast connects from basement to top. Staircase to fifth floor on left, approach to foyer of Playhouse on right

台中国家歌劇院

台湾中央部の大都市，台中市に計画された劇場コンプレックスである。2,014，800，200席の三つの劇場群と，豊富な練習室，バックスペースを持ち，さらに日常的なにぎわいのためのレストランや商業施設と，建物周辺の公園整備が要求されている。

当計画は，「せんだいメディアテーク」以降，最も複雑な構造システムを有している。すなわち単純なグリッドからなる幾何学を変形して生成される，3次元曲面RCシェルによる巨大な洞窟状の空間とし，その中に三つの劇場を内包することで，垂直，水平方向に展開する2組のチューブ状空間を形成している。この構造体を我々は「カテノイド」と命名している。2層を1組として開/閉を繰り返す空間を，垂直方向に繰り返した構成とした。

この空間原理は実現されなかった「ゲント市文化フォーラム」(pp.52-57)に基づいているが，いくつかの相異点もある。「ゲント」では周辺市街との密接な関係から，街路ネットワークを立体化した空間が意図され，外形も敷地に沿った多角の切断面となり，内外の連続感は強い。「台中国家歌劇院」の敷地は公園予定地であり，矩形に切断される四つのファサードは「せんだい」同様に，抽象性と自立性が強い。しかし，内部の歪曲した幾何学は外部へとあふれ出て，屋上庭園を含めてネットワーク化された庭園を形成することで，内外の連続を図っている。

劇場空間は完結性を求められるので，分節するための仕組みをより必要とした。これを我々は「プラグ」と称して，3次元カテノイド面に水平，垂直にはめ込まれた2次元面とした。水平プラグは床としての機能を大部分担うのだが，カテノイド空間に張られた水面のようであり，その水位を上下することによって連続したり，独立した床を構成した。垂直プラグもいわば，洞窟内に満たされた水のキューブの切断面と仮想され，ファサードや断面に繰り返し現れる。

いずれにしろ，ここでは洞窟のような自然を感じさせるプリミティブな場所を，有機的な空間ネットワークを通じて生き活きとつくり出すことが，演劇という根源的な人間の表現の場としてふさわしいと考えたのである。

Black Box

Playhouse

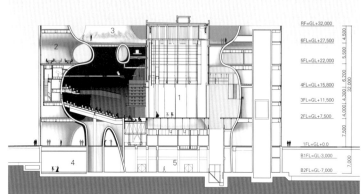

Section: Playhouse S=1:1000

1 PLAYHOUSE
2 RESTAURANT (TENANT)
3 SKY GARDEN
4 REHEARSAL ROOM
5 STORAGE

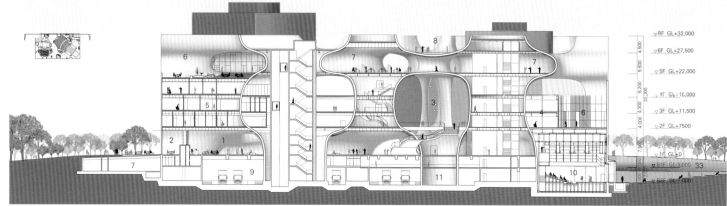

Longitudinal section S=1:1000

1 SHOP (TENANT)
2 CAFE (TENANT)
3 FOYER
4 DRESSING ROOM (PLAYHOUSE)
5 DRESSING ROOM (GRAND THEATER)
6 TERRACE
7 OFFICE
8 SKY GARDEN
9 LOADING
10 BLACK BOX
11 STORAGE

Fifth floor: book store (left) and spiral stair to beer bar on rooftop (center)

Pergola and bench at roof garden designed by Kazuko Fujie

Terrace on southeast at fifth floor

List of Works
2002–2016

2000–02
Brugge Pavilion
Bruges, Belgium

Program: pavilion
Total floor area: 96.6 m²
Structure: aluminum honeycomb panel
1 story

ブルージュ・パヴィリオン
所在地：ブルージュ、ベルギー
設計：200004-0110
工事：200111-0202
建築主：Brugge 2002
主要用途：パヴィリオン
構造：オーク構造設計
監理：bap
施工：Aelbrecht Maes, Depret, 他
主体構造・規模：アルミニウム造/地上1階
建築面積：96.6 m²

2001–
**Relaxation Park
in Torrevieja**
Torrevieja, Spain

Program: spa, etc.
Total floor area: 1,249 m²
Site area: 8 ha
Structure: steel & timber frame
1 story

リラクゼーション・パーク・イン・トレヴィエハ
所在地：トレヴィエハ、スペイン
設計：第1期/200104-0206, 第2期/200707-
工事：第1期/200307-0609
建築主：トレヴィエハ市
主要用途：公園、スパ附属施設
構造：SAPS/Sasaki and Partners, Masahiro Ikeda Architecture Studio, 第1期/Obiol & Moya Arquitectes Associates
設備：環境エンジニアリング, Fernando Lamas
設計協力：篠崎健一
施工：Grupo Enerala + Jost
主体構造・規模：鉄骨造、木造/地上1階
敷地面積：8 ha
建築面積：1,599 m²
延床面積：1,249 m²

2002
**Serpentine Gallery
Pavilion 2002**
London, U.K.

Program: pavilion
Total floor area: 309.76 m²
Structure: steel frame
1 story

サーペンタイン・ギャラリー・パヴィリオン 2002
所在地：ロンドン、イギリス
設計：200201-0206
工事：200204-0207
建築主：サーペンタイン・ギャラリー
主要用途：パヴィリオン
共同設計：Cecil Balmond (ARUP)
構造・環境：ARUP
施工：Sir Robert McAlpine Japan
主体構造・規模：鉄骨造/地上1階
建築面積：309.76 m²
延床面積：309.76 m²

2002
**Architects Competition
Vestbanen**
Oslo, Norway

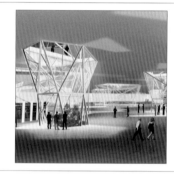

Program: library, museum, cinema, conference, office, residence, etc.
Total floor area: 168,950 m²
Site area: about 2,7000 m²
Structure: steel frame, reinforced concrete
8 stories, 2 basements

オスロ・ウェストバーネン再開発計画
コンペティション応募案
所在地：オスロ、ノルウェー
設計：2002
建築主：Statsbygg
主要用途：図書館、美術館、映画館、会議場、オフィス、住宅、店舗、他
構造：ARUP
設備：竹中工務店
主体構造：鉄骨造、鉄筋コンクリート造
規模：地上8階、地下2階
敷地面積：約27,000 m²
建築面積：27,440 m²
延床面積：168,950 m²

2003–
**Extention for "The Fair
of Barcelona Gran Via
Venue"**
Barcelona, Spain

Program: convention hall, office, restaurant, etc.
Total floor area: 185,800 m²
Site area: 450,000 m²
Structure: steel frame, reinforced concrete, steel reinforced concrete
1-6 stories, 1 basement

バルセロナ見本市 グランビア会場 拡張計画
所在地：バルセロナ市＋オスピタレット市、スペイン
設計：200306- 工事：200310-
建築主：FIRA2000
主要用途：見本市、コンベンションホール、オフィス、レストラン
構造：SAPS/Sasaki and Partners, IDOM
設備：環境エンジニアリング, IDOM
施工：DRAGADOS, FCC+COMSA, TIFERCA, ACCIONA, SACYR
主体構造：鉄骨造、鉄筋コンクリート造、鉄骨鉄筋コンクリート造
規模：地上1階〜6階、地下1階
敷地面積：450,000 m²
建築面積：108,200 m²
延床面積：185,800 m²

The Fair for the Barcelona Gran Via Venue is operated by FAIR OF BARCELONA

1999–2003
**Shinonome Canal Court
CODAN Block 2**
Koto, Tokyo, Japan

Program: housing
Total floor area: 35,465 m²
Site area: 7,076 m²
Structure: reinforced concrete
14 stories, 1 basement

東雲キャナルコート CODAN 2街区
所在地：東京都江東区
設計：199910-0307
工事：200105-0307
建築主：都市基盤整備公団（現UR都市機構）
主要用途：共同住宅、店舗、保育園、駐車場
共同設計：都市基盤整備公団、戸田建設
構造：中田捷夫研究室、都市基盤整備公団、戸田建設
設備：総合設備計画、EE設計、都市基盤整備公団、戸田建設
施工：戸田・五洋・錢高 建設工事共同企業体
主体構造・規模：鉄筋コンクリート造/地上14階、地下1階
敷地面積：7,076 m²
建築面積：4,719 m²
延床面積：35,465 m²

2000–03
Motomachi Chukagai Station, Minatomirai Line
Yokohama, Kanagawa, Japan

みなとみらい線 元町・中華街駅
所在地：神奈川県横浜市
設計：200009-0203
工事：200203-0312
建築主：横浜高速鉄道
設備用途：地下鉄駅舎
インテリア構造：佐々木睦朗構造計画研究所
グラフィックデザイン：マツダオフィス
設備：鉄道建設・運輸施設整備支援機構鉄道建設本部
施工：熊谷・東洋・相鉄建設工事共同企業体
主体構造：鉄筋コンクリート造、一部鉄骨造
規模：地上2階、地下4階
敷地面積：5,446m²
建築面積：885.2m²
延床面積：5,912m²

Program: station
Total floor area: 5,912 m²
Site area: 5,446 m²
Structure: reinforced concrete
2 stories, 4 basements

2003
S Project in Scotland
Scotland, U.K.

スコットランド・Sプロジェクト
所在地：スコットランド、イギリス
設計：200210-0312
主要用途：百貨店
共同設計：福嶋加津也、細谷浩美、Building Design Partnership(UK)
構造：ARUP
設備：Whitby Bird & Partners
主体構造・規模：鉄骨造／地上4階、地下1階
敷地・建築面積：5,000m²
延床面積：23,000m²

Program: department store
Total floor area: 23,000 m²
Site area: 5,000 m²
Structure: steel frame
4 stories, 1 basement

2000–04
Matsumoto Performing Arts Centre
Matsumoto, Nagano, Japan

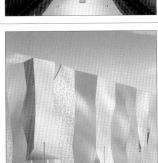

まつもと市民芸術館
所在地：長野県松本市
設計：200011-0110
工事：200111-0403
建築主：松本市
主要用途：劇場
構造：佐々木睦朗構造計画研究所
設備：環境エンジニアリング
施工：竹中・戸田・松本土建特定建設工事共同企業体
主体構造：鉄骨鉄筋コンクリート造
規模：地上7階、地下2階
敷地面積：9,142.50m²
建築面積：7,080.02m²
延床面積：19,184.38m²

Program: theater
Total floor area: 19,184.38 m²
Site area: 9,142.50 m²
Structure: steel reinforced concrete
7 stories, 2 basements

2002–04
Aliminum Cottage
Minamikoma, Yamanashi, Japan

アルミコテージ
所在地：山梨県南巨摩郡
設計：200206-0403
工事：200404-0406
建築主：日本軽金属
主要用途：別荘
構造：オーク構造設計
設備：イーエスアソシエイツ
施工：日軽産業
主体構造・規模：アルミニウム造／地上2階
敷地面積：8,300.00m²
建築面積：57.42m²
延床面積：75.19m²

Program: cottage
Total floor area: 75.19 m²
Site area: 8,300.00 m²
Structure: aluminum
2 stories

2002–04
TOD'S Omotesando Building
Shibuya, Tokyo, Japan

TOD'S 表参道ビル
所在地：東京都渋谷区
設計：200204-0305
工事：200306-0411
建築主：Holpaf B.V.
主要用途：店舗、事務所
構造：オーク構造設計
設備：イーエスアソシエイツ
施工：竹中工務店
規模：地上7階、地下1階
敷地面積：516.23m²
建築面積：401.55m²
延床面積：2,548.84m²

Program: retail, office
Total floor area: 2,548.84 m²
Site area: 516.23 m²
Structure: reinforced concrete, steel frame (partially)
7 stories, 1 basement

2004
Musashisakai Public Building Competition
Musashino, Tokyo, Japan

武蔵境新公共施設設計競技応募案
所在地：東京都武蔵野市
設計：200311-0401
建築主：武蔵野市
主要用途：図書館、ギャラリー、スタジオ、他
設計協力：鈴木明、菅谷明子
構造：佐々木睦朗構造計画研究所
設備：イーエスアソシエイツ
主体構造・規模：鋼板コンクリート造／地上G階、地下1階
敷地面積：2,162m²
建築面積：1,599m²
延床面積：9,790m²

Program: library, gallery, studio, etc.
Total floor area: 9,790 m²
Site area: 2,162 m²
Structure: steel panel and concrete
6 stories, 1 basement

2004
Forum for Music, Dance and Visual Culture Competition
Ghent, Belgium

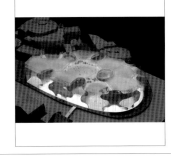

ゲント市文化フォーラム コンペティション応募案
所在地：ゲント、ベルギー
設計：200310-0404
建築主：ゲント市
主要用途：音楽ホール、劇場、スタジオ、等
共同設計：Andrea Branzi Architetto
構造：オーク構造設計
主体構造：鉄筋コンクリート造
規模：地上4階、地下2階
敷地面積：7,600m²
建築面積：5,706m²
延床面積：24,544m²

Program: music hall, theater, studio, etc
Total floor area: 24,544 m²
Site area: 7,600 m²
Structure: reinforced concrete
4 stories, 2 basements

2004
Fonds Régional d'Art Contemporain de Picaedie à Amiens Competition
Amiens, France

アミアンFRAC現代美術館 指名設計競技案
所在地：アミアン、フランス
設計：200312-04
建築主：Consiel Regional de Picardie
主要用途：美術館
共同設計：篠崎健一、Agence d'Architecture Deprick et Maniaque
構造：SAPS/Sasaki and Partners、0th Nord
設備：環境エンジニアリング、0th Nord.
Museography：Chantal Béret
主体構造・規模：鉄筋コンクリート造、一部プレキャストコンクリート造／地上2階、地下1階
敷地・建築面積：2,426m²
延床面積：4,770m²

Program: museum
Total floor area: 4,770 m²
Site area: 2,426 m²
Structure: reinforced concrete
2 stories, 1 basement

2001–05
Aluminum Brick Housing in Groningen
Groningen, the Netherlands

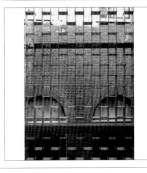

フローニンゲン アルミブリック ハウジング
所在地：フローニンゲン、オランダ
設計：200103-0403
工事：200404-0501
建築主：Ontwikketen IN
共同設計：Hosoya Schaefer Archiects
主要用途：ギャラリー、ゲストハウス
構造：オーク構造設計
施工：Keers Konstruktie Werken B.V.
主体構造・規模：アルミニウム造／地上3階
敷地面積：8,300m²
建築面積：57.42m²
延床面積：75.19m²

Program: gallery, guest house
Total floor area: 75.19 m²
Site area: 8,300 m²
Structure: aluminum bricks
3 stories

photo by © Wim te Brake

2002–05
Island City Central Park "GRIN GRIN"
Fukuoka, Japan

福岡アイランドシティ中央公園中核施設 ぐりんぐりん
所在地：福岡県福岡市
設計：200210-0311
工事：200403-0504
建築主：福岡市
主要用途：温室
構造：佐々木睦朗構造計画研究所
設備：環境エンジニアリング
施工：竹中工務店・高松組建設工事共同企業体
外構：総合設計研究所
主体構造：鉄筋コンクリート造、一部鉄骨造
規模：地上1階
敷地面積：129,170.00m²
建築面積：5,162.07m²
延床面積：5,033.47m²

Program: exhibition greenhouse
Total floor area: 5,033.47 m²
Site area: 129,170.00 m²
Structure: reinforced concrete, steel frame (partially)
1 story

2000–05
MAHLER 4 Block 5
Amsterdam, the Netherlands

オフィス・マーラー4・ブロック5
所在地：アムステルダム、オランダ
設計：200009-0208
工事：200301-0506
建築主：G&S VASTGOED
主要用途：事務所、店舗
構造：SAPS/Sasaki and Partners、Van Der Vorm Engineering
設備：Deems Raadgevende Ingenieurs BV
施工：G&S VASTGOED
主体構造：鉄筋コンクリート造、一部鉄骨造
規模：地上24階、地下2階
敷地面積：2,621m²
建築面積：2,621m²
延床面積：38,398m²

Program: office, retail
Total floor area: 38,398 m²
Site area: 2,621 m²
Structure: reinforced concrete
24 stories, 2 basement

2004–05
Dormitory for SUS Company Fukushima Branch
Sukagawa, Fukushima, Japan

SUS福島工場社員寮
所在地：福島県須賀川市
設計：200404-0408
工事：200411-0508
建築主：SUS
主要用途：寄宿舎
構造：オーク構造設計
設備：環境エンジニアリング
施工：戸田建設
主体構造・規模：アルミ合金造／地上1階
敷地面積：1,566.55m²
建築・延床面積：489.2m²

Program: dormitory
Total floor area: 489.2 m²
Site area: 1,566.55 m²
Structure: aluminum alloy
1 story

2003–05
MIKIMOTO Ginza 2
Chuo, Tokyo, Japan

Program: retail, office
Total floor area: 2,205.02 m²
Site area: 275.74 m²
Structure: steel panel and concrete
9 stories, 1 basement

MIKIMOTO Ginza 2
所在地：東京都中央区
設計：200308-0411
工事：200411-0511
建築主：ミキモト
主要用途：店舗、事務所
共同設計：大成建設
構造：佐々木睦朗構造計画研究所, 大成建設
設備：大成建設
施工：大成建設
主体構造・規模：鋼板コンクリート造,
一部壁式鉄筋コンクリート造/地上9階, 地下1階
敷地面積：275.74 m²
建築面積：237.69 m²
延床面積：2,205.02 m²

2004–06
'Meiso no Mori' Municipal Funeral Hall
Kakamigahara, Gifu, Japan

Program: crematorium
Total floor area: 2,264.57 m²
Site area: 6,695.97 m²
Structure: reinforced concrete, Steel frame (partially)
2 stories

瞑想の森 市営斎場
所在地：岐阜県各務原市
設計：200405-0503
工事：200504-0605
建築主：各務原市
主要用途：火葬場
構造：佐々木睦朗構造計画研究所
設備：環境エンジニアリング
ランドスケープ・デザイン：慶應義塾大学教授 石川幹子
施工：戸田・市川・天龍特定建設工事共同企業体
主体構造・規模：鉄筋コンクリート造, 一部鉄骨造
規模：地上2階
敷地面積：6,695.97 m²
建築面積：2,269.66 m²
延床面積：2,264.57 m²

2000–06
Hôpital Cognacq-Jay
Paris, France

Program: rehabilitation, hospice
Total floor area: 14,754 m² (except parking area)
Site area: 4,976 m²
Structure: reinforced concrete, Steel frame (partially)
6 stories, 2 basements

コニャック・ジェイ病院
所在地：パリ, フランス
設計：200001-0303
工事：200312-0609
建築主：コニャック・ジェイ財団
主要用途：リハビリテーション, ホスピス
共同設計：柳澤潤(コンテンポラリーズ),
マニュエル・ダルディッツ(みかんぐみ), Extra Muros
構造：SAPS/Sasaki and Partners, SETEC
設備：環境エンジニアリング, SETEC
躯体施工：Demathieu & Bard
ファサード施工：Bluntzer Sas/Rinaldi Structual
主体構造：鉄筋コンクリート造, 一部鉄骨造
規模：地上6階, 地下2階
敷地面積：4,976 m²
建築面積：3,207 m²
延床面積：14,754 m²（駐車場を除く）

2003–06
VivoCity
Singapore

Program: retail complex
Total floor area: 138,700 m²
Site area: 89,140 m²
Structure: reinforced concrete, prestressed concrete
3 stories, 2 basements

VivoCity
所在地：シンガポール
設計：200309-0610
工事：200401-0610
建築主：Mapletree Investments Pte Ltd.
主要用途：ショッピングモール
構造：SAPS/Sasaki and Partners
五洋建設＋Meinhardt(Singapore)Pte Ltd.
設備：五洋建設＋Parsons Brinckerhoff Pte Ltd.
施工：五洋建設
主体構造・規模：鉄筋コンクリート造,
プレストレスコンクリート造/地上3階, 地下2階
敷地面積：89,140 m²
建築面積：52,520 m²
延床面積：138,700 m²

2004–
Gavia Park in Madrid
Madrid, Spain

Program: park
Site area: 390,000 m²

ガヴィア公園
所在地：マドリード, スペイン
設計：200403-
工事：200701-
建築主：Madrid City, Empresa Municipal de la Vivienda y Suelo
主要用途：公園
Local architects : Antonio Marquerie Tamayo,
Dario Gazapo, Conchita Lapayese
設計：村井隆図, Jesas Jiménz Cañas,
Juan Azcasate
ランドスケープ・デザイン：慶應義塾大学教授 石川幹子,
Rafael Mata Olmo, Pedro Molina Holgado,
Luis Tejaro Encinao
設計協力：篠崎健一
施工：DICO
敷地面積：390,000 m²

2007
"Les Halles" Competition
Paris, France

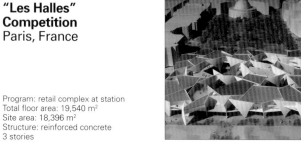

Program: retail complex at station
Total floor area: 19,540 m²
Site area: 18,396 m²
Structure: reinforced concrete
3 stories

レ・アール国際設計競技応募案
所在地：パリ, フランス
設計：200612-0705
建築主：パリ市
主要用途：駅複合施設
構造：ARUP
設備：ARUP, Setec TPI,
Transsolar Energietechnik GmbH
主体構造・規模：鉄筋コンクリート造/地上3階
敷地面積：18,396 m²
建築面積：12,850 m²
延床面積：19,540 m²

2004–07
Tama Art University Library (Hachioji campus)
Hachioji, Tokyo, Japan

Program: library
Total floor area: 5,639.46 m²
Site area: 159,184.87 m²
Structure: steel reinforced concrete
2 stories, 1 basement

多摩美術大学図書館（八王子キャンパス）
所在地：東京都八王子市
設計：200404-0510
工事：200511-0702
建築主：多摩美術大学
主要用途：図書館
構造：佐々木睦朗構造計画研究所, 鹿島建設
設備：鹿島建設
施工：鹿島建設
主体構造・規模：鉄骨鉄筋コンクリート造
規模：地上2階, 地下1階
敷地面積：159,184.87 m²
建築面積：2,224.59 m²
延床面積：5,639.46 m²

2007–08
SUMIKA PAVILION / SUMIKA PROJECT by TOKYO GAS
Utsunomiya, Tochigi, Japan

Program: pavilion
Total floor area: 81 m²
Site area: 6,522 m²
Structure: timber frame
1 story

SUMIKA パヴィリオン,
SUMIKA PROJECT by TOKYO GAS
所在地：栃木県宇都宮市
設計：200704-0803
工事：200807-0811
建築主：東京ガス
主要用途：パヴィリオン(見学用施設)
構造：オーク構造設計
設備：環境エンジニアリング
施工：トヨタウッドユーホーム
主体構造・規模：木造/地上1階
敷地面積：6,522 m²
建築・延床面積：81 m²

2005–08
ZA-KOENJI Public Theatre
Suginami, Tokyo, Japan

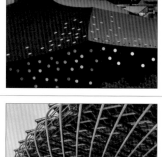

Program: theater
Total floor area: 4,977.74 m²
Site area: 1,649.26 m²
Structure: steel frame, reinforced concrete
3 stories, 3 basements

座・高円寺
所在地：東京都杉並区
設計：200506-0608
工事：200612-0811
建築主：杉並区
主要用途：劇場
構造：佐々木睦朗構造計画研究所
設備：環境エンジニアリング
施工：大成建設
主体構造・規模：鉄骨造, 鉄筋コンクリート造
規模：地上3階, 地下3階
敷地面積：1,649.26 m²
建築面積：1,107.86 m²
延床面積：4,977.74 m²

2006–09
Kaohsiung National Stadium
Kaohsiung, Taiwan, R.O.C.

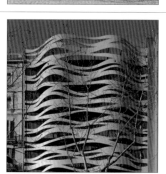

Program: stadium, park
Total floor area: 98,759.31 m²
Site area: 189,012.00 m²
Structure: steel frame, reinforced concrete
3 stories, 2 basements

高雄国家体育場
所在地：高雄, 台湾
設計：200601-0703 工事：200609-0901
建築主：台湾中央政府行政院體育委員會,
高雄市政府工務局
主要用途：競技場, 公園
共同設計：竹中工務店, 劉培森建築師事務所
構造：竹中工務店＋信業工程
設備：竹中工務店＋泰迪工程＋
玉堅冷凍空調工業技術事務所
外構：中冶環境造形
施工：互助營造
主体構造・規模：鉄骨造, 鉄筋コンクリート造
規模：地上3階, 地下2階
敷地面積：189,012.00 m²
建築面積：25,553.46 m²
延床面積：98,759.31 m²

2003–09
Facade Renovation "Suites Avenue Aparthotel"
Barcelona, Spain

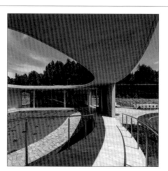

Program: aparthotel
Facade hight: about 24 m
Total floor area: 4,514 m²
Site area: 555 m²
Material: steel
8 stories

スイーツアベニュー・アパートホテル
ファサードリノベーション
所在地：バルセロナ, スペイン
設計：200312-0608
工事：200608-0903
建築主：Derby Hotels Collection
主要用途：ファサード・リノベーション
施工：Caldereria Dergado(ファサード鉄工)
Pai(本体)
主体構造・規模：鉄板造/地上8階
敷地面積：555 m²
建築面積：555 m²
延床面積：4,514 m²

2004–09
White O
Marbella, Chile

Program: villa
Total floor area: 400 m²
Site area: 2,500 m²
Structure: reinforced concrete
2 stories

White O
所在地：マルベーリャ, チリ
設計：200410-0701
工事：200801-0906
建築主・施工：Constructora Blanco Cero Ltda.
主要用途：別荘
構造：構造設計工房 デルタ, Luis Soler Piraces & Asociados
設備：Luis Soler Piraces & Asociados
主体構造・規模：鉄筋コンクリート造/地上2階
敷地面積：2,500 m²
建築面積：375 m²
延床面積：400 m²

2009
The New Deichman Main Library Competition
Oslo, Norway

オスロ市ダイクマン中央図書館 コンペティション応募案
所在地：オスロ, ノルウェー
設計：200811-0902
建築主：HAV Eiendom AS
主要用途：図書館, 劇場, オフィス, 他
構造：SAPS/Sasaki and Partners
設備：環境エンジニアリング
主体構造・規模：鉄骨造／地上8階, 地下1階
敷地面積：8,600 m²
建築面積：8,935 m²
延床面積：50,848 m²

Program: library, theater, office, etc.
Total floor area: 50,848 m²
Site area: 8,600 m²
Structure: steel frame
8 stories, 1 basement

2009
BAMPFA
University of California, Berkeley Art Museum and Pacific Film Archive
California, U.S.A.

カリフォルニア大学 バークレー美術館／パシフィック・フィルム・アーカイブ計画案
所在地：カリフォルニア州, アメリカ
設計：200609-0912
建築主：カリフォルニア大学 バークレー校
主要用途：ギャラリー, アーカイブ, ワークショップ
共同設計：EHDD | Architecture
構造：SAPS/Sasaki and Partners, FORELL/Elsesser Engineers, inc.
設備：環境エンジニアリング, IBE Consulting Engineers, inc.
主体構造・規模：鋼板コンクリート造／地上3階, 地下1階
敷地面積：5,200 m²
建築面積：3,400 m²
延床面積：12,900 m²

Program: gallery, archive, workshop
Total floor area: 12,900 m²
Site area: 5,200 m²
Structure: steel panel and concrete
3 stories, 1 basement

2004–10
TORRES PORTA FIRA
Barcelona, Spain

トーレス・ポルタ・フィラ
所在地：バルセロナ, スペイン
設計：200406-0607
工事：200604-1001
建築主：TORRES PORTA FIRA
主要用途：ホテル, オフィス
共同設計：Fermin Vázquez-B720 arquitectos
構造：IDOM Ingeniería y Sistema S.A.
設備：GRUPO JG
施工：FCC Construccion, S.A.
主体構造：鉄筋コンクリート造
規模：ホテル／地上26階, 地下2階
オフィス棟／地上24階, 地下3階
敷地面積：ホテル／5,755.55 m², オフィス棟／4,801.55 m²
建築面積：ホテル／4,810.08 m², オフィス棟／4,049.73 m²
延床面積：ホテル／34,688.10 m², オフィス棟／45,419.59 m²

Program: hotel, office
Total floor area: hotel / 34,688.10 m²
office / 45,419.59 m²
Site area: hotel / 5,755.55 m²
office / 4,801.55 m²
Structure: reinforced concrete
hotel / 26 stories, 2 basements
office / 24 stories, 3 basements

2006–10
Belle Vue Residences
Singapore

ベルビュー・レジデンシズ
所在地：オクスレーウォーク, シンガポール
設計：200603-0712
工事：200801-1009
建築主：Wing Tai Property Management
主要用途：集合住宅
構造：オーク構造設計, P&T Consultants, KTP Consultants
設備：United Project Consultant
施工：Tiong Aik Construction
主体構造・規模：鉄筋コンクリート造／地上5階, 地下1階
敷地面積：23,003.40 m²
建築面積：8,368.49 m²
延床面積：32,204.76 m²

Program: housing
Total floor area: 32,204.76 m²
Site area: 23,003.40 m²
Structure: reinforced concrete
5 stories, 1 basement

2010
Waalse Krook Competition
Ghent, Belgium

ゲント市図書館及びニューメディアセンター コンペティション応募案
所在地：ゲント, ベルギー
設計：200911-1005
建築主：CVBA Waalse Krook
構造：SAPS/Sasaki and Partners, Greisch Ingénierie
設備：Ingenium nv. Peutz bv. Takenaka Europe
主体構造・規模：鉄筋コンクリート造／地上4階, 地下1階
建築面積：5,550 m²
延床面積：20,070 m²

Program: library, new media center, auditorium
Total floor area: 20,070 m²
Built area: 5,550 m²
Structure: reinforced concrete
4 stories, 1 basement

2010
VEGA BAJA Museum Competition
Toledo, Spain

ベガ・バハ博物館 コンペティション応募案
所在地：トレド, スペイン
設計：201001-1006
建築主：Toletum Visigodo
主要用途：博物館, 研究センター, 他
構造：SAPS/Sasaki and Partners, BOMA
設備：環境エンジニアリング
主体構造・規模：鉄筋コンクリート造／地上2階, 地下1階
敷地面積：31,900 m²
建築面積：13,414 m²
延床面積：15,017 m²

Program: museum, research center, etc.
Total floor area: 15,017 m²
Site area: 31,900 m²
Structure: reinforced concrete
2 stories, 1 basement

2010
Taipei Pop Music Center Competition
Taipei, Taiwan, R.O.C.

台北POPミュージックセンター・コンペティション応募案
所在地：台北市, 台湾
設計：200908-1010
建築主：台北市政府
主要用途：ホール, 博物館, スタジオ, 他
構造：SAPS/Sasaki and Partners
設備：竹中工務店
主体構造：鉄骨鉄筋コンクリート造
規模：地上6階, 地下3階
敷地面積：76,500 m²
延床面積：約68,000 m²

Program: hall, museum, studio, etc.
Total floor area: about 68,000 m²
Site area: 76,500 m²
Structure: reinforced concrete
6 stories, 2 basements

2008–11
Toyo Ito Museum of Architecture, Steel Hut
Imabari, Ehime, Japan

今治市伊東豊雄建築ミュージアム, スティールハット
所在地：愛媛県今治市
設計：200807-0908
工事：201008-1103
建築主：今治市
主要用途：美術館
構造：佐々木睦朗構造計画研究所
設備：イーエスアソシエイツ, 大瀧設備事務所
施工：大成建設
主体構造：鉄骨造, 一部鉄筋コンクリート造
規模：地上2階
敷地面積：ミュージアム全体／6,295.36 m²
建築面積：194.92 m²
延床面積：168.99 m²

Program: museum
Total floor area: 168.99 m²
Site area: 6,295.36 m²
Structure: steel frame
2 stories

2009–11
Toyo Ito Museum of Architecture, Silver Hut
Imabari, Ehime, Japan

今治市伊東豊雄建築ミュージアム, シルバーハット
所在地：愛媛県今治市
設計：200904-1008
工事：201009-1105
建築主：今治市
主要用途：美術館
構造：O.R.S.事務所
設備：イーエスアソシエイツ, 大瀧設備事務所
施工：大成建設
主体構造：鉄筋コンクリート造, 一部鉄骨造（屋根）
規模：地上2階
敷地面積：ミュージアム全体／6,295.36 m²
建築面積：168.32 m²
延床面積：188.32 m²

Program: museum
Total floor area: 188.32 m²
Site area: 6,295.36 m²
Structure: reinforced concrete, steel frame
2 stories

2009–11
Ken Iwata Mother and Child Museum, Imabari City
Imabari, Ehime, Japan

今治市岩田健母と子のミュージアム
所在地：愛媛県今治市
設計：200909-1003
工事：201010-1105
建築主：岩田健, ギャラリー長谷川
主要用途：美術館
構造：佐々木睦朗構造計画研究所
設備：イーエスアソシエイツ, 大瀧設備事務所
施工：大成建設
主体構造・規模：鉄筋コンクリート造／地上1階
敷地面積：1,912 m²
建築面積：197.29 m²
延床面積：197.29 m²

Program: museum
Total floor area: 197.29 m²
Site area: 1,912 m²
Structure: reinforced concrete
1 story

2009–11
House H
Hokkaido, Japan

洞爺湖 H邸
所在地：北海道
設計：200902-1009
工事：201010-1105
主要用途：別荘
構造：佐々木睦朗構造計画研究所
設備：環境エンジニアリング
共同設計：横田歴男建築設計事務所
施工：平almost建設
主体構造・規模：鉄筋コンクリート造／地上1階
敷地面積：1,150.49 m²
建築面積：148.74 m²
延床面積：148.46 m²

Program: house
Total floor area: 148.46 m²
Site area: 1,150.49 m²
Structure: reinforced concrete
1 story

photo by © Reo Yokota

2010–11
TOKYO GAS Ei-WALK CONCEPT ROOM
Arakawa, Tokyo, Japan

東京ガス 千住見学サイト Ei-WALK CONCEPT ROOM
所在地：東京都荒川区
設計：201009-1012
工事：201102-1106
建築主：東京ガス
主要用途：ヴィジター・センター
構造：佐藤淳構造設計事務所
設備：環境エンジニアリング
施工：内藤建設
主体構造・規模：鉄骨造／地上1階
敷地面積：32,010.94 m²
建築面積：124.12 m²
延床面積：119.38 m²

Program: visiter center
Total floor area: 119.38 m²
Site area: 32,010.94 m²
Structure: steel frame
1 story

2009–11
Tokyo Mother's Clinic
Setagaya, Tokyo, Japan

Program: clinic
(obstetrics and gynecology)
Total floor area: 980.29 m²
Site area: 878.75 m²
Structure: reinforced concrete,
steel reinforced concrete (partially)
2 stories

東京マザーズクリニック
所在地：東京都世田谷区上用賀
設計：200911-1012
工事：201101-1111
建築主：医療法人準和会
主要用途：診療所（産婦人科）
構造：オーク構造設計
設備：環境エンジニアリング、大成建設
施工：大成建設
主体構造・規模：鉄筋コンクリート造、
一部鉄骨鉄筋コンクリート造／地上2階
敷地面積：878.75m²
建築面積：527.11m²
延床面積：980.29m²

2009–11
Yaoko Kawagoe Museum
(Yuji Misu Memorial Hall)
Kawagoe, Saitama, Japan

Program: museum
Total floor area: 464.30 m²
Site area: 1,824.19 m²
Structure: box frame type reinforced concrete, steel frame (partially)
1 story

ヤオコー川越美術館（三栖右嗣記念館）
所在地：埼玉県川越市
設計：200904-1009
工事：201012-1112
建築主：ヤオコー
主要用途：美術館
構造：佐々木睦朗構造計画研究所
設備：イーエスアソシエイツ、大誠設備事務所
施工：大成建設
主体構造：壁式鉄筋コンクリート造、一部鉄骨造
規模：地上1階
敷地面積：1,824.19m²
建築面積：471.36m²
延床面積：464.30m²

2011
Centre Culturel et Touristique du Vin á Bordeaux, Concours
Bordeaux, France

Program: gallery, marche, office, auditorium, panoramic restaurant
Total floor area: 15,870 m²
Site area: 12,450 m²
Structure: reinforced concrete
4 stories

rendering by © Studio Cyrulle Thomas

ボルドーワイン文化・観光センター コンペティション応募案
所在地：ボルドー、フランス
設計：201012-201104
建築主：ボルドー市
主要用途：ギャラリー、マルシェ、事務所、オーディトリアム、パノラマレストラン
構造：COTEBA, SAPS/Sasaki and Partners
設備：COTEBA
主体構造・規模：鉄筋コンクリート造／地上4階
敷地面積：12,450m²
建築面積：7,410m²
延床面積：15,870m²

2012
New National Stadium Japan International Design Competition
Shinjuku, Tokyo, Japan

Program: stadium, sports museum and library
Total floor area: 292,200 m²
Site area: 113,000 m²
Structure: reinforced concrete (stand), steel frame (roof), roof isolation system
7 stories, 2 basements

新国立競技場基本構想国際デザイン競技応募案
所在地：東京都新宿区
設計：2012
建築主：独立行政法人日本スポーツ振興センター
主要用途：スタジアム、スポーツ博物館、図書館
構造：佐々木睦朗構造計画研究所
主体構造・規模：鉄筋コンクリート造（スタンド）＋鉄骨造（屋根）、屋根免震／地上7階、地下2階
敷地面積：113,000m²
建築面積：72,000m²
延床面積：292,200m²

2010–13
Katsushika ni'ijukumirai Parks
Katsushika, Tokyo, Japan

Program: park
Site area: 71,309.44 m²
Structure: pergola / steel frame, public lavatory / reinforced concrete

葛飾にいじゅくみらい公園
所在地：東京都葛飾区
設計：201004-1103
工事：201110-1303
建築主：葛飾区
主要用途：公園
ランドスケープ・デザイン：中央大学教授 石川幹子
主体構造：パーゴラ／鉄骨造、公衆トイレ棟／鉄筋コンクリート造
敷地面積：71,309.44m²

2011–13
Hermès Pavilion
Basel, Switzerland

Program: pavilion
Total floor area: 1,040 m²
Structure: steel frame
2 stories

photo by © Iwan baan

エルメス パヴィリオン
所在地：バーゼル、スイス
設計：201109-1212
製作：201203-1303
設営：201303-1304
建築主：La Montre Hermès
主要用途：パヴィリオン
構造：SAPS/Sasaki and Partners, WGG Schnetzer Puskas Ingenieure
設備：ETAVIS Kriegel + Schaffner
施工：ファサード／Daniel Fournier、鉄骨／Jakem
主体構造・規模：鉄骨造／地上2階
建築面積：646m²
延床面積：1,040m²

2006–13
National Taiwan University, College of Social Sciences
Taipei, Taiwan, R.O.C.

Program: educational facility (university)
Total floor area: 53,231.69 m²
Site area: 869,491 m²
Structure: reinforced concrete, steel frame (partially)
8 stories, 2 basements

台湾大学社会科学部棟
所在地：台北市、台湾
設計：200608-0910
工事：201002-1305
建築主：國立臺灣大學
主要用途：教育施設（大学）
構造：SAPS/Sasaki and Partners, 超偉工程
設備：竹中工務店、冠遠工程、巽茂工程
施工：互助營造
主体構造・規模：鉄筋コンクリート造、一部鉄骨造
規模：地上8階、地下2階
敷地面積：869,491m²
建築面積：6,776.89m²
延床面積：53,231.69m²

2012–13
ITO JUKU Ebisu Studio
Shibuya, Tokyo, Japan

Program: workshop, lecture space and residence
Total floor area: 131.77 m²
Site area: 191.01 m²
Structure: steel frame
2 stories

伊東建築塾 恵比寿スタジオ
所在地：東京都渋谷区
設計：201204-1212
工事：201303-1306
建築主：伊東豊雄
主要用途：学習塾兼用住宅
構造：佐々木睦朗構造計画研究所
設備：環境エンジニアリング
施工：内藤建設
主体構造・規模：鉄骨造／地上2階
敷地面積：191.01m²
建築面積：114.59m²
延床面積：131.77m²

2008–13
Songshan Taipei New Horizon Building
Taipei, Taiwan, R.O.C.

Program: office, hotel, retail, hall, etc.
Total floor area: 105,742.55 m²
Site area: 12,000 m²
Structure: steel reinforced concrete, steel frame, reinforced concrete
14 stories, 5 basements

松山 台北文創ビル
所在地：台北市、台湾
設計：200810-1112
工事：201107-1309
建築主：台北文創
主要用途：オフィス、ホテル、店舗、ホールなど
構造：SAPS/Sasaki and Partners, 信辰工程
設備：環境エンジニアリング、A-bl、正弦工程、林伸環境設計、萬泰工業
施工：中産營造
主体構造・規模：鉄骨鉄筋コンクリート造、鉄骨造、鉄筋コンクリート造／地上14階、地下5階
敷地面積：12,000m²
建築面積：6,378.30m²
延床面積：105,742.55m²

2013
Museum + / West Kowloon Cultural District Competition
Hongkong, China

Program: museum, retail, etc.
Total floor area: 70,000 m²
Structure: steel panel and reinforced concrete
7 stories, 1 basement

render by © LIFANG Comuputer Graphics Limited

Museum + / West Kowloon Cultural District Competition
所在地：香港、中華人民共和国
設計：201301-1306
建築主：West Kowloon Cultural District Authority (WKCDA)
主要用途：美術館複合施設
構造：SAPS/Sasaki and Partners + ARUP
設備：イーエスアソシエイツ
主体構造・規模：鋼板コンクリート造／地上7階、地下1階
建築面積：12,860m²
延床面積：70,000m²

2012–14
K-port / Isoya Suisan Minatomachi 1chome Branch
Kesen'numa, Miyagi, Japan

Program: restaurant / house, retail
Total floor area: 125.55 m² / 427.22 m²
Site area: 626.90 m² / 788.07 m²
Structure: steel frame, 1 story + steel frame, 3 stories

K-port / 磯屋水産港町一丁目店
所在地：宮城県気仙沼市
設計：201209-1305
工事：201306-1310, -1402（磯屋水産）
建築主：K-port／渡邉謙、磯屋水産／安藤竜司
主要用途：K-port／飲食店、磯屋水産／店舗兼住宅
構造：佐々木睦朗構造計画研究所
設備：エービル
施工：みちのく建設工業
主体構造・規模：K-port／鉄骨造 地上1階、磯屋水産／鉄骨造 地上3階
敷地面積：K-port／626.90m²、磯屋水産／788.07m²
建築面積：K-port／125.55m²、磯屋水産／180.13m²
延床面積：K-port／125.55m²、磯屋水産／427.22m²

2011–14
Residential Hall at Nanyang Drive, Nanyang Technological University
Singapore

Program: student's dormitory, staff & professor's residence
Total floor area: 31,300 m²
Site area: 27,600 m²
Structure: reinforced concrete
7 stories, 1 basement

photo by © Kai Nakamura

南洋理工大学学生寮
所在地：シンガポール
設計：201112-1212
工事：201301-1406
建築主：南洋理工大学
主要用途：学生寮
構造：SAPS/Sasaki and Partners, KTP Consultants
設備：ARUP, Mott Macdonald
施工：Santarli-Zheng Keng JV
主体構造・規模：鉄筋コンクリート造
規模：地上7階、地下1階
敷地面積：27,600m²
建築面積：8,860m²
延床面積：31,300m²

2007–14
CapitaGreen
Singapore

Program: office
Total floor area: 82,003.07 m²
Site area: 5,478.5 m²
Structure: reinforced concrete,
steel reinforced concrete
40 stories, 3 basements

photo by © Kai Nakamura

2013–15
Yamanashi Gakuin University International College of Liberal Arts
Kofu, Yamanashi, Japan

Program: lecture room, office, student's dormitory
Total floor area: 9,972.16 m²
Site area: 7,484.54 m²
Structure: reinforced concrete, steel frame (partially)
7 stories

2011–15
'Minna no Mori' Gifu Media Cosmos
Gifu, Japan

Program: library, community center, gallery
Total floor area: 15,444.23 m²
Site area: 14,848.34 m²
Structure: reinforced concrete, steel frame, timber frame (beam)
2 stories, 1 basement

2015
New National Stadium Japan Proposal
Shinjuku, Tokyo, Japan

Program: stadium
Total floor area: 185,673 m²
Site area: 113,040 m²
Structure: wood column + reinforced concrete (stand), steel frame (roof), mid-story isolation system
3 stories, 2 basements

2012–16
Museo Internacional del Barroco
Puebla, México

Program: museum
Total floor area: 18,149 m²
Site area: 50,000 m²
Structure: prestressed concrete wall
2 stories

2005–16
National Taichung Theater
Taichung, Taiwan, R.O.C.

Program: theater, gallery, restaurant
Total floor area: 51,152.19 m²
Site area: 57,020.46 m²
Structure: reinforced concrete
6 stories, 2 basements

National Taichung Theater is built by the Taichung City Government, Republic of China (Taiwan).

2014–16
Miyagi Gakuin Preschool "Mori no Kodomo-en"
Sendai, Miyagi, Japan

Program: preschool
Total floor area: 998.84 m²
Site area: 190,665 m²
Structure: timber frame
1 story

2010–16
Fubon Sky Tree
Taichung, Taiwan, R.O.C.

Program: residence
Total floor area: 52,279.95 m²
Site area: 9,108 m²
Structure: steel frame
42 stories, 4 basements

2011–
Fubon Life Insurances Taichung Wenxin Office Building
Taichung, Taiwan, R.O.C.

Program: office
Total floor area: 17,100 m²
Site area: 1,500 m²
Structure: steel frame, steel reinforced concrete
20 stories, 5 basements
2 stories, (penthouse)

render © Kuramochi + Oguma

2011–
Crematorium and Akayama Historic Nature Park in Kawaguchi
Kawaguchi, Saitama, Japan

Program: crematorium
Total floor area: 7,901.42 m²
Site area: 19,800.32 m²
Structure: reinforced concrete, steel frame (partially)
2 stories, 1 basement

2011–
Crematorium and Akayama Historic Nature Park in Kawaguchi [2]
Kawaguchi, Saitama, Japan

Program: reference library, retail, etc.
Total floor area: reference / 483.09 m²
retail / 406.90 m²
Site area: 62,049.17 m²
Structure: reference / steel frame
retail / steel reinforced concrete, etc.
1 story

2013–
New Athletic Field and Sports Park in Aomori
Aomori, Japan

Program: stadium
Total floor area: 28,812.59 m²
Site area: 847,841.80 m²
Structure: reinforced concrete, steel frame, steel reinforced concrete
4 stories, 1 basement

Model by © Toyo Ito & Associates, Architects + Chuo University, Department of Integrated Science and Engineering for Sustainable Society Environmental Design Laboratory

2013–
The Crest
Singapore

Program: housing (469 units)
Total floor area: 49,950.00 m²
(include balcony)
Site area: 23,785.40 m²
Structure: reinforced concrete
3 Towers / 23 stories,
4 Villas / 5 stories

The Crest
所在地：シンガポール
設計：201310-　工事：201406-
建築主：Wingcrown Investment,
Jointly developed by Wing Tai Land, Metro
Australia Holdings & Maxdin
主要用途：集合住宅
構造：P&T Consultants
設備：United Project Consultants
環境：ARUP
施工：GREATEARTH CONSTRUCTION
主体構造：鉄筋コンクリート造
規模：高層棟3棟／地上23階、地下1階
低層棟4棟／地上5階、地下1階
敷地面積：23,785.40m²
建築面積：6,215.79m²
延床面積：49,950.00m²（バルコニー部含む）

2013–
Interior Design for the Reconstruction Project of Jikido in Yakushiji Temple
Nara, Japan

Program: temple
Total floor area: 629.79 m²
Site area: 44,722.00 m²
Structure: steel frame

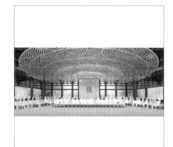

薬師寺食堂復興計画（内部）
所在地：奈良県奈良市
設計：201310-
工事：201504-1705（予定）
建築主：宗教法人　薬師寺
主要用途：寺院
監修：鈴木嘉吉
復元設計：文化財保存計画協会
構造・設備及び実施設計：竹中工務店
施工：竹中工務店
絵画：田渕俊夫
照明計画：LIGHTDESIGN
主体構造・規模：鉄骨造／地上1階
敷地面積：44,722.00m²
建築面積：1037.37m²
延床面積：629.79m²

2014–
Sports Hall, Nanyang Technological University
Singapore

Program: sports hall
Total floor area: 9,774.94 m²
Site area: 2,008,344.70 m²
Structure: timber frame,
steel frame (partially)
3 stories

南洋理工大学　スポーツホール
所在地：シンガポール
設計：201401-1501
工事：201506-1610（予定）
建築主：南洋理工大学
主要用途：体育館
構造：SAPS/Sasaki and Partners,
T.Y. Lin International
設備：T.Y. Lin International
施工：B19 Technologies
主体構造・規模：木造、一部鉄骨造／地上3階
敷地面積：2,008,344.70m²
建築面積：4,692.87m²
延床面積：9,774.94m²

2014–
The Shinano Mainichi Shimbun Matsumoto Head Office
Matsumoto, Nagano, Japan

Program: office, retail
Total floor area: 8,101 m²
Site area: 3,940 m²
Structure: steel frame, reinforced concrete, steel reinforced concrete
5 stories, 1 basement

信濃毎日新聞社松本本社
所在地：長野県松本市
設計：201410-1611
工事：201612-1803（予定）
建築主：信濃毎日新聞社
主要用途：事務所、店舗
構造：佐々木睦朗構造計画研究所
設備：イーエスアソシエイツ、大瀧設備事務所
施工：北野建設
主体構造・規模：鉄骨造、鉄筋コンクリート造、鉄骨鉄筋コンクリート造／地上5階、地下1階
敷地面積：3,940m²
建築面積：1,555m²
延床面積：8,101m²

2015–
Onomichi City Momoshima Branch Office
Onomichi, Hiroshima, Japan

Program: office
Total floor area: 180.41 m²
Site area: 429.96 m²
Structure: timber frame
1 story

尾道市百島支所庁舎
所在地：広島県尾道市
設計：201510-1603
建築主：尾道市
主要用途：事務所（庁舎）
構造：オーク構造設計
設備：建築エネルギー研究所
主体構造・規模：木造／地上1階
敷地面積：429.96m²
建築面積：212.09m²
延床面積：180.41m²

2016–
Mito Civic Hall
Mito, Ibaraki, Japan

Program: theater, gallery, retail
Total floor area: 21,630 m²
Site area: 8,300 m²
Structure: reinforced concrete, steel frame, timber frame
4 stories, 1 basement

（仮称）水戸市民会館
所在地：茨城県水戸市
設計：201608-1803（予定）
工事：2018-（予定）
建築主：泉町1丁目北地区市街地再開発（準備）組合
主要用途：劇場、ギャラリー、店舗等
共同設計：横須賀満夫建築設計事務所
構造：ARUP
主体構造：鉄筋コンクリート造、鉄骨造、木造
規模：地上4階、地下1階
敷地面積：8,300m²
建築面積：6,980m²
延床面積：21,630m²

Monograph and Published Writing

1986	「SD8609　伊東豊雄：風の変様体」　鹿島出版会
1988	「日本現代建築家シリーズ12　伊東豊雄」　新建築社
1989	「風の変様体」　青土社
1995	「EL croquis 71: Toyo Ito」　El Croquis Editorial，スペイン
2000	「透層する建築」　青土社
2001	「GA ARCHITECT 17　Toyo Ito 1970-2001」　A.D.A. EDITA Tokyo
2003	「PLOT 03　伊東豊雄：建築のプロセス」　A.D.A. EDITA Tokyo
2005	「EL croquis 123: Toyo Ito 2001-2005 beyond modernism」　El Croquis Editorial，スペイン
	「みちの家」（子どもたちに伝えたい家の本 08）　インデックス・コミュニケーションズ
2008	「伊東豊雄　最新プロジェクト」　A.D.A. EDITA Tokyo
2009	「TOYO ITO」　Phaidon Press Limited，イギリス
	「EL croquis 147: Toyo Ito 2005-2009 liquid space」　El Croquis Editorial，スペイン
2011	「Architecture Words 8 "Tarzans in the Media Forest"」　AA Publications, U.K.
2012	「建築の大転換」中沢新一共著　筑摩書房
	「Toyo Ito Forces of Nature」　Princeton Architecture Press, U.S.A.
	「あの日からの建築」　集英社新書
2013	「伊東豊雄の建築 1　1971-2001」　TOTO出版
2014	「伊東豊雄の建築 2　2002-2014」　TOTO出版
	「ArchiCreation／建築創作 No.176 伊東豊雄 2014」　Archicreation Journal，中国
	「伊東豊雄　自然の力」　丸善出版
	「伊東豊雄　子ども建築塾」　LIXIL出版
2016	「『建築』で日本を変える」　集英社新書

Toyo Ito & Associates, Architects

Current Staff Members

伊東豊雄　Toyo Ito
泉洋子　Yoko Izumi
東建男　Takeo Higashi
古林豊彦　Toyohiko Kobayashi
藤江航　Wataru Fujie
大宮由紀子　Yukiko Omiya
澤村圭介　Keisuke Sawamura
水沼靖昭　Yasuaki Mizunuma
庵原義隆　Yoshitaka Ihara
矢部倫太郎　Rintaro Yabe
小針修一　Shuichi Kobari
大賀淳史　Junji Oga
福田誠　Makoto Fukuda
樽谷敦　Atsushi Tarutani
ニルス・ベッカー　Nils Becker
南俊允　Toshimitsu Minami
近藤奈々子　Nanako Kondo
伊東美也　Miya Ito
磯田和明　Kazuaki Isoda
大原央行　Takayuki Ohara Martinez
竹内啓　Kei Takeuchi
郷野正広　Masahiro Gouno
木下栄理子　Eriko Kinoshita
池田耕三　Kozo Ikeda
山田有吾　Yugo Yamada
井上智香子　Chikako Inoue
福田陽之輔　Yonosuke Fukuda
方薇雅　Wei-ya Fang
ジュリア・リー・カ・イ　Julia Li Ka Yee
中村裕太　Yuta Nakamura
矢吹光代　Mitsuyo Yabuki
長曽我部亮　Ryo Chosokabe
高塚順旭　Nobuaki Takatsuka
山田明子　Meiko Yamada
中島成隆　Shigetaka Nakajima
林盛　Sei Hayashi
孫豪聰　Andy Sun
青柳有依　Yui Aoyagi
太田由真　Yuma Ota
井上裕之　Hiroyuki Inoue
高垣麻衣花　Maika Takagaki
長塚幸助　Kosuke Nagatsuka
桝永絵理子　Eriko Masunaga
神崎夏子　Natsuko Kanzaki
大澤智美　Satomi Osawa
杉山由香　Yuka Sugiyama
山崎拓野　Takuya Yamazaki
王乾　Qian Wang
エレナ・ハスブン　Elena Hasbun

Former Staff Members

祖父江義郎　Yoshiro Sofue
柴田牧子　Makiko Shibata
石田敏明　Toshiaki Ishida
柴田いづみ　Izumi Shibata
片倉保夫　Yasuo Katakura
飯村和道　Kazumichi Iimura
妹島和世　Kazuyo Sejima
小宮功　Isao Komiya
桑原立郎　Tatsuo Kuwahara
城戸崎和佐　Nagisa Kidosaki
二瓶稔　Minoru Nihei
佐々木勉　Tsutomu Sasaki
佐藤光彦　Mitsuhiko Sato
小池ひろの　Hirono Koike
奥瀬公子　Kimiko Okuse
曽我部昌史　Masashi Sogabe
手塚義明　Yoshiaki Tezuka
徳永照久　Teruhisa Tokunaga
アストリッド・クライン　Astrid Klein
マーク・ダイサム　Mark Dytham
鈴木優子　Yuko Suzuki
横溝真　Makoto Yokomizo
篠崎健一　Kenichi Shinozaki
冨永謙　Ken Tominaga
伊藤文子　Fumiko Ito
上條美枝　Yoshie Kamijo
佐藤京子　Kyoko Sato
石津麻里子　Mariko Ishizu
伊藤淳　Atsushi Ito
中村康造　Kozo Nakamura
ムーン・ギュー・チョイ　Moongyu Choi
柳澤潤　Jun Yanagisawa
桜本まゆみ　Mayumi Sakuramoto
堀達浩　Tatsuhiro Hori
竹内申一　Shinichi Takeuchi
田畑美穂　Miho Tabata
福島加津也　Katsuya Fukushima
安田光男　Teruo Yasuda
奥矢恵　Megumi Okuya
瀬尾拓広　Takuhiro Seo
高山正行　Masayuki Takayama
赤松純子　Junko Akamatsu
井上雅宏　Masahiro Inoue
高橋直子　Naoko Takahashi
荒木研一　Kenichi Araki
塚田修大　Nobuhiro Tsukada
久保田顕子　Akiko Kubota
関口惠津　Etsu Sekiguchi
松原弘典　Hironori Matsubara
平田晃久　Akihisa Hirata
式地香織　Kaori Shikichi
横田歴男　Leo Yokota
西村麻利子　Mariko Nishimura
細谷浩美　Hiromi Hosoya
中山英之　Hideyuki Nakayama
多羅尾希　Nozomi Tarao
高塚章夫　Akio Takatsuka
金本智香子　Chikako Kanamoto
赤崎光基　Koki Akasaki
末光弘和　Hirokazu Suemitsu
三好隆之　Takayuki Miyoshi
青島琢治　Takuji Aoshima
横川雄一　Yuichi Yokokawa
中原英隆　Hidetaka Nakahara
白川在　Zai Shirakawa
篠崎弘之　Hiroyuki Shinozaki
橋本朋子　Tomoko Hashimoto
クリストフ・セラリウス　Christoph Cellarius
アンドリュー・バーリー　Andrew Barrie
森畑孝幸　Takayuki Morihata
錦織真也　Maya Nishikori
平山高康　Takayasu Hirayama
足立拓　Taku Adachi
木上理恵　Rie Kigami
秋山隆浩　Takahiro Akiyama
フロリアン・ブッシュ　Florian Busch
佐野健太　Kenta Sano
御手洗龍　Ryu Mitarai
魚野美紀　Miki Uono
渡邉弾　Dan Watanabe
鵜飼恵三子　Emiko Ukai
岡野道子　Michiko Okano
田邊曜　Hikaru Tanabe
森山ちはる　Chiharu Moriyama
前田健太郎　Kentaro Maeda
星島美完　Minori Hoshijima
喜多裕　Yutaka Kita
アンドレ・ギモンド　Andre Guimond
髙橋麻実　Asami Takahashi
髙池葉子　Yoko Takaike
百田有希　Yuki Hyakuda
玉木浩太　Kota Tamaki
花岡徳秋　Noriaki Hanaoka
林俐廷　Lin Li-Ting
林宜佩　Lin Yi Pei
福西健太　Kenta Fukunishi
高橋真未　Mami Takahashi
ルイ・イギェホン　Ruyi Igiehon
劉明璋　Ming-Chang David Liu

Credits

Photography Credits

Yukio Futagawa: *p.30, pp.32-33, pp.38-47, p.68 right, p.69, p.88, p.89 left, p.91 top, pp.92-99, p.105 right, pp.106-107, p.115, p.116 left bottom, pp.116-117, p.118 right middle, right bottom, p.119, p.280 second and third from top, p.281 third from left top, p.282 third from left top, right top*
Yoshio Futagawa: *p.89 right, p.91 middle, bottom, pp.108-111, pp.132-137, pp.138-139, pp.140-147, pp.152-155, pp.192-194, pp.196-199, pp.200-203, pp.232-236, pp.238-239, p.241, pp.246-249, pp.254-263, pp.268-279, p.280 second from bottom, p.281 fifth from right top, p.282 fourth, fifth and sixth from right top, p.283 third from left top, p.284 right top, third from right top, p.285 third, fifth sixth from left top, second from right top,*
Makoto Yamaguchi: *p.177 right top*
Ayane Hirose: *pp.172-173, p.284 left top,*
Nohara Yamazaki: *pp.174-175, pp.188-189, pp.204-205, p.214, pp.224-225, pp.226-227, pp.230-231, pp.250-253, pp.264-265, p.284 second and fifth from right top, p.285 fourth from left top, right top, fourth and sixth from right top, p.286 fourth and sixth from top*
GA photographers: *p.5, pp.22-23, p.24 right top, p.25, pp.34-37, pp.48-51, pp.52-53, p.55, pp.56-57, pp.60-62, p.63 bottom, pp.64-65, pp.66-67, p.68 left, pp.70-73, pp.74-76, pp.78-79, pp.80-87, pp.100-101, pp.112-114, p.116 left top, p.118 left, right top, pp.120-121, p.126, pp.128-129, pp.148-151, pp.156-161, p.162 bottom, pp.164-167, pp.168-170, pp.242-245, p.280 top, bottom, p.281 left top, fourth and fifth from left top, p.281 right top, fourth and sixth from right top, p.282 left top, second, fourth and sixth from left top, second and third from right top, p.283 second and fourth from left top, right top, second, third and fourth from right top, second and fifth from left top, p.285 second from right top,*
–
Tomio Ohashi: *p.26*
Takenaka Corporation: *p.63 right top, p.213*
Leo Yokota: *p.162 top, p.163*
Toru Ito: *p.176 right top*
Koichi Torimura: *p.177 left top, left bottom*
fog: *p.177 center bottom*
Photo516 Koichiro Sato: *p.177 center top*
Iwan Baan: *pp.180-181*
Hiroshi Yoda: *p.182 right bottom*
Makoto Fujii: *p.182 left bottom*
Kumamoto Prefecture: *p.178, p.179 bottom*
Kai Nakamura: *pp.216-222*
Photos provided by the architect except as noted above

Drawing and Rendering Credits

Michiko Okano Architects: *p.179 (plan and elevation)*
Mikiko Ishikawa: *p.188 left top (site plan), p.229 right bottom (first floor plan)*
Toyo Ito & Associates, Architects + Chuo University, Department of Integrated Science and Engineering for Sustainable Society Environmental Design Laboratory: *pp.204-205 (model production)*
LIFANG Computer Graphics limited: *p.208 (rendering)*
Kuramochi+Oguma: *p.211 (rendering), p.267 bottom (section)*
Drawing and rendering provided by the architect except as noted above

English Translation

Lisa Tani: *p.23, p.89*
Kei Sato: *p.26, p.53, p.58, p.101, p.104, p.113, p.120, p.129, p.138, p.141, p.149, p.152, p.194, p.269*
Satoko Hirata: *p.162*
Erica Sakai: *p.35, p.39, p.60, p.66, p.92, p.165, p.168, p.171, p.180, pp.182-183, p.184, pp.220-221, pp.226-227, p.229, p.236, p.256*
Nanami Kawashima: *p.123, pp.176-178, pp.188-189, p.200, p.204, p.209, pp.213-214, p.224, p.264*
Joyce Lam: *p.31, p.48, p.70, p.74, p.81, p.157, p.172, pp.174-175, p.216, p.246, p.250*
Haruki Mikio: *p.132*

伊東豊雄作品集　2002－2016

2016年11月25日発行

企画・編集：二川由夫
編集：杉田義一
撮影：GA photographers
序文：伊東豊雄
ロゴ・デザイン（GA）：細谷巌
デザイン：関拓弥
発行者：二川由夫
印刷・製本：大日本印刷株式会社
制作：GA design center
発行：エーディーエー・エディタ・トーキョー
151-0051 東京都渋谷区千駄ヶ谷3-12-14
TEL.(03)3403-1581(代)

禁無断転載

ISBN978-4-87140-435-8 C1352